*PARTY IDENTIFICATION,
POLITICAL BEHAVIOR,
AND THE AMERICAN ELECTORATE*

**Recent Titles in
Contribution in Political Science**
Series Editor: Bernard K. Johnpoll

The Myth of Inevitable Progress
Franco Ferrarotti

A Philosophy of Individual Freedom: The Political Thought of F. A. Hayek
Calvin M. Hoy

Roots of Failure: United States Policy in the Third World
Melvin Gurtov and Ray Maghroori

Disarmament Without Order: The Politics of Disarmament at the United Nations
Avi Beker

The Liberty Lobby and the American Right: Race, Conspiracy, and Culture
Frank P. Mintz

The Liberal Future in America: Essays in Renewal
Philip Abbott and Michael B. Levy, editors

A Change of Course: The West German Social Democrats and NATO, 1957–1961
Stephen J. Artner

Power and Policy in Transition: Essays Presented on the Tenth Anniversary of the National Committee on American Foreign Policy in Honor of Its Founder, Hans J. Morgenthau
Vojtech Mastny, editor

Ideology and Soviet Industrialization
Timothy W. Luke

Administrative Rulemaking: Politics and Processes
William F. West

Recovering from Catastrophes: Federal Disaster Relief Policy and Politics
Peter J. May

Judges, Bureaucrats, and the Question of Independence: A Study of the Social Security Administration Hearing Process
Donna Price Cofer

Party Identification, Political Behavior, and the American Electorate

SHELDON KAMIENIECKI

Introduction by Heinz Eulau

CONTRIBUTIONS IN POLITICAL SCIENCE, NUMBER 125

Greenwood Press
WESTPORT, CONNECTICUT · LONDON, ENGLAND

Library of Congress Cataloging in Publication Data

Kamieniecki, Sheldon.
  Party identification, political behavior, and the American electorate.

  (Contributions in political science, ISSN 0147-1066 ; no. 125)
  Bibliography: p.
  Includes index.
  1. Party affiliation—United States. I. Title.
II. Series.
JK2271.K36   1985   324.973   84-15692
ISBN 0-313-24358-1 (lib. bdg.)

Copyright © 1985 by Sheldon Kamieniecki

All rights reserved. No portion of this book may be reproduced, by any process or technique, without the express written consent of the publisher.

Library of Congress Catalog Card Number: 84-15692
ISBN: 0-313-24358-1
ISSN: 0147-1066

First published in 1985

Greenwood Press
A division of Congressional Information Service, Inc.
88 Post Road West
Westport, Connecticut 06881

Printed in the United States of America

10 9 8 7 6 5 4 3 2 1

To G. Barbot, M. Bogard, M. Clarke, S. Cohen, R. O'Brien, T. Roskin, and N. Shargel; *for their friendship and support*

CONTENTS

Figures and Tables	ix
Preface	xiii
Introduction: On the Search for Party Identification in the National Election Studies Heinz Eulau	3
1. A Reassessment of Party Identification	14
2. Social Background and Party Identification	37
3. Party Identification and Orientation toward the Political System	81
4. Views on Groups and Issues	118
5. Party and Candidate Evaluations	147
6. Electoral Behavior	168
7. Observations and Conclusions	201
Bibliography	211
Index	223

FIGURES AND TABLES

FIGURES

1-1	The Seven-Point Party Identification Scale	16
1-2	Three Dimensions of Party Identification	29
2-1	The Results of Weisberg's Factor Analysis of Fourteen Party Identification Measures, January–February, 1980	40
2-2	Values of Eleven Party Identification Measures	45

TABLES

1-1	Stability and Change in Party Identification, 1956	17
1-2	Percentage of Electorate Identifying with a Political Party, 1952–1980	18
2-1	Factor Loadings of Weisberg's Party Identification Measures, Pre-Election Survey, 1980	42
2-2	Factor Loadings of Eleven Different Party Identification Measures, Pre-Election Survey, 1980	44
2-3	Pearson Correlations between Race, Age, and Party Identification, Pre-Election Survey, 1980	48
2-4	Pearson Correlations between Age and Party Identification for Blacks and Whites, Pre-Election Survey, 1980	52
2-5	Statistical Significance of Region by Party Identification, Pre-Election Survey, 1980	55

2-6	Statistical Significance of Religion and Opinion on the Bible by Party Identification, 1980	59
2-7	Pearson Correlations between Importance of Religion and Party Identification for Protestants and Catholics, 1980	61
2-8	Pearson Correlations between Party Identification and Attitudes toward the Moral Majority, Post-Election Survey, 1980	62
2-9	Pearson Correlations between Party Identification and Attitudes toward the Moral Majority for Protestants and Catholics, Post-Election Survey, 1980	64
2-10	Pearson Correlations between Parents' and Respondents' Party Identification, Pre-Election Survey, 1980	65
2-11	Pearson Correlations between Family Income, the Duncan SEI, Education, and Party Identification, Pre-Election Survey, 1980	68
2-12	Tau-C Correlations between Class Self-Identification and Party Identification, Pre-Election Survey, 1980	71
2-13	Multivariate Analysis between Social Background and Party Identification, Pre-Election Survey, 1980	72
3-1	Tau-C Correlations between Party Identification and Interest in Political Campaign, Post-Election Survey, 1980	83
3-2	Pearson Correlations between Party Identification and Concern over Election Outcome, Pre-Election Survey, 1980	85
3-3	Tau-C Correlations between Party Identification and Attentiveness to Printed Media, Post-Election Survey, 1980	89
3-4	Tau-C Correlations between Party Identification and Attentiveness to Electronic Media, Post-Election Survey, 1980	90
3-5	Pearson Correlations between Party Identification and Knowledge about Presidential Candidates, Pre-Election Survey, 1980	92
3-6	Pearson Correlations between Party Identification and Whether People Watched the Carter-Reagan Debate, Post-Election Survey, 1980	94
3-7	Statistical Significance of Party Identification by Perceived Outcome of the Carter-Reagan Debate, Post-Election Survey, 1980	96
3-8	Pearson Correlations between Party Identification and Whether Carter or Reagan Won the Debate, Post-Election Survey, 1980	97
3-9	Pearson Correlations between Party Identification and Party System Support, Pre-Election Survey, 1980	101
3-10	Pearson Correlations between Party Identification and Attitudes toward the Parties, Pre-Election Survey, 1980	103
3-11	Tau-C Correlations between Party Identification and How Often People Can Trust Government in Washington to Do What Is Right, Pre-Election Survey, 1980	108

3-12	Pearson Correlations between Party Identification, for Whom Is Government Run, and Whether Government Is Run by Mostly Smart People, Pre-Election Survey, 1980	109
3-13	Pearson Correlations between Party Identification and Political Efficacy, Post-Election Survey, 1980	110
4-1	Pearson Correlations between Party Identification and Attitudes toward Hispanics and Blacks, Post-Election Survey, 1980	120
4-2	Pearson Correlations between Party Identification and Attitudes toward Labor Unions and Big Business, Post-Election Survey, 1980	122
4-3	Pearson Correlations between Party Identification and Attitudes toward Older People and People on Welfare, Post-Election Survey, 1980	124
4-4	Pearson Correlations between Party Identification and Attitudes toward Civil Rights Leaders, Post-Election Survey, 1980	126
4-5	Pearson Correlations between Party Identification and Government Spending, Pre-Election Survey, 1980	130
4-6	Pearson Correlations between Party Identification, Aid to Minorities, and Government Power, Post-Election Survey, 1980	132
4-7	Pearson Correlations between Party Identification and Public Opinion on Employment, 1980	134
4-8	Tau-C Correlations between Party Identification and Civil Rights, Post-Election Survey, 1980	136
4-9	Tau-C Correlations between Party Identification and the Equal Rights Amendment, Post-Election Survey, 1980	137
4-10	Pearson Correlations between Party Identification and Ideology, Pre-Election Survey, 1980	140
5-1	Tau-C Correlations between Party Identification and Handling of War and the Economy by Parties, Pre-Election Survey, 1980	149
5-2	Tau-C Correlations between Party Identification and Carter's Handling of Inflation and Unemployment, Pre-Election Survey, 1980	152
5-3	Tau-C Correlations between Party Identification and Carter's Handling of the Soviet Union's Invasion of Afghanistan and the Iranian Hostage Crisis, Pre-Election Survey, 1980	154
5-4	Tau-C Correlations between Party Identification and Carter's Job Approval Rating, Pre-Election Survey, 1980	156
5-5	Pearson Correlations between Party Identification and Personal Qualities of Reagan, Pre-Election Survey, 1980	158
5-6	Pearson Correlations between Party Identification and Personal Qualities of Carter, Pre-Election Survey, 1980	159

xii   Figures and Tables

5-7   Tau-C Correlations between Party Identification and Qualifications of Reagan, Pre-Election Survey, 1980   161
5-8   Tau-C Correlations between Party Identification and Qualifications of Carter, Pre-Election Survey, 1980   162
5-9   Pearson Correlations between Party Identification and Perceived Outcome of the Presidential Election, Pre-Election Survey, 1980   163
6-1   Pearson Correlations between Party Identification and Whether Respondents Tried to Persuade Others to Vote a Certain Way, Post-Election Survey, 1980   171
6-2   Pearson Correlations between Party Identification and Campaign Contributions, Post-Election Survey, 1980   172
6-3   Pearson Correlations between Party Identification and Campaign Activity, Post-Election Survey, 1980   173
6-4   Tau-C Correlations between Party Identification and Past Frequency of Voting, Pre-Election Survey, 1980   177
6-5   Pearson Correlations between Party Identification and Voter Registration, Validation Study, 1980   178
6-6   Pearson Correlations between Party Identification and Voting Behavior in Primaries, Validation Study, 1980   180
6-7   Pearson Correlations between Party Identification and Voter Turnout in General Election, Validation Study, 1980   181
6-8   Pearson Correlations between Party Identification and Two-Party Vote Choice, Post-Election Survey, 1980   184
6-9   Proportion of Variance in Two-Party Presidential Vote Accounted for by Seven-Point Party Identification Scale and Party Difference Index, 1964–1980   185
6-10 Pearson Correlations between Party Identification and Past Party Voting for President, Pre-Election Survey, 1980   187
6-11 Pearson Correlations between Party Identification and Vote Switching, Post-Election Survey, 1980   189
6-12 Pearson Correlations between Party Identification and Split Ticket Voting at the State and Local Level, Post-Election Survey, 1980   192
6-13 Pearson Correlations between Party Identification and Split Ticket Voting at the National Level, Post-Election Survey, 1980   194

PREFACE

I was first introduced to the concept of party identification in the early 1970s when I was an undergraduate at the State University of New York at Buffalo. I was taking a course on voting behavior from Jim Stimson at the time, and *The American Voter* was one of the assigned readings. Several class discussions centered on Angus Campbell and his associates' notion of party identification. Their theory and data suggested that a psychological attachment to a political party was formed in early adulthood, was deeply rooted, and endured throughout one's life. The empirical evidence offered by Campbell and his colleagues linking party identification with the vote choice was impressive, and both their conceptualization and operationalization of the concept seemed compelling. I soon embraced their seven-point party identification scale and, like most other researchers, have used it regularly in my work.

Within the last few years a number of political scientists have challenged the Michigan school's operationalization and conceptualization of party identification. Because of my earlier training and socialization, it was difficult for me to question the assumptions on which the concept and standard measure were based. However, John Petrocik's study pointing to the intransitivities of the standard seven-point scale and Richard Katz's findings suggesting that party identification might actually be multidimensional rather than unidimensional (as first thought) forced me to begin rethinking the theoretical and empirical premises on which the concept was based. My doubts about the validity and reliability of the traditional party identification measure grew after reading articles by other well-respected scholars in the field. Herbert Weisberg's formulation and application of a new multidimensional model of party orientation, in particular, had a tremendous impact on my beliefs concerning the concept. It was his excellent

Political Behavior article that led me to explore the debate over the conceptualization and measurement of party identification more closely.

This book reports the findings of a broad and extensive study on the validity of the standard seven-point party identification and four-point partisan strength scales. The book begins with a comprehensive review of the literature in the area, with particular attention paid to the criticisms of the Michigan school's earlier work. Using data collected in the 1980 SRC/CPS pre- and post-election surveys, Weisberg's multidimensional model is reexamined and restructured. Criterion variable analysis is used to assess the external validity of his alternative party identification measures versus the standard measures. A wide range of variables considered to be theoretically related to party affiliation are examined, including demographic, socioeconomic, attitudinal, and behavioral factors. In short, there are three major findings: (1) party identification consists of three dimensions—partisan direction, partisan strength, and party independence, (2) a party difference index and not the standard seven-point scale is the best measure of partisan direction, while the old four-point partisan strength scale and a new strength of independence scale are the best indicators of strength of identification and political independence, respectively, and (3) partisan strength and independence do not fall along the same continuum as commonly assumed and, rather, represent two separate dimensions. As the reader will see, the empirical evidence supporting these conclusions is overwhelming.

I would like to take this opportunity to thank several individuals and institutions for their help. I would like to thank Heinz Eulau for publishing Weisberg's article in *Political Behavior* and writing the book's Introduction which explains the development of the new party identification questions included in the 1980 SRC/CPS study. His Introduction draws upon his firsthand experience while Chair of the National Board of Overseers for the 1980 election study. I am also deeply indebted to Robert O'Brien and Herbert Weisberg for carefully reading and commenting on a draft of the book. Their suggestions were insightful and helpful. It was Weisberg who persuaded me to place greater emphasis on the bidimensionality of partisan strength and independence. Jody Battles must be rewarded for her diligent typing and patience, especially after the diskette containing the first chapter was destroyed by a faulty disk drive. A Haynes Foundation Fellowship facilitated my analysis and writing. The book could not have been completed without the aid of the computer center's staff at the University of Southern California. And, most of all, I owe a great deal of gratitude to my wife, Eliz Sanasarian, for tolerating my moodiness throughout the project.

*PARTY IDENTIFICATION,
POLITICAL BEHAVIOR,
AND THE AMERICAN ELECTORATE*

INTRODUCTION: ON THE SEARCH FOR PARTY IDENTIFICATION IN THE NATIONAL ELECTION STUDIES

HEINZ EULAU

Big research is cooperative research. It also is expensive. If in the social sciences most research is neither big nor cooperative, it is because it has been and largely continues to be underfunded. One of the few big and cooperative research projects in the social sciences, supported by the National Science Foundation, is the National Election Studies, conducted by the Center for Political Studies (CPS), University of Michigan, in collaboration, at any given point in time, with several dozen investigators at many universities and, over time, hundreds of other scholars who make use of the survey data on citizen behavior during the country's biennial congressional and quadrennial presidential elections. Sheldon Kamieniecki's *Party Identification, Political Behavior, and the American Electorate* is one of the book-length studies made possible by the National Election Studies. As, over the last eight years, I served on the Board of Overseers for the Studies and gained some insight into the conduct of big and cooperative social science research, it gives me great pleasure to introduce Professor Kamieniecki's book.[1]

I want to take this opportunity to make some observations especially on the collaborative aspects of the enterprise. While, in text and footnotes, Kamieniecki generously acknowledges the published contributions of many scholars to our understanding of electoral behavior and electoral processes, there exists an "underworld" of contributors to the design and execution of the National Election Studies that deserves some public recognition. This is particularly true in regard to the central topic of this book, an exploration of the causes and consequences of party identification in the voting behavior of the American electorate. Both as a concept in political theory and as an instrument in electoral research, the "party identification scale" (PID scale) long used in the National

Election Studies (NES) has been the target of scientific criticism, the object of possible improvement, and a topic for defense. Kamieniecki reviews some aspects of this matter in his first chapter.

My task here is to report and reflect on PID-related discussions which occurred within the NES Board of Overseers and its work groups, and between the Board and the relevant national community of scholars, in the four years prior to the 1980 election. This review, I hope, will provide more insight than published research can into the complex of considerations that culminated in the treatment of PID in the 1980 NES survey. Although some of these considerations are implicit or explicit in Kamieniecki's book and in the publications of many other scholars, telling the "whole story" requires a step-by-step report on the proceedings behind the story.

National election studies, as Kamieniecki indicates, were conducted by a team of Michigan-based social scientists from 1948 on, and their books and numerous articles reporting on their findings had an enormous impact on the scientific study of electoral behavior and elections in the United States and abroad.[2] While occasionally a few other scholars participated in designing the earlier studies, on the whole the scholarly community was primarily a consumer and not a direct participant in the research conducted by Angus Campbell, Philip E. Converse, Warren E. Miller, and Donald E. Stokes. It was not until 1976 that the idea of making NES a truly "national resource" in all phases of research, from design to ultimate execution, became a new reality. To make it so required not only long-range funding of an order of magnitude that would guarantee the continuity of NES but also an effort to draw the relevant national community of scholars into its organizational ambit. In fact, long-range funding by the National Science Foundation (NSF) was predicated on the cooptation of a very large cadre of scientists into the enterprise. Big research and cooperative research were seen to go hand-in-hand.

In retrospect, the effort required to organize the national scholarly community for collaborative work may seem relatively easy, but at the time the road ahead was less than clear. I remember receiving in late spring, 1976, a call from Warren Miller, then and now the driving force in NES, asking me to serve on a committee or "board" that would have to "oversee" the NES if NSF funding on a long-term basis were to be obtained. "What kind of board?" I asked. "Not at all clear," he said. "How much work will it involve?" I asked. "Not at all clear," he again said. The "board" was something NSF wanted, but I think that neither the Foundation, nor Miller as principal investigator, nor those of us invited to serve on this "board," had a clear idea of just what it was supposed to do. There are, in the academic world as in the worlds of business and government, all kinds of boards—some running things and others rubber-stamping them. What this NES board would be doing was a matter in a future that was not known.

I shall concentrate on that part of the "whole story" especially germane to the topic of Kamieniecki's book, at the risk of neglecting the larger context of other concerns within which the early discussions about PID took place.[3] The story begins in late summer, 1976, when a national advisory group of social scientists was convened in Ann Arbor to aid in formulating and drafting a proposal for long-term NSF support of NES.[4] In a first effort to permit the relevant research community to have an "input" into the proposal, members of the advisory group individually contacted a great number of research scholars across the country for suggestions on their needs and priorities in the field of electoral studies. Some seventy scholars responded, including many who were sensitive to some of the problems with the PID scale and other measures of partisanship—a sensitivity that had also become evident in various publications cited by Kamieniecki. As a result, and not surprisingly, the proposal submitted to NSF in January, 1977, took cautious note of the problems involved: "A ready remedy may not be forthcoming, but an attempt to create new measures relevant to the several different dimensions of party identification would seem to be a reasonable responsibility of the CPS election studies."

The proposal then recommended that, with the data available from prior studies, "a small group of substantively interested and methodologically talented researchers should be commissioned to design exploratory research directed at improving our measurement of the many-faceted concept that is so important to most electoral analysis." Indeed, the proposal budget included an item for theory-driven methodological research on PID, but at its June, 1977, meeting the advisory group, soon to become the NES Board of Overseers, decided not to begin with a "small group" addressing the problems involved but rather, as part of an effort to draw the entire research community into the design of the 1980 study, to hold a series of major research conferences, including one on PID, to be held in the course of the 1977–78 academic year.

In preparation for the PID conference, Board members Kristi Andersen (Ohio State University) and Heinz Eulau (Stanford University) wrote a "stimulus memorandum" which was sent to several hundred investigators who were asked to respond with relevant "idea memos." On the basis of these memos some twenty persons were to be selected for a conference on PID to be held at Florida State University in Tallahassee in February, 1978. The stimulus memorandum suggested four conference sessions on these topics: (1) the problem of conceptualization as "a necessary first step in a reexamination of relevant research and of the theoretical and technical questions that have been raised in recent years"; (2) the findings concerning party identification "in comparative transnational research which have been the source of much discomfort to political analysts"; (3) the question of "how changes in research design might help to untangle the causal and temporal relationship among partisan preference, attitudes on issues, group identifications and vote choice"; and (4) "some of the more immediately technical issues of concern in regard to voting behavior. . . . Because the measure of party identification is so simple and has 'worked' so well in many instances, some of the very simple technical questions have not been asked."

Altogether, thirty-two memoranda on PID, several co-authored, were received in response to the stimulus letter, and twenty-one persons could be invited.[5] (Budget limitations did not permit inviting all those who had responded.) On the basis of the responses received, Andersen and I prepared a second memorandum that summarized all comments and suggestions under four new headings which also constituted the final conference agenda: (1) "On the Conceptualization of Party Identification"; (2) "On the Measurement of Party Identification"; (3) "On Research Design Problems and Strategies"; and (4) "On Loose Ends and Future Possibilities." Some quotations from the summary memorandum convey the flavor of prevailing concerns:

. . . while it is unlikely that the discussion of theory and conceptualization can altogether avoid reference to the NES/CPS scale and other relevant variables, we would like to proceed in the first session as if these measures had never been invented, and as if new concepts and instruments had to be built from the ground up.

. . . we would hope that the critique of current familiar measures will not be an end in itself but rather the jumping-off point either for improvement and specification of the measures or for recommendations as to new measures.

. . . perusal of the memoranda shows that questions of research design, broadly conceived, are anchored in considerations of both theory and measurement. Vice versa, it is also quite clear that the solution of the most vexing theoretical and empirical measurement problems depends on alternatives of research design, notably the use of one or another form of panel design and possibly sub-sampling.

We have set aside the last session to pick up unexplored themes and to take a long look at the future of our joint enterprise as a whole. We hope that this session will contribute to overcoming the now familiar distinction between "they" (the Michigan crowd) and "us" (the rest of us).

I daresay that most of the PID conference participants significantly contributed to and benefited from the proceedings which were lively and informative. At the conclusion of the conference and again in a follow-up letter the participants were asked for "some very specific suggestions, either in regard to modifications of present measurement instruments or in regard to new questions which you would like to see included in the interview schedule. Please accompany each suggestion with a brief theoretical statement that would be helpful in appraising your suggestion." In fact, the Board received seventeen "priority memoranda" which met its request for very specific recommendations. The new set of memoranda was in turn summarized by Kristi Andersen who, interestingly, noted that while the memoranda suggested a host of innovations, "many conferees, in their post-Tallahassee communications, emphasized the importance of continuity in this area. Several defenses of the measure (the traditional PID scale) were provided, as well as some criticisms. Many of the memoranda also repeated a feeling, expressed at the conference, that the data we presently have has not been sufficiently exploited."[6]

With a wealth of ideas, suggestions, criticisms, and reaffirmations, the NES Board found itself in a kind of quandary on how to proceed next. Obviously, not all of the PID conference participants or others interested in PID could be individually consulted on every step of the research process. Moreover, the complex of problems connected with PID was part of a much larger configuration of concerns on the NES research agenda, including congressional elections, the measurement of policy issues, the question of candidate images and characteristics, and other matters. It became clear to the Board that its conference program might actually lead to counter-productive frustrations in the research community if no "research and development" (R and D) effort were made "in the field" that would constitute a follow-up to the conferences and a tryout of at least some of the suggestions made by conference participants.

As a R and D program would have to accommodate a heterogeneity of research interests, the Board decided to hold a workshop during the summer of 1978 that would bring together a number of scholars who had participated in one or another of the conferences and could be spokespersons for the various interests with a stake in NES. The workshop, it was thought, would also make the participants aware of the difficult choices that had to be made among competing interests if a R and D "pilot study" was to be fielded in time to be useful in preparing for the 1980 presidential election study. A Board subcommittee composed of John E. Jackson (then at the University of Pennsylvania), David O. Sears (University of California, Los Angeles), and Merrill Shanks (University of California, Berkeley) made arrangements for a R and D workshop that was held in Ann Arbor during August, 1978. The Tallahassee PID conference participants were represented by Richard Brody (Stanford), Jack Dennis (University of Wisconsin), Richard Niemi (Rochester), and Herbert Weisberg (Ohio State University). Again, in preparation for the workshop, the national research community was informed of the design options for the 1980 study which by now included the possibility of a year-long panel study beginning in January, 1980. A panel study was particularly pleasing to PID investigators because it might shed some light on the controversy concerning PID as a long- or short-term electoral force. In response to this latest communication the Board received ten more memoranda which, along with the dozens of others received earlier, gave the R and D workshop much to chew on. The workshop strongly recommended a pilot study that would be fielded in early 1979, provided funds (not then budgeted) could be found, as in fact they were.[7]

Following the R and D workshop, the participants were expected to submit concrete proposals for the pilot study, including interview time and personnel and budget estimates, and they were encouraged to seek the cooperation of other scholars, especially those who had attended one or another of the earlier conferences. At the same time, in October, 1978, the wider research community was informed of the impending pilot study and asked to make recommendations "for particular questions or measures which scholars may wish to see incorporated in the pre-test, pilot study or the 1980 schedule." This invitation yielded another nine memoranda, in addition to those prepared by the R and D workshop participants.

The R and D group reassembled in Ann Arbor in January, 1979, to finalize the contents of the Pilot Study (then written with capital letters). By this time the Board had come to the conclusion that the Pilot Study should emphasize new substantive content over sheer methodological experimentation because this seemed to promise more research payoff in the 1980 study. While some methodological work would have high priority, the focus of the Pilot Study thus shifted somewhat from what had been envisaged earlier. However, PID and partisanship-related questions were given some methodological priority.

The Pilot Study was crucial for the evolution of the partisanship measures that were used in the 1980 study. The pilot survey itself was conducted in two waves, the first between March 5 and 16, 1979, and the second (a reinterview wave) between March 26 and April 13, 1979. To accommodate as many new questions as possible, each wave provided for two half-samples.[8]

Of only concern here are the questions concerning PID and related matters that were in the Pilot Study or, finally, in the 1980 study that provides the data for Kamieniecki's analyses. It is important to point out that by no means all or most questions survived the Pilot Study test. But they are also not merely of archival interest. While some "bombed out" on being found inadequate, others had to be excluded from the 1980 study because of time restrictions in the interviews. Even the Pilot Study itself could not accommodate all suggestions. To appreciate individual contributions, let me briefly connect the new Pilot Study items with the post-workshop memoranda of the four R and D investigators who were mainly responsible for the party-related questions. While Kamieniecki properly credits Herbert Weisberg with influencing his own work on PID, the contributions of the R and D investigators should be recognized as well. In turn, it should be kept in mind that the four PID investigators—Brody, Dennis, Niemi, and Weisberg—benefited from the many memoranda received by the Board in the previous years and from the discussions at the Tallahassee PID conference as well as the R and D workshop. The whole operation was an overtime collaborative enterprise.

Several of the party-related questions in the Pilot Study were questions asked in earlier NES surveys, and I shall not deal with them. The most important innovations were the following:

1. Brody recommended a series of probes following the traditional PID scale. As inspection of the interview schedule shows, several other closed items attached to the scale also satisfied some of Dennis' recommendations for open-ended probes, notably on "partisan support" and "partisan behavior." Some of these items also met Niemi's (and his collaborator Richard Katz's) quest for more information on the parental partisanship of the respondents and past party switching—the so-called recall questions (Wave I, Form A; Wave II, Form B).

2. Brody recommended exploration of partisan attitudes by way of a pair-

wise semantic differential technique which also, in part, met a Dennis recommendation for "projective tests" on partisan symbols and respondent reactions to reference words associated with the parties. For instance, respondents were confronted with terms like "fair-unfair," "weak-strong," or "honest-dishonest," and so on, and were asked to locate Democrats, Republicans, or Independents in one of seven boxes along a continuum from one extreme to the other (Wave II, Forms A and B).

3. Finally, Brody persuaded the R and D group to include two items which would get at what is called "affective preference." In their Pilot Study version these items were (Wave II, Form A):

When it comes to politics, would you say that most of your friends are Republicans, Democrats, independents, or what?

If you're free to choose, would you say that you would rather discuss politics with a Republican, a Democrat, or an independent?

4. Dennis argued for a distinction to be made between "party identification" and "party support," and the battery of new questions used in the Pilot Study reflected his and others' concerns. The battery first asked the respondent whether he/she thought of himself/herself as a "supporter of one of the political parties," then about which party, and finally about the degree of support (on a seven-point scale). Non-supporters were asked to locate themselves on a seven-point "closeness scale." Similar questions were asked of Independents. The battery sought to separate partisanship and independence in connection with "support" but not, it should be emphasized, "identification." A slightly revised version of the battery was included in the 1980 study and is used by Kamieniecki in his research (Wave I, Form B; Wave II, Form A).

5. Dennis also recommended inclusion of a series of Likert-type agree-disagree scale items related to partisanship previously used in a number of Wisconsin surveys. Eleven of these items were included in the Pilot Study (Wave I, Form B; Wave II, Form A), and a few survived testing and found their way into the 1980 study.

6. Dennis and Weisberg advocated experimentation with an application of the "feeling thermometer" technique in the partisan context. Earlier NES surveys had asked respondents to express their feelings on the thermometer concerning "Democrats" and "Republicans" but not concerning the "Democratic *party*" and "Republican *party*." The Pilot Study, to make comparison of these versions possible, included both the older version concerning "persons" (Wave I, Form A) and the new "party version" (Wave I, Form B). As it turned out, the change in stimuli did not reveal systematic or significant differences between the two versions. While cognitive differentiation was expected, the difference in stimuli was evidently too small to discriminate in the responses of the public. Nevertheless, the new "party version" was taken over into the 1980 study and is used by Kamieniecki.

7. As Weisberg's work on the problem of dimensionality in the traditional PID scale shows, the technical issues involved are several and, in fact, had been topics of discussion in many of the memoranda received by the Board and at the Tallahassee PID conference. There is no need for me to rehearse these issues, referred to by Kamieniecki in his text, except to point out that Weisberg, in the article reporting results from the first 1980 NES panel, generously acknowledges the contributions made by such Tallahassee participants as John Van Wingen, David Valentine, Richard Katz, Randall Guynes, and others working in the field.[9] Weisberg thus acted as an agent for many others by introducing a simple seven-point scale—ranging from "strong Republicans" at one end to "strong Democrats" at the opposite end. "Some people think of themselves as strong Democrats, some as strong Republicans, and others somewhere in between. Where would you place yourself on this scale?" (See Waves I and II, Forms A and B.) Two things should be noted. First, the concept of "independents" is not used, so that it can only be inferred that respondents clustering around the scale's "neutral" midpoint might be "independents." Second, the Pilot Study investigators evidently thought the question important enough to be included in both waves and on both forms. The measure did not "work" and was not included in the 1980 study. In fact, Weisberg, and now Kamieniecki, construct a "party difference" measure based on respondent scores on the feeling thermometers.

There were, of course, many other ideas about question wording and about alternative or new questions which, throughout the R and D period, were discussed by the Board, the workshop group, and, finally, the 1980 study committee including, in addition to Board members Jackson, Sears, and Shanks, also Brody, Dennis, and Donald Kinder (then of Yale). To be a bit jocular about it all, I formulated at the time "Eulau's Law of Variable Proliferation." The law states that the greater the number of investigators in a research project, the greater the number of variables that enter the agenda of discovery. In fact, the law may have a polynomial function. As the reader will find, Kamieniecki "takes off" from thirteen different party-related measures made available by the 1980 NES study, reduces the number to eleven when two measures presumably linked to "party system support" do not pan out and, mercifully, comes back to three "factors" (partisan direction and strength, and independence). What all this disguises is that any number of good ideas did not get into the Pilot Study and others, included there, did not make their way into the 1980 surveys.

In any case, the 1980 Study Committee was considered the most suitable instrumentality for coordinating the work of all the R and D teams and evaluating their reports which were ready by the end of summer, 1979. In regard to the latter, the Study Committee's task was to develop a comprehensive and theoretically integrated interview schedule. The Committee, perhaps unbelievable to believe, met six times to accomplish its work. It had at its disposal, as far as PID is concerned, four reports analyzing the Pilot Study data. The reports were written by: Brody, "Measuring of Party Identification in the 1979 Pilot

Study," July 29, 1979; Dennis, "An Analysis of Some Measures of Partisanship Using the Pilot Study Data," August 10, 1979; Niemi, Katz, and Newman, "Reconstructing Past Partisanship: The Failure of the Party Identification Recall Questions," August 7, 1979; and Weisberg and Boyd, "Report on Party Identification Questions in Pilot Study," August 7, 1979. I mention these reports to point out, especially to those not familiar with the ways in which a collaborative national research project progresses, that the inclusion or exclusion of questions is not whimsical but based on the most careful scrutiny of test results.

While not whimsical, decisions concerning inclusion or exclusion must to a certain degree be "arbitrary" in the sense of being discretionary; they are arbitrated decisions following certain decision rules. It may be useful to quote here from the NES Board's *Annual Report for 1979–80*:

> In making its decisions concerning new study content or changes in the measurement of "old" variables, the Board was guided by a number of decision rules that should be clearly understood. First, relevant proposals concerning new content had to have passed the iron test of having been pretested and having been demonstrated to yield valid and reliable analytic results. Findings from the Pilot Study but also findings from other studies served as bases for judgment as to whether a questionnaire item or series of items should be included or omitted. Second, changes in the wording of "old" items, especially those defined as core, were made only if the results of pretesting indicated that change would improve measurement without losing conceptual equivalence—the latter being necessary to safeguard the continuity and integrity of the NES time series. Third, if time constraints on the questionnaire seemed to call for the elimination of an item, the implications of omission for the research interests of particular individuals in the research community were considered with great seriousness. . . . The Board does not expect that all scholars will agree with its decisions, and it may well be that, on some exclusions, the Board erred in its "judgment calls." We can only assure the scholarly community that the 1980 Study Committee and the Board tried to arrive at their own best judgments, even if some others might have arrived at other judgments.[10]

The rest is now history. As Kamieniecki's book and many other publications show, the study of American elections, electoral processes, and electoral behavior has been well served by a project that, like NES, is both big and cooperative. This is not to say that NES can or should take responsibility for all the research based on the data, or that there do not remain numerous theoretical, methodological, and substantive problems to be tackled. Kamieniecki's book is a further contribution to the collaborative enterprise in electoral research. As he makes abundantly clear, his own work would have been impossible without the big and collaborative "national resource" that NES is. If I stress this theme so much, it is because in no other of the many fields of political science has so much progress been made, not only because the necessary resources have not been mobilized, but also because research has not been collaborative.

In conclusion I should also mention that work on this scale would be impossible without the assistance of a skilled and devoted staff. In connection with the Pilot and 1980 surveys, Maria Sanchez was mainly responsible for the proper formatting of the questions, Jeanne Castro for supervising the field operations, and Ann Robinson, as study manager, for keeping the total enterprise together. In the end, all students of electoral behavior are in deep debt to Warren Miller who, as Director of the Center for Political Studies and principal investigator of the National Election Studies for three decades, has had the rare ability to "think big and cooperative." Anyone interested in understanding what "thinking big and cooperative" in research means should read Miller's presidential address to the American Political Science Association.[11]

NOTES

1. For a recent appraisal of the importance of electoral research, see Philip E. Converse, Heinz Eulau, and Warren E. Miller, "The Study of Voting," in Robert McC. Adams, Neil J. Smelser, and Donald J. Treiman, eds., *Behavioral and Social Science Research* (Washington, D.C.: National Academy Press, 1982), Vol. 2, pp. 33–75.

2. See Angus Campbell, Gerald Gurin, and Warren E. Miller, *The Voter Decides* (Evanston, Ill.: Row Peterson, 1954); Angus Campbell, Philip E. Converse, Warren E. Miller, and Donald E. Stokes, *The American Voter* (New York: John Wiley and Sons, 1960); Angus Campbell, Philip E. Converse, Warren E. Miller, and Donald E. Stokes, *Elections and the Political Order* (New York: John Wiley and Sons, 1966); Philip E. Converse, *The Dynamics of Party Support* (Beverly Hills, Calif.: Sage Publications, 1976); and Warren E. Miller and Teresa E. Levitin, *Leadership and Change: The New Politics and the American Electorate* (Cambridge, Mass.: Winthrop Publishers, 1976).

3. Interested readers can get a feeling for this context by consulting the *Annual Reports* of the NES Board of Overseers for 1977–78, 1978–79, and 1979–80, obtainable from the Center for Political Studies, University of Michigan, P. O. Box 1248, Ann Arbor, Michigan, 48106.

4. Members of the advisory group were Kristi Andersen, Ohio State University; James Davis, Dartmouth College; Heinz Eulau (Chair), Stanford University; Richard F. Fenno, University of Rochester; Benjamin I. Page, University of Chicago; David O. Sears, University of California, Los Angeles; J. Merrill Shanks, University of California, Berkeley; John Sprague, Washington University; and Edward R. Tufte, Princeton University. Some of these members have since changed their university affiliations.

5. Actually, in addition to Board members, twenty-five persons attended. The invited participants were: Herbert B. Asher, Ohio State University; Paul Allen Beck, University of Pittsburgh; Richard A. Brody, Stanford University; William Claggett, University of Mississippi; Jack Dennis, University of Wisconsin; Bernard Grofman, University of California, Irvine; Randall Guynes, Emory University; John E. Jackson, University of Pennsylvania; Kenneth Janda, Northwestern University; J. Paul Johnston, University of Alberta; Richard S. Katz, Johns Hopkins University; David Knoke, Indiana University; Milton Lodge, State University of New York, Stony Brook; William T. McAllister, University of Chicago; Richard G. Niemi, University of Rochester; Helmut Norpoth, University of Arizona; Jerry Perkins, Georgia State University; Gerald M. Pomper, Rutgers State University; Bradley Richardson, Ohio State University; Steven Rood, Boston University; W. Phillips Shively, University of Minnesota; James A. Stimson, Florida State University; David Valentine, Missouri Senate Research; John R. Van Wingen,

University of Southern Mississippi; and Herbert F. Weisberg, Ohio State University. Several of these persons have since changed their institutional affiliation.

    6. For a report on the Tallahassee Party Identification Conference, see *PS* Vol. 11 (Spring 1978), pp. 241–42.

    7. For "Report on Workshop Preparing for 1980 Presidential Election," see *PS* Vol. 11 (Fall 1978), pp. 504–5.

    8. For a report on the Pilot Study, see *PS* Vol. 12 (Spring 1979), pp. 210–11.

    9. Herbert F. Weisberg, "A Multidimensional Conceptualization of Party Identification," *Political Behavior* Vol. 2 No. 1 (1980), pp. 33–60.

    10. Board of Overseers, National Election Studies, *Annual Report for 1979–80* (June 1, 1980), pp. 12–13.

    11. Warren E. Miller, "The Role of Research in the Unification of A Discipline," *American Political Science Review* Vol. 75 (March 1981), pp. 9–16.

1
A REASSESSMENT OF PARTY IDENTIFICATION

Survey findings are being reported in the media more often now than ever before. Obviously, the media gatekeepers believe that Americans are interested in learning about what is on the public's mind. An increase in the accuracy of survey results also explains why reporters are willing to communicate such information. Improvements in questionnaire design, selection of samples, and the administration of surveys over the last three decades have enhanced the precision of surveys. In addition, recent breakthroughs in computer technology allow researchers to analyze huge data bases quickly and efficiently. These developments helped the television networks declare Ronald Reagan the winner in the 1980 presidential race even before the polls had closed in many western states.

Perhaps no other institution has contributed more to the advancement of survey research than the University of Michigan at Ann Arbor. Since 1948 the Survey Research Center (SRC) and, more recently, the Center for Political Studies (CPS) at the University of Michigan have conducted national surveys during each presidential and (since 1958) congressional election year.[1] These in-depth studies seek to elicit the political attitudes and behavior along with the demographic background of a scientifically selected random sample of adults. Although each survey represents only a snapshot of the political mood of the country at one point in time, when analyzed together these studies can provide us with insights into past, present, and future trends. Political scientists have recognized the tremendous value of the SRC/CPS surveys and have written hundreds of convention papers, journal articles, and books using the data collected in these studies.

THE ORIGIN OF PARTY IDENTIFICATION

From the beginning the Michigan researchers believed that people's psychological attachment to a political party could tell us a great deal about their political orientations and behavior.[2] In explaining the concept of party identification in *The American Voter* (published in 1960), Angus Campbell, Philip Converse, Warren Miller, and Donald Stokes wrote:

Only in the exceptional case does the sense of individual attachment to party reflect a formal membership or an active connection with a party apparatus. Nor does it simply denote a voting record, although the influence of party allegiance on electoral behavior is strong. Generally this tie is a psychological identification, which can persist without legal recognition or evidence of formal membership and even without a consistent record of party support . . . the strength and direction of party identification are facts of central importance in accounting for attitude and behavior.[3]

They went on to discuss how party identification was related to the way people psychologically attach themselves to a group.[4] The group in their study, of course, was a political party.

A measure of party identification was included in the 1952 and 1956 SRC/CPS National Election Studies. Campbell and his colleagues analyzed the data collected in these two surveys in *The American Voter* and found that party identification was an accurate predictor of the vote and that it was rather stable across people's lives. As they demonstrated in their book, these findings had important implications for a wide variety of political questions. The results of their investigation had a profound impact on democratic theory and on voting behavior research for the next twenty years. Their findings concerning party identification catapulted them into the forefront of the behavioral revolution in political science.

Recently, however, a number of political scientists have questioned the manner in which party identification has been conceptualized and measured by the Michigan research team. The purpose of this chapter is to review the characteristics of the present measure and criticisms against it. This book has three main objectives. First, we want to learn more about the social background, attitudes, and behavior of partisans and Independents. In other words, we wish to discover who they are, what they think, and how they behave. Second, this study examines whether strength of identification and political independence are one component of party identification as commonly believed, or whether they are two separate entities. Third, we want to determine whether a rival conceptualization leads to a better measure of party identification. This will be done by comparing various measures of this concept throughout the study. As will soon be shown, the standard model has certain definite advantages. Thus, if the new measures are more accurate, a judgment will be made at the conclusion of the book as to whether the amount of improved measurement achieved justifies the replacement of the traditional model with a revised one.

THE STANDARD OPERATIONALIZATION OF PARTY IDENTIFICATION

The standard operationalization of party identification is fairly straightforward. Interviewers first ask respondents: "Generally speaking, do you usually think of yourself as a Republican, a Democrat, an Independent, or what?" Respondents who say they are either Republicans or Democrats are then asked if they would call themselves "strong" or "not very strong" identifiers. Those who consider themselves to be Independents are asked if they feel closer to either the Republican or Democratic parties. (Respondents who are neither partisans nor Independents are classified as such.) The resulting seven-point party identification scale appears in Figure 1–1. This measure was used extensively to explain public attitudes and electoral behavior in *The American Voter* and subsequent works.

Figure 1-1
The Seven-Point Party Identification Scale

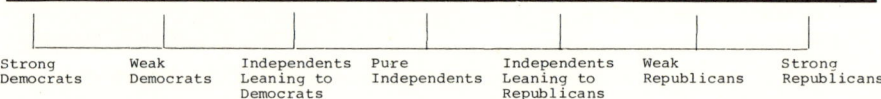

THE STABILITY OF PARTY IDENTIFICATION

Campbell and his associates also showed how Americans' party identification remains relatively stable over time. As Table 1–1 reveals, those who identified with a political party rarely switched their affiliation. The greatest propensity to switch was found among those individuals whose party attachment was weakest.

The authors of *The American Voter* pointed out that "not all members of the electorate form strong party attachments . . . and they make up a sufficiently large proportion of the population to permit the short-term influence of political forces associated with issues and candidates to play a significant role in determining the outcome of specific elections."[5] Indeed, this was the case during the 1952 and 1956 presidential elections which they studied. As Table 1–2 shows, even though Democrats outnumbered Republicans in the electorate by a wide margin during the 1950s, the Republican presidential candidate, Dwight D. Eisenhower, was elected in 1952 and 1956. The General's tremendous popularity as a World War II hero led many people who were weak identifiers with the Democratic party to abandon their party temporarily and vote for him. In spite of this, the authors of *The American Voter* were able to demonstrate the stability of party identification and the strong influence it had on voting. They believed it was a "standing decision" which was not directly tied to immediate political events. It was considered to be a "long-term electoral force" as op-

Table 1-1
Stability and Change in Party Identification, 1956

	Strong Dem.	Weak Dem.	Ind. Dem.	Ind.	Ind. Rep.	Weak Rep.	Strong Rep.
Have not changed from one party to other*	93%	89%	69%	68%	55%	74%	85%
Were Rep., changed to Dem.	7	11	—	—	—	—	—
Were Rep., changed to Ind.	—	—	13	10	8	—	—
Were Dem., changed to Ind.	—	—	18	22	37	—	—
Were Dem., changed to Rep.	—	—	—	—	—	26	15
Number of cases	364	397	108	145	144	250	261

*Included here may be some people who moved from an Independent position to one of the parties. The interview does not permit the isolation of such cases.

Source: Angus Campbell, Philip E. Converse, Warren E. Miller, and Donald E. Stokes, *The American Voter* (New York: John Wiley and Sons, 1960), p. 148. Reprinted with permission of the publisher.

Table 1-2
Percentage of Electorate Identifying with a Political Party, 1952–1980

	1952	1956	1960	1964	1968	1972	1976	1980
Strong Democrat	22%	21%	21%	26%	20%	15%	15%	18%
Weak Democrat	25	23	25	25	25	25	25	23
Independent Leaning Democrat	10	7	8	9	10	11	12	11
Independent	5	8	8	8	11	13	14	13
Independent Leaning Republican	7	8	7	6	9	11	10	10
Weak Republican	14	14	13	13	14	13	14	14
Strong Republican	13	15	14	11	10	10	9	8
Apolitical/Don't know	4	3	4	2	1	2	1	2
Total percent	100%	100%	100%	100%	100%	100%	100%	99%*
Number of cases	1,614	1,772	3,021	1,571	1,553	2,705	2,869	1,613

Source: SRC/CPS Election Studies.

*Due to rounding error.

posed to a "short-term force," such as the state of the economy or various domestic and foreign policy issues.

These findings led Campbell, Converse, Miller, and Stokes to develop three classifications of presidential elections: maintaining, deviating, and realigning elections.[6] In a maintaining election "the pattern of partisan attachments prevailing in the preceding period persists" and the presidential candidate representing the majority party in the electorate wins as a result of partisan support.[7] Since the Great Depression in the early 1930s there have been more Democratic than Republican party identifiers among the population. Thus, the election of Democrat Jimmy Carter to the White House in 1976 was a maintaining one. A deviating election is one in which the presidential candidate representing the minority party in the electorate wins because short-term forces temporarily override standing partisan loyalties. The election of Republican Ronald Reagan to the presidency in 1980 was a deviating election.

Finally, in a realigning election politics is extremely salient.[8] The minority party in the electorate becomes the majority party and its presidential candidate is elected. Since this transformation does not take place suddenly but only after some time has passed, it is probably more accurate to refer to this unusual occurrence as a realigning electoral *era* instead of a realigning election. Prior to the Depression the Republican party was the majority party in the electorate. However, a large number of Americans blamed President Herbert Hoover and the Republican party for bringing about the Panic of 1929 and the economic strife that followed. Franklin Roosevelt, a Democrat, defeated President Hoover in 1932 and soon became known as the one who lifted America out of its severe economic condition. At the same time, a sufficient number of citizens developed a strong loyalty to the Democratic party to make it the majority party.[9] In summary, the suggestion of three classifications of presidential elections by Campbell and his colleagues underscored the confidence they had in both the predictive power and stability of party identification.

On the basis of survey data reflecting the stability of party identification and its high predictive character, Philip Converse developed the concept of the "normal vote" in 1966.[10] He recommended that researchers use party identification as a baseline against which to gauge variations in behavior. If there was a complete absence of short-term forces, one would expect the final vote in an election to represent directly the percentage of Republican and Democratic identifiers in the electorate. This would be a "normal" or "baseline" vote. Deviations from the norm would occur as a result of short-term forces in a specific election. Such short-term forces could be treated as residuals and studied for their unique contribution to the vote.

Returning to Table 1-2, however, one notices a change in the percentage of those calling themselves Independents beginning to take place between 1964 and 1968. While 22–23 percent of the electorate said they were Independents or leaning Independents between 1952 and 1964, 30 percent of the electorate reported they were Independents or leaning Independents in 1968. Moreover, this figure continues to rise after 1968. A decline in the percentage of party identifiers accompanies this trend. Today over one-third of the electorate do not identify with either of the two major parties.

The rise in the number of Independents beginning in the mid–1960s led some scholars to speculate that perhaps the turbulent civil rights movement, the strong opposition to America's involvement in the Vietnam War, and the general social unrest which characterized that period loosened party attachments. Clearly, these events touched the lives of a large number of Americans, generally in a negative way. Perhaps many felt that these incidents represented a failure on the part of the political parties and their candidates in particular, and the political system in general, to develop and implement acceptable and effective public policies. The younger generation especially seemed to feel this way, possibly explaining the sharp rise in the proportion of Independents among those first entering the electorate beginning in the mid–1960s.[11] Accompanying this trend was an increase in the number of people who were voting more on the basis of issues and less on the basis of their party affiliation. Party identification could no longer be considered the sole major determinant of the vote as it was in the 1950s. It now appeared to be a more immediate political variable than was first thought.[12]

The changes in party identification depicted in Table 1–2 forced researchers to reconsider the characteristics of the variable, especially the one concerning the stability of individuals' party attachments. Douglas Dobson and Douglas St. Angelo, for example, found that movements of party identifiers between parties or between strengths of identification were politically motivated.[13] Despite the fact that the level of party identification was stable from 1952 to 1964, there were still hidden shifts in the percentage identifying with each of the two major parties.[14] Edward Dreyer, however, concluded that changes in party affiliation were due to crude techniques of measurement.[15] Norman Nie, Sidney Verba, and John Petrocik believed that switching in party orientation was also due to the shortcomings of the measure as well as the inattentiveness of respondents.[16] But in three separate studies, Kenneth Meier, Richard Brody, and W. Phillips Shively uncovered patterns in party identification movements similar to those found by Dobson and St. Angelo.[17] Moreover, Richard Brody and Lawrence Rothenberg's analysis showed that voters' party identification is influenced by their evaluation of the candidates and the policy performance of the parties even during an election.[18] Research in the field indicates that party identification does respond to political stimuli.

There has also been research on the relationship between party identification and the presidential vote since 1952. John Kessel presented data that showed a continued close relationship between the two variables over time.[19] The strong association between party identification and presidential vote since 1952, however, hides the switching that has taken place among party identifiers and Independents. He also showed that strong Republicans have been more likely to support their presidential candidate than strong Democrats. Overall, the relationship between party affiliation and the vote "has been quite strong and remarkably stable in view of the variety of candidates and circumstances" that have characterized the elections over the years.[20]

SOCIALIZATION AND PARTY IDENTIFICATION

How do people come to identify with a political party? It is commonly believed that party identification originates in childhood and is largely acquired from one's parents. Although adults often identify with their parents' party, it remains unclear whether this is the result of direct transmission or because the children share their parents' social conditions along with many of their basic values. Admittedly, both of these processes might lead children to adopt the same party identification as their parents, however, in the latter case the affiliation (chosen at adulthood) might have greater political content.[21]

According to Shively, children and adult reports of party identification are fairly stable over time.[22] Yet, researchers have been unable to show a direct link between childhood party identification and adult party identification. M. Kent Jennings and Richard Niemi addressed this question in a panel study which followed a sample of adolescents aged 17 to 18 in 1965 through to 1973, when they were 25 to 26.[23] Along with this group, they studied a panel of respondents' parents over the same period of time. This strategy allowed them to learn the degree to which the party identification of individuals in their late childhood carried over into the early years of their adulthood. They found a moderate relationship between adolescent party identification and young adult party identification, and a strong relationship in the parents' party identification over the eight-year period. Although the moderate relationship indicates an association between childhood and adult party identification, it is still weak enough, compared to the stronger relationship for the sample of parents, to suggest that much of the formation of adult party identification may take place during the adult years.[24] Precisely how much of adult party identification can be traced to childhood is still uncertain, and other factors (such as important political events) appear to affect the formation of adult party identification.[25]

RETHINKING PARTY IDENTIFICATION

The discussion above suggests that the manner in which the Michigan researchers originally characterized party identification in *The American Voter* and other works was flawed. This is particularly true concerning the political nature of the variable. Anomalies found in the stability of party identification have sparked various attempts to reconsider the variable.

Positive Versus Negative Identification

Michael Maggiotto and James Piereson's investigation focused on the attitudes of Americans toward the opposition party.[26] They proposed a "hostility hypothesis"; party identification is inversely related to the degree of hostility left toward the opposition party.[2;,s7] The two researchers used the party "feeling thermometer" questions included in the SRC/CPS election surveys conducted between 1964 and 1974 to measure people's hostility toward the opposition party. The "feeling thermometer" questions permit respondents to rate the Republican and Democratic parties on scales ranging from zero to 100. Respondents who feel "cold" or unfavorable toward a party are asked to rate it between zero and 50 degrees while those who feel "warm" or favorable toward a party are asked to rate it between 50 and 100 degrees.[28] They found that evaluations of the opposition party—something the traditional seven-point scale did not pick up—were independent, long-term factors which enhance our ability to explain and predict voting behavior. Based on this finding they concluded that the standard measure has left the concept of party identification only partly specified and incompletely measured, and that an approach consisting of several items and not just one would be more appropriate.

Although Shively agreed that hostility influences voting behavior, he had reservations about including it conceptually as part of identification with a party.[29] He feared that adding hostility toward a party "might come dangerously close to transforming party identification simply into a bundle of important independent variables, which would predict well how people would vote but would not be sufficiently distinct from the vote itself to help much in the development of theory."[30]

A Weighted Sum of Past Political Experiences

A large body of research on elections has employed theories of rational political behavior.[31] Scholars working in this area assume that voters have specific goals in mind and will make decisions only after weighing the benefits and costs of alternatives. However, those in this field have encountered difficulty incorporating party identification as a long-term factor in their research since it was not clear how such a predisposition could further any specific aim. Partly because of this, Morris Fiorina proposed a conception of party identification based on a weighted average of past experiences with the Republican and Democratic parties.[32] His conception takes into account that people will have different experiences that will vary in influence on the decision to identify with either party. The role of adult political experiences is included in his approach. He has therefore

proposed a model of the individual voting decision that depends on the notion that citizens monitor party promises and performances over time, encapsulate their observations in a summary judgment termed 'party identification,' and rely on this core of previous experience when they assign responsibility for current societal conditions and evaluate ambiguous platforms designed to deal with uncertain futures.[33]

More explicitly, Fiorina defined party identification as:

Party identification with Democrats = Past political experiences with Democrats − Past political experiences with Republicans + gamma.

The term "gamma" represents "the effects not included directly in an individual's political experiences (e.g., parents' party ID)."[34] While he included hostility to the opposite party in his model, he did not recommend that hostility be a separate dimension. After analyzing his definition of party identification Shively said, "Casting the definition in a way which lets the variable be included easily in rational models is an important step forward, which may help to lessen the estrangement between theory and empirical research in this area."[35]

Party Identification Only as a Political Response

As stated earlier, any conception of party identification should include some element of response to immediate political stimuli. Some researchers, most of them European, have argued that party identification consists solely of an immediate political response, that it is only a restatement of how the person being interviewed intends to vote. We already knew that reports of party identification tended to be less stable in Europe than reports of party identification in the United States. David Butler and Donald Stokes, for example, found this to be true for the electorate in England.[36] They also found British voters were more likely than American voters to shift their partisan self-images in line with their electoral choice. For this and other reasons, condemned the use of the concept and measure in England.[37] Jacques Thomassen wrote that Ivor Crewe reports of party identification among the Dutch should be treated as the respondents' choice of which party they will vote for rather than the reverse.[38] Kenneth Meier suggested the same phenomenon was probably occurring even in the United States.[39]

It would be a mistake to treat party identification *only* as an immediate political response. Shively provided good evidence that "voting fluctuates much more than party identification does" and that "voting choice would not be an especially good predictor of party identification" in the United States.[40] As far as the European context is concerned, one must realize that unique historical circumstances have made it unnecessary for European voters to develop party affiliations as American voters have done. Certain events in European history have led to greater political and social class polarization there than in the United States. Consequently, many Europeans are class-conscious voters who have different class parties to choose from and support. Shively noted this was changing and that "we might expect in the future to see European voters develop (an) American style of party identification."[41] Kendall Baker observed this may now be happening in Germany.[42]

Party Identification in Behavioral Terms

Another way to conceptualize party identification is in behavioral terms. People could be classified as partisans and Independents based on their actual voting behavior rather than on their responses to survey questions. For instance, political scientists could define Independents as people who voted for a presidential candidate of a particular party in one election and voted for the presidential candidate of another party in the previous election. Those who voted for the presidential candidates of the same party in two succeeding elections would be partisans.[43] Or, researchers could classify people based on whether they voted for candidates of different parties in the same election. Those who ticket split would be categorized as Independents while those who voted a straight party ticket would be categorized as partisans. Walter DeVries and V. Lance Tarrance adopted this approach in their study on ticket splitting and found the social and demographic background of "Independents" to differ from previous descriptions of Independents.[44] This should not be surprising given the way in which they conceived party identification at the outset of their investigation.

Everett Ladd and Charles Hadley explained that in times of rapid social change and partisan realignment, self-identification with a party may lag behind actual voting behavior.[45] In other words, individuals may continue to identify with a party even though they no longer vote for its presidential candidates. This appears to be happening in the South today where Democratic party identifiers generally support Republican presidential candidates. Perhaps it makes sense to define party identification in behavioral terms under such conditions. However, events could always arise to alter this trend before the realignment actually occurs.[46] A severe recession or another Watergate scandal during a Republican administration, for example, could resolidify Democratic support in the South. This would seriously hamper efforts to understand present conditions and forecast future trends.

There are two other problems with defining party identification in behavioral terms. First, as Herbert Asher pointed out, "if party identification was measured by how a person voted, then it could not be used to explain voting behavior since it would be synonymous with voting behavior."[47] Second, such an approach would severely confine empirical analysis of the entire electorate because it would be directly linked to voter turnout rates. In the 1980 and 1984 presidential elections only slightly more than half of the electorate voted. If researchers adopted a behavioral definition of party identification, they would be forced to exclude a large number of Americans from their analyses. This problem will become even more serious if turnout rates continue to decline. Given these problems, it would be wiser to conceptualize party identification in attitudinal terms.

Controversies Involving Independents

One criticism of the SRC/CPS party identification questions is that they do not accurately measure people's independence of the two major parties. It is suspected that an increased emphasis on individualism and the positive value placed on independence by our society have prompted many to say they are pure Independents when they actually are partisans. Asher, however, provided compelling evidence which showed that the amount of concealed partisanship was probably very low.[48] He found that 23 percent of pure Independents, representing only 2 percent of the 1976 election study sample, have always or mostly always voted for the same party. Since younger people have had fewer opportunities to vote, it is likely that a significant portion of the 23 percent have always or mostly always voted for the same party merely by coincidence. A further examination of the data by him revealed that when Independents only over 35 were considered, the percentage of Independents frequently voting for the same party dropped to 15 percent. Based on this finding, "the problem of the undercover partisan is not a very worrisome one."[49]

In another study, Shively found leaning Independents exhibited a high degree of loyalty to their party's nominee.[50] He argued that leaners were genuine Independents who, in response to the follow-up party identification question, were simply stating their intended vote in the upcoming election. Additional analyses are necessary before we can determine whether he is correct. Other problems concerning the ability of the standard party identification questions to measure independence are discussed in the next section.

Dimensionality of Party Identification

The most serious challenge to the way Campbell and his associates originally conceptualized and measured party identification involves the dimensionality of the concept. In light of new evidence there is the possibility that the concept, which was first introduced as a unique entity having a single meaning or dimension, actually contains more than one meaning or dimension. When a concept is thought to have more than one dimension, researchers try to capture the different dimensions by using more than one indicator. This strategy is often referred to as a "multiple indicators" approach. The objective of this approach is to capture the various meanings of the concept as accurately as possible. When this is done successfully, the different indicators together can explain more variation in other theoretically related variables than can a single indicator. The price paid for increased accuracy, however, is that it is more cumbersome to use several indicators in data analysis than just one. Since researchers never have perfect measurement they must decide how much error they are willing to tolerate. Moreover, additional survey items cost more money, especially over the long run. As will be seen, these concerns are particularly relevant in light of this study's findings. One question addressed at the conclusion of the book is whether it is worth replacing the traditional unidimensional measure of party identification with a new multidimensional one. Let us first take a closer look at the arguments surrounding the concept's dimensionality.

John Petrocik was among the first researchers to raise the question of whether the seven-point party identification scale actually represents a single dimension, or whether in fact the scale represents a mix of various dimensions.[51] After examining the relationship between party identification and ten political involvement variables, he found that in eight of ten cases leaning Independents were more politically involved than weak party identifiers. One would have expected monotonicity in the association between partisanship and involvement, i.e., increased party loyalty accompanied by greater political involvement. According to him, these "intransitivities" occurred because leaning Independents possessed higher incomes and, in particular, higher levels of education than weak party identifiers. At the end of his study he suggested that perhaps alternative measures of party identification could alleviate these intransitivities.

David Valentine and John Van Wingen later argued that Petrocik's study did not explain why leaning Independents appear to be more partisan than weak partisans on some measures of political involvement, but neither more nor less partisan on other measures of involvement.[52] Since the SRC/CPS party identification question asks respondents who already have stated they are Independents to say whether they lean toward either the Republican or Democratic party, "we have no a priori reason to suspect that the partisan independents will be either less or more partisan than the weak partisans."[53] Yet, we can surmise, a priori, that the partisan independents will tend to be more independent than the weak partisans. Therefore, according to them, "any differences in the behavior of the two groups should stem from the difference in the strength of their independence, *not* the differences in the strength of their partisanship."[54] Their analysis of weak partisans and leaners participation in different activities between 1952 and 1976 revealed:

When the values associated with independence conflict with the values of partisanship, the partisan independents *appear* to be less partisan than the weak partisans; when the two sets of values are harmonious, partisan independents *appear* to be more partisan than the weak partisans; and when the values of independence provide no guide to behavior, the partisan independents *appear* to be neither less partisan nor more partisan than the weak partisans.[55]

Hence, leaning Independents are more independent, not more partisan, than are weak party identifiers. Their results explain why Petrocik found the standard party identification scale to have an intransitivity in its ordering. Based on their findings, the traditional party identification scale is actually bidimensional and not unidimensional. Thus, they recommended that researchers develop separate unidimensional measures of partisanship and independence.[56]

Bruce Keith and his colleagues also analyzed leaning Independents; however, their findings differed sharply from those reported by Valentine and Van Wingen.[57] Keith and his associates studied leaners' participation in presidential primaries, the stability over time of their party identification and voting choices, and their views on the two parties. Their investigation showed that leaners' attitudes and behavior closely resemble the attitudes and behavior of weak partisans in the same party. Pure Independents, in contrast, did exhibit a different pattern of attitudes and behavior. They therefore argued that most leaning Independents vote the way they do because they are more partisan than politically independent.[58]

In an effort to add further insight into the phenomenon of political independence, Jack Dennis put forth a theory of independence which suggests that the concept may be multidimensional.[59] According to him, there are four possible reasons why voters call themselves Independents:

1. Voters feel that they are nonpartisan.
2. They hold a negative feeling toward the two parties or partisanship.
3. They positively identify with the ideals of independence.
4. They are closet partisans.

Separating Independents into these groups may help to explain better their attitudes and behavior. Unfortunately, the standard party identification questions do not allow us to differentiate among these four types of Independents (if they do exist), and it will be necessary to develop new questions that more directly address these possible reasons for independence.

From a somewhat different perspective, Richard Katz discovered an anomaly which suggested that the standard scale may be bidimensional.[60] Upon examining the 1956–1958–1960 National Election Panel Study conducted by the Michigan researchers, he found that strong identifiers who changed parties from one election to another were more likely to become strong identifiers of the *new* party than weak identifiers or leaning Independents. In other words, those who were strong Democrats and switched parties must have felt closer to strong Republicans than to weak Republicans or leaning Republican Independents. He therefore concluded that the standard measure really includes two dimensions—strength and direction of identification—and not one.

The most devastating attack on the dimensionality of the standard measure was launched by Herbert Weisberg.[61] He argued that the group attachment notion, first suggested by Campbell, Converse, Miller, and Stokes, unnecessarily confines the interpretation of party identification in three ways: (1) it assumes that people can identify with only one party rather than investigating more fully their attitudes toward both parties; (2) it assumes that political independence is exactly the opposite of partisanship; and (3) it assumes the importance of parties rather than examining Americans' identification with the party system.[62]

At the heart of his criticism was that voters can have multiple and varied identifications, and these identifications can differ in nature and degree. In the world of sports, for example, people do identify with more than one team. Many New Yorkers probably like the Yankees (baseball), the Jets (football), and the Islanders (hockey) at the same time. Also, people can feel differently about two supposedly rival teams. Californians may like both the Los Angeles Dodgers (baseball) and the San Francisco Giants (baseball); others may like one team more than the other; and still others may not like baseball at all because they believe it has become too business oriented or because other sports are more exciting for them to watch. Thus, any study about which baseball teams Americans root for would have to include attitudes toward the individual teams, the possibility of multiple identifications, diverse meanings of nonidentification, and attitudes toward the sport of baseball as a whole.

In the political world, this analogy also pertains to party identification. According to Weisberg:

> Some people might actually consider themselves both Republicans and Democrats. Some people might be Independents because they dislike both parties, while others might be Independents because they like both parties equally, and still others might be Independents because they positively value political independence. Indeed, some people might consider themselves both Republicans (or Democrats) and Independents, particularly if they generally support Republican issue stands but feel that one should vote on the basis of issues rather than party labels. And some people might be so alienated from the political system that they negatively identify both with political parties and with independence as traditionally conceived.[63]

Hence, a measure of party identification would have to encompass attitudes toward the separate parties, the possibility of multiple identifications, diverse meanings of nonidentification, and attitudes toward the party system.

Weisberg introduced a three-dimensional interpretation of party identification along these lines. As shown in Figure 1-2, his three-dimensional model included one dimension representing attitude toward the Republican party, another representing attitude toward the Democratic party, and the third representing attitude toward political independence.[64] Using survey data collected in the January-February segment of the 1980 National Election Study, he operationalized each of these three dimensions by selecting questions that closely resembled the dimensions in Figure 1-2 either separately or in combination with one another. The standard seven-point party identification scale was also included in his investigation as was the often used four-point strength of identification scale. The latter measure is constructed from the SRC/CPS party identification questions and is comprised of pure Independents, leaning Independents, weak partisans, and strong partisans. He conducted a factor analysis, a statistical technique which helps to identify individual dimensions, on fourteen items to determine the accuracy of his three-dimensional model. He found four separate components: a strength of partisanship factor, an independence factor, a partisan direction factor, and a party system factor.[65] The traditional seven-point and four-point measures fell on the partisan direction and partisan strength factors, respectively.

Weisberg's findings are suggestive for at least two reasons. First, they appear to support Katz's argument that there are distinct direction and strength elements in party identification. Second, his findings also seem to support Valentine and Van Wingen's assertion that independence is a separate dimension. This is especially significant because most researchers have assumed that partisan strength and independence fall along the same continuum, and they have used

Figure 1-2
Three Dimensions of Party Identification

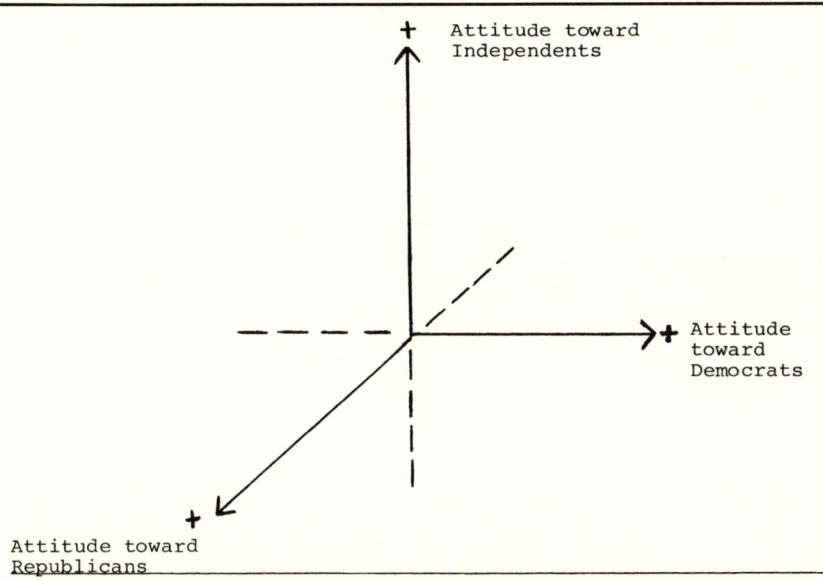

Source: Herbert F. Weisberg, "A Multidimensional Conceptualization of Party Identification," Political Behavior Vol. 2 No. 1 (1980), p. 37. Reprinted with permission of the publisher, Agathon Press.

the standard four-point partisan strength scale—ranging from pure Independents to strong partisans—as a measure of both. Weisberg's analysis, however, implies that this assumption is incorrect. Accordingly, this study addresses this question. At the very least, a multidimensional approach such as his deserves serious consideration.

DETERMINING EXTERNAL ASSOCIATION

Findings by Weisberg and others suggest the concept of party identification is more complex than first thought. However, since every study on political attitudes and electoral behavior adopted Campbell and his colleagues' unidimensional conceptualization, there is a good chance that previous findings have been influenced by the cloudy conceptual nature of the standard seven-point scale. Because Weisberg's model is by far the most encompassing one developed to date, I have decided to explore the relationships between his new party identification measures, the standard partisan direction and partisan strength scales, and other theoretically related variables. The central issue is whether the different party identification measures are "equivalent" or "interchangeable."[66] In other words, if these measures represent party identification empirically, the relationships between these measures and the external theoretically relevant variables—"criterion" variables—should be similar in terms of direction, strength, and consistency. Yet, if the standard and alternative items relate differentially to the same criterion variables, then these items are not interchangeable. The results of such an analysis provide evidence about the theoretical meaning that can be attributed to the individual party identification measures.[67] Researchers, of course, will want to exclude nonequivalent items from future investigations.

As far as this study is concerned, it is possible that the individual elements of Weisberg's multidimensional model are associated with other variables in different ways. For instance, perhaps different racial, class, or religious groups relate to the political parties in distinct ways. Moreover, separate party identification measures may be associated differently with attitudinal and behavioral variables such as issue positions, political cynicism, party and candidate evaluations, voter turnout, voter defection, and the vote choice. These are among the criterion variables analyzed in this study.

OUTLINE OF THE BOOK

This book seeks to help students better comprehend the dynamics of party identification by comparing and analyzing two different conceptualizations of the concept, one unidimensional and the other multidimensional. This is done by reanalyzing previous theoretical and empirical research involving party identification. Because of limited space, the author cannot reexamine every single investigation which included the concept. Thus, only the most direct and important relationships between the concept and other variables are addressed in this study.

This book was written with the idea that most students of politics do not have a strong background in statistics and methodology. Consequently, I explain statistics and complicated techniques simply in the text. Sophisticated readers will be able to find formulas, documentation, and other technical information concerning the analysis in the footnotes.

A potential problem with this investigation is that it only focuses on one point in time, the 1980 presidential election year. The authors of *The American Voter* received considerable criticism for generalizing their findings, including those about party identification, beyond the 1950s. We certainly do not want to make the same mistake. Let us therefore keep in mind that the results of this study pertain to the 1980 election year. Although a longitudinal analysis would have been preferable, the exclusion of certain items comprising Weisberg's multidimensional model from previous election surveys makes this impossible. Future researchers will be able to build on the findings reported in this study as more data become available.

The second chapter begins by briefly describing how Weisberg constructed his party identification measures. A primary purpose of the chapter is to determine the social characteristics of partisans and Independents (as they are defined in unidimensional and multidimensional terms). A brief review of previous theory and findings is presented prior to introducing each section in this and subsequent chapters. Also, a summary of the findings is provided at the conclusion of every chapter.

The next three chapters explore the relationships between the standard and alternative measures and political attitudes. The third chapter examines orientations toward the political system, and the fourth chapter addresses views on groups and issues. Party and candidate evaluations are covered in the fifth chapter.

The sixth chapter analyzes party identification and electoral behavior. The last chapter discusses the implications of the study's findings for future research. We begin by taking a closer look at Weisberg's model.

NOTES

1. For an excellent description of the role and preeminence of the SRC/CPS in electoral research see: David B. Hill and Norman R. Luttbeg, *Trends in American Electoral Behavior*, Second Edition (Itasca, Ill.: F.E. Peacock Publishers, 1983), pp. 14–22.

2. The concept of party identification was first introduced and discussed in: George Belknap and Angus Campbell, "Political Party Identification and Attitudes Toward Foreign Policy," *Public Opinion Quarterly* Vol. 15 (Winter 1952), pp. 601–23.

3. Angus Campbell, Philip E. Converse, Warren E. Miller, and Donald E. Stokes, *The American Voter* (New York: John Wiley and Sons, 1960), p. 121.

4. Ibid.

5. Ibid., p. 149.

6. Ibid., pp. 531–38.

7. Ibid., p. 531.

8. This classification was actually an extension of V.O. Key's theory of critical elections first proposed in 1955. V.O. Key, "A Theory of Critical Elections," *Journal of Politics* Vol. 17 (February 1955), pp. 3–18. A thorough treatment of party realignments can be found in: Jerome M. Clubb, William H. Flanigan, and Nancy H. Zingale, *Partisan Realignment: Voters, Parties, and Government in American History* (Beverly Hills, Calif.: Sage Publications, 1980).

9. Kristi Andersen argued that Democratic gains during the New Deal era came largely from a mobilization of new voters previously uninvolved in politics. Kristi Andersen, "Generation, Partisan Shift, and Realignment: A Glance Back to the New Deal," in *The Changing American Voter* by Norman Nie, Sidney Verba, and John R. Petrocik, Enlarged Edition (Cambridge: Harvard University Press, 1979), Chap. 5; and Kristi Andersen, *The Creation of a Democratic Majority, 1928–1936* (Chicago: University of Chicago Press, 1979). Richard Niemi, Richard Katz, and David Newman questioned Andersen's methodological approach in assessing changes in party identification across generations. Richard G. Niemi, Richard S. Katz, and David Newman, "Reconstructing Past Partisanship: The Failure of the Party Identification Recall Questions," *American Journal of Political Science* Vol. 24 (November 1980), pp. 633–51. Also, contrary to Andersen's position, Robert Erikson and Kent Tedin maintained that the realignment occurred because many Republicans began to identify with the Democratic party. Robert

S. Erikson and Kent L. Tedin, "The 1928–1936 Partisan Realignment: The Case for the Conversion Hypothesis," *American Political Science Review* Vol. 75 (December 1981), pp. 951–62.

10. Philip E. Converse, "The Concept of a Normal Vote," in *Elections and the Political Order*, ed. Angus Campbell et al. (New York: John Wiley and Sons, 1966), pp. 9–39.

11. This idea was elaborated in: Nie, Verba, and Petrocik, *The Changing American Voter*, pp. 59–73.

12. Converse found evidence to support the claim that the decline in party identification was rooted in the events which took place during the mid–1960s. Philip E. Converse, *The Dynamics of Party Support* (Beverly Hills, Calif.: Sage Publications, 1976). Also consult: Arthur H. Miller, "Partisanship Reinstated? A Comparison of the 1972 and 1976 U.S. Presidential Elections," *British Journal of Political Science* Vol. 8 (April 1978), pp. 129–52.

13. Douglas Dobson and Douglas St. Angelo, "Party Identification and the Floating Vote: Some Dynamics," *American Political Science Review* Vol. 69 (June 1975), pp. 481–90.

14. W. Phillips Shively, "The Nature of Party Identification: A Review of Recent Developments," in *The Electorate Reconsidered*, ed. John C. Pierce and John L. Sullivan (Beverly Hills, Calif.: Sage Publications, 1980), pp. 219–36.

15. Edward C. Dreyer, "Change and Stability in Party Identification," *Journal of Politics* Vol. 35 (August 1973), pp. 712–23.

16. Nie, Verba, and Petrocik, *The Changing American Voter*, pp. 419–22.

17. Kenneth J. Meier, "Party Identification and the Vote Choice: The Causal Relationship," *Western Political Quarterly* Vol. 28 (September 1975), pp. 496–505; Richard A. Brody, "Stability and Change in Party Identification: Presidential to Off-Years," presented at the 1977 Annual Meeting of the American Political Science Association, Washington, D.C.; Shively, "The Nature of Party Identification"; and Dobson and St. Angelo, "Party Identification and the Floating Vote." The reader should also consult: Douglas Dobson and Duane A. Meeter, "Alternative Markov Models for Describing Change in Party Identification," *American Journal of Political Science* Vol. 18 (August 1974), pp. 487–500; and Niemi, Katz, and Newman, "Reconstructing Past Partisanship."

18. Richard A. Brody and Lawrence S. Rothenberg, "Dynamics of Partisanship During the 1980 Election," presented at the 1983 Annual Meeting of the American Political Science Association, Chicago, Illinois.

19. John H. Kessel, *Presidential Campaign Politics: Coalition Strategies and Citizen Response* (Homewood, Ill.: The Dorsey Press, 1980), especially Chap. 9.

20. Ibid., p. 225.

21. For further discussion of this question refer to: Arthur S. Goldberg, "Social Determinism and Rationality as Bases of Party Identification," *American Political Science Review* Vol. 63 (March 1969), pp. 5–25; and Shively, "The Nature of Party Identification." Also see: Campbell, Converse, Miller, and Stokes, *The American Voter*; David Butler and Donald E. Stokes, *Political Change in Britain* (New York: St. Martin's Press, 1969); M. Kent Jennings and Richard G. Niemi, "The Transmission of Political Values from Parent to Child," *American Political Science Review* Vol. 62 (March 1968), pp. 169–84; Jack Dennis and Donald J. McCrone, "Pre-Adult Development of Political Party Identification in Western Democracies," *Comparative Political Studies* Vol. 3 (July 1970),

pp. 243–63; David Knoke and Michael Hunt, "Social and Demographic Factors in American Party Affiliation: 1952–1972," *American Sociological Review* Vol. 39 (October 1974), pp. 700–713; Philip E. Converse and George Dupeux, "The Politicization of the Electorate in France and the United States," in *Elections and the Political Order*, ed. Angus Campbell et al., pp. 269–91; Donald D. Searing, Joel J. Schwartz, and Alden E. Lind, "The Structuring Principle: Political Socialization and Belief Systems," *American Political Science Review* Vol. 67 (June 1973), pp. 415–32; Kent L. Tedin, "The Influence of Parents on the Political Attitudes of Adolescents," *American Political Science Review* Vol. 68 (December 1974), pp. 1579–92; and Kent L. Tedin, "Assessing Peer and Parent Influence on Adolescent Political Attitudes," *American Journal of Political Science* Vol. 24 (February 1980), pp. 136–54.

22. Shively, "The Nature of Party Identification," p. 224. He also said that the process by which party identification was acquired probably differed from the process by which it was strengthened (p. 232). This was demonstrated in: William Claggett, "Partisan Acquisition Versus Partisan Intensity: Life-Cycle, Generation, and Period Effects, 1952–1976," *American Journal of Political Science* Vol. 25 (May 1981), pp. 193–214.

23. M. Kent Jennings and Richard G. Niemi, "The Persistence of Political Orientations: An Over-Time Analysis of Two Generations," *British Journal of Political Science* Vol. 8 (July 1978), pp. 333–63; and M. Kent Jennings and Richard G. Niemi, *Generations and Politics: A Panel Study of Young Adults and Their Parents* (Princeton: Princeton University Press, 1981).

24. In a follow-up study conducted between 1973 and 1982 Gregory Markus and M. Kent Jennings found that the party identification of the offspring stabilizes over time to the point where the stability of their partisanship rivals that of their parents. Electoral participation is identified as a major contributor to the increased durability of partisanship among the younger cohort. Gregory B. Markus and M. Kent Jennings, "Partisan Orientations over the Long Haul: Results from the Three-Wave Political Socialization Panel Study," presented at the 1983 Annual Meeting of the American Political Science Association, Chicago, Illinois.

25. An issue that received considerable attention in the literature was whether people begin to identify with a political party, and become more strongly partisan, as they move through the life cycle, whether generational differences among the public account for changes in direction and strength of party identification, or whether political events or "period effects" explain changes in direction and strength of party identification. This question is beyond the scope of this chapter; however, interested readers can refer to: Campbell, Converse, Miller, and Stokes, *The American Voter*, Chap. 7; Philip E. Converse, "Of Time and Partisan Stability," *Comparative Political Studies* Vol. 2 (July 1969), pp. 139–71; Norval D. Glenn, "Aging, Disengagement and Opinionation," *Public Opinion Quarterly* Vol. 33 (Spring 1969), pp. 17–34; Neal E. Cutler, "Generation, Maturation and Party Affiliation: A Cohort Analysis," *Public Opinion Quarterly* Vol. 33 (Winter 1970), pp. 583–88; Norval D. Glenn and Michael Grimes, "Aging, Voting and Political Interest," *American Sociological Review* Vol. 33 (September 1968), pp. 563–75; Norval D. Glenn and Ted Hefner, "Further Evidence on Aging and Party Identification," *Public Opinion Quarterly* Vol. 36 (Spring 1972), pp. 31–47; Paul Allen Beck, "A Socialization Theory of Partisan Realignments," in *The Politics of Future Citizens*, ed. Richard G. Niemi et al. (San Francisco: Josey-Bass, 1974), pp. 200–206; Paul R. Abramson, "Generational Change in the American Electorate," *American Political Science Review* Vol. 68 (March 1974), pp. 93–105; Paul R. Abramson, "Gen-

erational Change and the Decline of Party Identification in America: 1952–1974,'' *American Political Science Review* Vol. 70 (June 1976), pp. 469–78; Converse, *The Dynamics of Party Support*; Paul R. Abramson, "Developing Party Identification: A Further Examination of Life-Cycle, Generational, and Period Effects," *American Journal of Political Science* Vol. 23 (February 1979), pp. 78–96; Philip E. Converse, "Rejoinder to Abramson," *American Journal of Political Science* Vol. 23 (February 1979), pp. 97–100; W. Phillips Shively, "The Relationship between Age and Party Identification: A Cohort Analysis," *Political Methodology* Vol. 6 No. 4 (1979), pp. 437–46; and Claggett, "Partisan Acquisition Versus Partisan Intensity."

26. Michael Maggiotto and James Pierson, "Partisan Identification and Electoral Choice: The Hostility Hypothesis," *American Journal of Political Science* Vol. 21 (November 1977), pp. 745–67.

27. Ibid., p. 746.

28. In the 1980 SRC/CPS election study respondents were asked to rate political figures and other objects as well as the parties. The exact wording of the question was:

I'd like to get your feelings toward some of our political leaders and other people who are in the news these days. I'll read the name of a person and I'd like you to rate that person using this feeling thermometer. You may use any number from zero to 100 for a rating. Ratings between 50 and 100 degrees mean that you feel favorable and warm toward the person. Ratings between zero and 50 degrees mean that you don't feel too favorable toward the person. If we come to a person whose name you don't recognize, you don't need to rate that person. Just tell me and we'll move on to the next one. If you do recognize the name, but don't feel particularly warm or cold toward the person, you would rate that person at the 50 degree mark. Our first person is Jimmy Carter. How would you rate him using the thermometer?

29. Shively, "The Nature of Party Identification," pp. 224–25.

30. Ibid., p. 225.

31. The best example of this approach is: Anthony Downs, *An Economic Theory of Democracy* (New York: Harper, 1957). Also see: Morris Fiorina, "Formal Models in Political Science," *American Journal of Political Science* Vol. 19 (February 1975), pp. 133–59.

32. Morris Fiorina, "An Outline for a Model of Party Choice," *American Journal of Political Science* Vol. 21 (August 1977), pp. 601–25; and Morris Fiorina, *Retrospective Voting in American National Elections* (New Haven: Yale University Press, 1981), Chap. 5.

33. Fiorina, *Retrospective Voting in American National Elections*, p. 83.

34. Ibid., p. 89. For a more detailed explanation of this equation consult: Fiorina, "An Outline for a Model of Party Choice."

35. Shively, "The Nature of Party Identification," p. 226.

36. Butler and Stokes, *Political Change in Britain: Forces Shaping Electoral Choice*.

37. Ivor Crewe, "Party Identification Theory and Political Change in Britain," in *Party Identification and Beyond: Representations of Voting and Party Competition*, ed. Ian Budge, Ivor Crewe, and Dennis Farlie (New York: John Wiley and Sons, 1976), pp. 33–61. Warren Miller defended the Michigan school's conception and measure of party identification in: Warren E. Miller, "The Cross-National Use of Party Identification," in *Party Identification and Beyond*, ed. Ian Budge et al., pp. 21–31.

38. Jacques Thomassen, "Party Identification As A Cross-Cultural Concept: Its Meaning in the Netherlands," in *Party Identification and Beyond*, ed. Ian Budge et al., pp. 63–79.

39. Meier, "Party Identification and Voter Choice."
40. Shively, "The Nature of Party Identification," pp. 222–23, 226.
41. Ibid., p. 226. Also refer to: W. Phillips Shively, "The Development of Party Identification among Adults: Exploration of A Functional Model," *American Political Science Review* Vol. 73 (December 1979), pp. 1039–54.
42. Kendall Baker, "Generational Differences in the Role of Party Identification in German Political Behavior," *American Journal of Political Science* Vol. 22 (February 1978), pp. 106–29.
43. An analysis of these types of voters was conducted in: V.O. Key, *The Responsible Electorate: Rationality in Presidential Voting, 1936–1960* (Cambridge: Harvard University Press, 1966).
44. Walter DeVries and V. Lance Tarrance, *The Ticket-Splitter: A New Force in American Politics* (Grand Rapids: William B. Eerdmans Publishing Company, 1972).
45. Everett C. Ladd and Charles D. Hadley, "Party Definition and Party Differentiation," *Public Opinion Quarterly* Vol. 37 (Spring 1973–74), p. 32.
46. Herbert Asher made this point in: Herbert B. Asher, *Presidential Elections and American Politics: Voters, Candidates, and Campaigns Since 1952*, Revised Edition (Homewood, Ill.: The Dorsey Press, 1980), p. 65.
47. Ibid., p. 65.
48. Ibid., pp. 65–66.
49. Ibid., p. 66.
50. W. Phillips Shively, "Identification Costs and the Partisan Cycle," presented at the 1977 Annual Meeting of the American Political Science Association, Washington, D.C., pp. 16–20.
51. John R. Petrocik, "An Analysis of Intransitivities in the Index of Party Identification," *Political Methodology* Vol. 1 (Summer 1974), pp. 31–47.
52. David C. Valentine and John R. Van Wingen, "Partisanship, Independence, and the Partisan Identification Question," *American Politics Quarterly* Vol. 8 (April 1980), pp. 165–86.
53. Ibid., p. 169.
54. Ibid.
55. Ibid., p. 179.
56. Ibid., p. 181. William Jacoby also found that the standard party identification questions measure two dimensions, partisanship and independence. William G. Jacoby, "Unfolding the Party Identification Scale: Improving the Measurement of An Important Concept," *Political Methodology* Vol. 8 No. 2 (1982), pp. 33–59.
57. Bruce E. Keith, David B. Magleby, Candice J. Nelson, Elizabeth Orr, Mark C. Westlye, and Raymond E. Wolfinger, "Further Evidence on the Partisan Affinities of Independent 'Leaners'," presented at the 1983 Annual Meeting of the American Political Science Association, Chicago, Illinois.
58. But also see: Arthur H. Miller and Martin P. Wattenberg, "Measuring Party Identification: Independent or No Partisan Preference?," *American Journal of Political Science* Vol. 27 (February 1983), pp. 106–21. Their analysis suggests that the traditional party identification question concerning Independents should be changed so that researchers can differentiate between voters who are "true" Independents and those who are "no preference" nonpartisans.
59. Jack Dennis, "Toward A Theory of Political Independence," presented at the 1983 Annual Meeting of the American Political Science Association, Chicago, Illinois.

60. Richard S. Katz, "The Dimensionality of Party Identification: Cross-National Perspectives," *Comparative Politics* Vol. 11 (January 1979), pp. 147–63.

61. Herbert F. Weisberg, "A Multidimensional Conceptualization of Party Identification," *Political Behavior* Vol. 2 No. 1 (1980), p. 33–60.

62. Ibid., p. 35.

63. Ibid., p. 36.

64. Ibid., pp. 37–38.

65. Ibid., pp. 53–55.

66. Paul F. Lazarsfeld, "Problems in Methodology," in *Sociology Today: Problems and Prospects*, ed. Robert K. Merton et al. (New York: Harper and Row, 1959), pp. 39–78.

67. Richard A. Zeller and Edward G. Carmines, *Measurement in the Social Sciences: The Link between Theory and Data* (Cambridge: Cambridge University Press, 1980), pp. 916–17. A similar procedure is employed in: Sheldon Kamieniecki and Robert O'Brien, "Are Social Class Measures Interchangeable?," *Political Behavior* Vol. 6 No. 1 (1984), pp. 41–59.

2
SOCIAL BACKGROUND AND PARTY IDENTIFICATION

The next five chapters examine the extent to which unidimensional and multidimensional party identification measures are empirically related to certain criterion variables. The criterion variables included in the analysis are thought to be theoretically associated with party identification. As stated in the first chapter, one objective of this study is to learn more about partisans and Independents. A second objective is to investigate whether partisan strength and political independence comprise one dimension of party identification as assumed in the literature, or whether they represent two separate dimensions. A third aim is to compare the standard seven-point party identification and four-point strength of identification scales with Herbert Weisberg's alternative measures, and to determine which approach is preferable for future analyses.[1]

This chapter is divided into two main sections. The first section discusses the components of Weisberg's model and reports on an attempt to replicate his work. The results of this effort lead to the development of a substantially modified multidimensional model of party identification which is used throughout the study. The second section examines the relationships between social background variables, including race, age, region, place of residence, religion, parents' party affiliation, social status and class, and party identification. This is followed by a multivariate analysis of party identification. A summary of the investigation's findings is presented at the end of the chapter.

WEISBERG'S MODEL IN DETAIL

Weisberg originally theorized that there are three dimensions inherent in party identification: attitude toward the Republican party, attitude toward the Democratic party, and attitude toward political independence.[2] To test this theory he used a sophisticated statistical technique called factor analysis. This technique helps researchers to identify underlying patterns among a number of variables which are thought to be theoretically related in some way. Variables that are correlated and cluster together are said to represent a particular factor or dimension. Although a factor analysis can show researchers which items cluster together empirically, it cannot determine the theoretical meaning of a factor. Investigators themselves must interpret and label factors by carefully examining the size and direction of the factor loadings. Factor loadings can range from −1.00 to zero to 1.00, and they indicate the direction and degree to which items are correlated with an entire factor. Items that have something in common and load "high" on a factor (and low on other factors) help one interpret the factor's meaning.[3]

As discussed in Chapter One, Weisberg's factor analysis of the standard and new party identification questions in the January-February segment of the 1980 National Election Study generated four separate factors: partisan direction, strength of partisanship, party system support, and political independence.[4] Let us examine the items which comprise each factor.

Partisan Direction

According to Weisberg, the first factor represents direction of partisanship and consists of six measures: a party difference index, the traditional seven-point party identification scale, a party support scale, a party closeness scale, and the Democratic party and Republican party feeling thermometers. The party difference index measures how much more a person likes the Republican party than the Democratic party. The index scores are obtained by subtracting the feeling thermometer for Democrats from that for Republicans. As explained in the last chapter, the feeling thermometer questions permit respondents to rate the two parties on scales ranging from zero (cold) to 100 (warm) degrees. The resulting scores are first collapsed (by Weisberg) into five categories: strong Republicans (31 to 100), weak Republicans (1 to 30), neutrals (zero), weak Democrats (−30 to −1), and strong Democrats (−100 to −31). The traditional party identification question is then used to divide the neutral category into Republican neutrals, pure neutrals, and Democratic neutrals. The result is an index of party difference ranging from 1 (for strong Republicans) to 7 (for strong Democrats).

In the 1980 election study respondents were asked whether they thought of themselves as supporters of one of the major parties. If they responded "yes," they were asked which party they supported and how strongly they supported that party on a scale from 1 ("not very strongly") to 7 ("very strongly").[5] These questions were used by Weisberg to construct a party support scale ranging from +7 for strong Republican support to zero for not supporting either party to +7 for strong Democratic support.

In addition, all respondents were asked how close they felt to the two parties.[6] People were requested to place themselves on a scale ranging from 1 (very close to the Republican party) to 7 (very close to the Democratic party). Those who did not feel closer to either party were coded 4. This led to a seven-point party closeness scale.

Strength of Partisanship

Weisberg's strength of partisanship factor consists of the absolute value of the difference in thermometer ratings given the two parties, a folded party closeness scale, a folded party support scale, the standard four-point strength of identification scale, and the maximum of the thermometer ratings given the Republican and Democratic parties. The folded party closeness measure is constructed by collapsing the values of the party closeness scale into a new scale ranging from +7 for very close to one's own party to +4 for equally close to the two major parties. Similarly, the party support measure is folded into a scale ranging from +7 for strong support of one's own party to +1 for weak support of one's own party and zero for not supporting either party. Finally, the seven-point party identification measure is transformed into the standard four-point strength of identification scale where pure Independents are scored (coded) 1, leaning Independents 2, weak identifiers 3, and strong identifiers 4.

Party System Support

His third factor contains the Republican and Democrat feeling thermometers, a thermometer question addressing "political parties, in general," and the maximum thermometer score assigned to a party. He felt that the interpretation of this factor was difficult, though a pro-party/anti-party label seemed "reasonable."[7] He believed the inclusion of another variable measuring attitude toward the party system in a subsequent factor analysis would be useful in confirming this interpretation. Further clarification of this factor was pursued as part of an effort to replicate his work, and the findings will be discussed shortly.

Political Independence

The fourth factor in Weisberg's study is party independence and it consists of two measures, a strength of independence scale and a thermometer rating of Independents. In the 1980 study respondents were asked:

Do you ever think of yourself as a political independent, or not? (If yes) on this scale from 1 to 7 (where 1 means "not very strongly," and 7 means "very strongly"), please choose the number that describes how strongly independent in politics you feel.

This question was used to construct a strength of independence scale. Respondents who did not think of themselves as Independents were assigned a zero on

Figure 2-1
The Results of Weisberg's Factor Analysis of Fourteen Party Identification Measures, January–February, 1980

Factor 1 - Partisan Direction

    Party Difference Index
    Party Closeness Scale
    Party Support Scale
    Democratic Party Feeling Thermometer
    Republican Party Feeling Thermometer
    Seven-Point Party Identification Scale

Factor 2 - Strength of Partisanship

    Absolute Value of Difference in Thermometer Ratings Given Two Parties
    Folded Party Closeness Scale
    Folded Party Support Scale
    Maximum Thermometer Score Assigned to A Party
    Four-Point Strength of Party Identification Scale

Factor 3 - Party System Support

    Republican Party Feeling Thermometer
    Political Parties Feeling Thermometer
    Maximum Thermometer Score Assigned to A Party
    Democratic Party Feeling Thermometer

Factor 4 - Independence

    Strength of Independence Scale
    Independents Feeling Thermometer

this scale. As in the Republican, Democrat, and political parties thermometer questions, respondents were asked to rate political Independents from zero to 100 degrees.

Figure 2–1 summarizes the results of his factor analysis of fourteen different party identification measures included in the January-February segment of the 1980 election study. Unfortunately, he did not provide the factor loadings for the fourteen items, and he only indicated that the Republican party and political parties thermometers loaded higher than the maximum thermometer score and the Democratic party thermometer on factor three.[8] Nevertheless, he did supply enough information to permit a replication of his study.[9]

THE DATA BASE

The data analyzed throughout this investigation were drawn from a national survey of Americans taken immediately before and after the November 1980 presidential election by the SRC/CPS. The pre- and post-election panel study was part of an ambitious, eight-stage survey research project funded by the National Science Foundation. Congressional districts constituted the primary sampling areas (Washington, D.C., was excluded) and people 18 years of age and older (by election day, 1980) were personally interviewed. The pre-election study consisted of a multi-stage probability sample of 1,614 respondents. The post-election study contained 1,408 respondents, representing an 87 percent reinterview rate.

The comprehensive pre- and post-election surveys sought to obtain data on four specific topics: new measures of party identification, the measurement of voter attitudes toward public policy issues, the public's perception of and response to political leadership, and the relationship between social networks and the vote choice. Respondents were also questioned about their social and demographic background. In addition, a vote validation study was conducted in February 1981. Investigators were sent to electoral offices throughout the nation to determine whether respondents were actually registered to vote in 1980 and, if registered, whether they had visited the polls to vote on election day. In summary, the 1980 National Election Study represents a bold and exciting attempt by the SRC/CPS to collect in-depth information about Americans' political attitudes, values, and behavior.[10]

As already noted, Weisberg's findings were based on an analysis of the January-February segment of the 1980 election study (designated P-1 by the SRC/CPS). Our investigation uses the 1980 pre- and post-election surveys (designated C-3PO by the SRC/CPS) to replicate his work, primarily because they contain the new party identification questions as well as important criterion variables (for example, turnout and vote choice) not found in the January-February segment. Furthermore, the February 1981 validation study permits us to check the accuracy of respondents' reports concerning their voter registration status and their visit to the polls on election day.

REPLICATING WEISBERG'S STUDY

A factor analysis of Weisberg's party identification measures in the 1980 pre-election survey generated the same four factors.[11] As Table 2-1 shows, the seven-point party identification scale (which ranges from zero to 6, strong Republican to strong Democrat) and the four-point strength of identification scale load high on the partisan direction and strength of partisanship factors, respectively, and appear to be tapping the same dimensions as the new measures. It is still possible, however, that the new items are better measures of partisan direction and strength of partisanship than the two standard scales. The best way to determine this is to see how closely all the party identification measures are related to important external variables, something this study does. In addition, Table 2-1 reveals that the items which load high on Weisberg's factors also load high on our factors with two exceptions. First, the maximum thermometer score as-

Table 2-1
Factor Loadings of Weisberg's Party Identification Measures, Pre-Election Survey, 1980[a]

Items	Partisan Direction	Strength of Partisanship	Party System Support	Independence
Party Difference Index	.92799			
Seven-Point Party Identification Scale	.87916			
Party Closeness Scale	.85048			
Party Support Scale	.78719			
Democratic Party Feeling Thermometer	.75351		.49342	
Republican Party Feeling Thermometer	-.65989		.53153	
Folded Party Closeness Scale		.76007		
Folded Party Support Scale		.75179		
Four-Point Strength of Identification Scale		.58634		
Maximum Thermometer Score Assigned to A Party			.78788	
Political Parties Feeling Thermometer			.41058	
Strength of Independence Scale				.79848
Independents Feeling Thermometer				.41233

a - Based on 1162 cases. Factor loadings not included in the table were below .40.

signed to a party has a low loading on the strength of partisanship factor and a high loading on the party system support factor, suggesting that it best measures the latter component. Second, and more significantly, the inclusion of the absolute value of the difference in thermometer ratings given the two major parties severely distorted the entire factor structure and was therefore excluded from the analysis. Exactly why this happened is unknown. Aside from these two exceptions, our factor solution resembles his quite closely.

An effort was made to confirm Weisberg's speculation that the third factor represents party system support. In a section of the pre-election study respondents were read five general statements about political parties and asked to state how strongly they agreed or disagreed with each one on a scale of 1 ("disagree very strongly") to 7 ("agree very strongly"). Responses to three of the five statements were found to be unidimensional and were summed to form a "party system support scale."[12] This scale was placed in a factor analysis along with the thirteen party identification items in Table 2-1 and failed to load high on any factor.

Questions addressing party system support were also included in the post-election questionnaire. Respondents were asked how good a job the political parties were doing "for the country as a whole" on a scale ranging from zero ("very poor job") to 8 ("very good job").[13] Respondents were also asked whether the political parties pay "a good deal, some, or not much" attention to what they think.[14] The first measure was included in a factor analysis along with the thirteen party identification items and did not load high on any factor. In addition, low correlations were found between the second measure and the four items comprising the third factor.[15] These findings suggest that his four dimensional model, especially its so-called "party system support" component, deserves rethinking.

Based on the results of our investigation, it could be that the items which comprise the third factor do not represent party system support but something else. One possibility is that the items are actually indicators of another concept, trust in government. Perhaps many view the political parties as a formal part of the national government and support for one means support for the other. Those who hold such a perception may believe that the parties and government operate in the same manner and strive for similar goals. If this were true, we would expect to find fairly high correlations between the items on the third factor and trust in the government.

Those interviewed in the pre-election survey were asked how much of the time they can trust "the government in Washington" to do what is right.[16] Possible responses included "none of the time" (if volunteered), "only some of the time," "most of the time," and "just about always." The data show that only weak relationships exist between the Democrat, Republican, and political parties thermometers, the maximum thermometer score, and the trust in government question.[17] Thus, we still do not know the exact meaning of Weisberg's third factor.

An equally important issue is whether support for the party system as a whole is really a theoretical component of party identification. Certainly, Angus Campbell and his colleagues never considered party system support to be part of their group attachment notion.[18] Even if we are willing to reject their unidimensional conceptualization of party identification in favor of a multidimensional one, it is difficult to explain compellingly how party system support is an indicator of party affiliation. It is likely that party system support is a much broader concept. If anything, logic dictates that party identification is an indicator of party system support. In that case, one's orientation toward independence and the individual parties is conceptually distinct from one's orientation towards the entire party system. If this argument is valid, any attempt to combine the two concepts empirically will introduce considerable measurement error in our analysis.

Given the above empirical and theoretical concerns, the wisest strategy is to eliminate the "party system support" component, and relevant items, from the model. But to what extent will this disturb the rest of the factor structure?

The results of a factor analysis of eleven party identification measures appear in Table 2-2.[19] As one can see, the Democrat and Republican thermometers

Table 2-2
Factor Loadings of Eleven Different Party Identification Measures, Pre-Election Survey, 1980[a]

	FACTORS		
Items	Partisan Direction	Strength of Partisanship	Independence
Party Difference Index	.93669		
Seven-Point Party Identification Scale	.88918		
Party Closeness Scale	.86220		
Party Support Scale	.79794		
Democratic Party Feeling Thermometer	.71198		
Republican Party Feeling Thermometer	-.60788		
Folded Party Closeness Scale		.77763	
Folded Party Support Scale		.77169	
Four-Point Strength of Identification Scale		.63032	
Strength of Independence Scale			.78731
Independents Feeling Thermometer			.40518

a - Based on 1193 cases. Factor loadings not included in the Table were below .40.

were not dropped from the analysis, primarily because of their significant contribution to the partisan direction dimension. The removal of the political parties thermometer and the maximum thermometer score from the analysis yields a three factor solution with the position of the items and the size of the loadings remaining about the same. The three dimensional model in Table 2–2 is believed to be superior to Weisberg's four dimensional model and will therefore be used in our investigation. Readers can refer to the list of measures and codes in Figure 2–2 to help them interpret the results of subsequent analyses.

Points of Reference

Even though the preceding analysis shows that the items within each dimension are empirically related to one another, each item has a unique point of reference. This is evident in the wording of the questions used to construct the individual measures. For example, while respondents' party *identity* is referred to in the questions used to construct the standard party identification measures, respondents' *closeness to* and *support for* a party is addressed in the questions embodied in the party closeness scale, the party support scale, and their partisan strength derivatives. Similarly, the feeling thermometer items attempt to tap voters' *separate attitudes toward* the Republican and Democratic parties and Independents. Attitudes toward each party are incorporated in the party difference index. The question used to create the strength of independence scale asks

Figure 2-2
Values of Eleven Party Identification Measures

Items	Dimensions	Values
Party Difference Index	Partisan Direction	1 to 7 (strong Republican to strong Democrat)
Party Closeness Scale	Partisan Direction	1 to 7 (very close to Republicans to very close to Democrats)
Party Support Scale	Partisan Direction	-7 to +7 (strong Republican supporter to strong Democrat supporter)
Democratic Party Feeling Thermometer	Partisan Direction	0 to 100 (cold to warm)
Republican Party Feeling Thermometer	Partisan Direction	0 to 100 (cold to warm)
Seven-Point Party Identification Scale	Partisan Direction	0 to 6 (strong Republican to strong Democrat)
Folded Party Closeness Scale	Strength of Partisanship	4 to 7 (equally close to two parties to very close to one's own party)
Folded Party Support Scale	Strength of Partisanship	0 to 7 (not a party supporter to a strong supporter of one's own party)
Four-Point Strength of Identification Scale	Strength of Partisanship	1 to 4 (pure Independent to strong identifier)
Strength of Independence Scale	Independence	0 to 7 (not independent to very strongly independent)
Independents Feeling Thermometer	Independence	0 to 100 (cold to warm)

respondents how independent from politics *they feel* rather than *how they feel about* Independents in general. These reference points are distinct enough to warrant an investigation of the interchangeability of the various party identification measures.

EXPLAINING CORRELATIONS AND STATISTICAL SIGNIFICANCE

Tau-b, Tau-c, and Pearson Product-Moment correlations will be used to show the strength and direction of the relationships between criterion variables and party identification.[20] Tau-b and Tau-c correlations will be reported when the cross-tables on which they are based are either square (i.e., the number of rows and columns are equal) or rectangular (i.e., the number of rows and columns are unequal), respectively, and the outside variable has ranked or ordered values. Pearson correlations will be reported when the outside variable's values have equal intervals. These correlations can range from -1.00 (a perfect negative relationship) to zero (no relationship) to 1.00 (a perfect positive relationship) and can differ in their level of statistical significance. Level of significance tells us the probability that a correlation is due to sampling fluctuation or chance. It is determined by the size of the correlation and the number of cases involved. Generally speaking, as the correlation and the number of cases increase, so does the probability that the correlation is significant. Most researchers consider a significance level of .05 or higher to be an acceptable level.

Another concern will be whether the differences between the correlations for the criterion variables and the standard and alternative party identification measures are statistically significant. For example, suppose a particular criterion variable is found to be more highly correlated with the seven-point party identification scale than with the party closeness scale. We will want to know whether the distance between the two correlations is due to sampling fluctuation or is statistically significant. Thus, significant differences between correlations will be noted during the analysis.

As discussed in Chapter One, Weisberg's multidimensional model of party identification implies that partisan strength and political independence are two separate dimensions. This directly challenges the assumption of previous researchers that both of these elements fall along a single continuum, best reflected in the standard four-point partisan strength measure. My revised version of Weisberg's model also implies that partisan strength and independence are two distinct elements. If this part of the model is valid, then we should find correlations with the *same* signs between the partisan strength and independence measures and the criterion variables. However, if these two entities do in fact comprise a single dimension, then we should find correlations with *opposite* signs between the partisan strength and independence measures and the criterion variables. Correlations that have opposite signs but *noticeably differ in size* will suggest that partisan strength and independence are bidimensional. We begin with an analysis of social background and party identification.

SOCIAL BACKGROUND

Angus Campbell, Philip Converse, Warren Miller, and Donald Stokes thought that research on the relationships between different social and demographic variables and party identification could tell us a lot about Americans' partisan ties. As explained in *The American Voter*, the social environment has a strong influence on the formation and duration of attachments to political parties.[21] The four investigators examined the relationship between social background and partisanship during the 1950s and found them to be closely connected. Whether citizens were black or white, young or old, Protestant, Catholic, or Jewish, working class or middle class, lived in the North or South, or in a city or a rural area, or had Republican or Democratic parents affected their party identification. Although partisan shifts have been detected among social groups and within demographic categories since the 1950s, few today deny the effect of the social environment on party identification.[22]

Race

Prior to the 1930s, election statistics suggest that blacks tended to prefer the Republican party.[23] This was due to the Civil War and the actions taken by President Lincoln, a Republican, which helped blacks. Their party preference, however, changed during the Depression years. The Roosevelt Administration and its New Deal politics contained strong elements of social equalitarianism which attracted minorities who had felt discriminated against. Although FDR was never a public supporter of racial equality, his economic policies deviated sharply from those of previous Republican administrations and were perceived by blacks as aiding them. Consequently, many of them threw their support behind the Democrats.[24]

The Democratic party gained additional black support in the 1960s when it adopted a more "pro-civil rights" image. The enactment of the 1964 Civil Rights Act and various War on Poverty programs during President Johnson's Administration was welcomed by blacks. These actions also tended to personify the different issue positions of the two parties, though southern Democrats opposed such policies. Gallup Poll data analyzed by Robert Erikson, Norman Luttbeg, and Kent Tedin clearly showed that blacks have voted for Democratic presidential candidates in overwhelming numbers since the 1960s.[25] President Reagan's well-publicized budget cuts in social programs and ambiguous stand on minority rights will probably guarantee the continuation of this trend.

Naturally, party identification and vote choice are not the same thing. Still, based on history and previous research, we would expect blacks to feel more

Table 2-3
Pearson Correlations between Race, Age, and Party Identification, Pre-Election Survey, 1980[a]

Items and Dimensions	Race	Age
Partisan Direction		
Party Difference Index	-.27*** (1370)	.02 (1388)
Party Closeness Scale	-.27*** (1118)	.08** (1130)
Party Support Scale	-.23*** (1536)	.07** (1553)
Democratic Party Feeling Thermometer	-.27*** (1497)	.14*** (1515)
Republican Party Feeling Thermometer	.11*** (1493)	.06** (1511)
Seven-Point Party Identification Scale	-.26*** (1557)	.04* (1575)
Strength of Partisanship		
Folded Party Closeness Scale	-.16*** (1118)	.22*** (1130)
Folded Party Support Scale	-.12*** (1536)	.19*** (1553)
Four-Point Strength of Identification Scale	-.16*** (1557)	.23*** (1575)
Independence		
Strength of Independence Scale	.13*** (1545)	-.16*** (1565)
Independents Feeling Thermometer	.05* (1377)	-.11*** (1396)

a - Figures in parentheses are numbers of cases.

* Significant at the .05 level.
** Significant at the .01 level.
*** Significant at the .001 level.

closely affiliated with the Democratic party than whites. Table 2–3 shows this to be the case in 1980. Overall, the correlations between race (coded zero for blacks and 1 for whites) and the partisan direction items are in the anticipated direction. The reason the correlations between race, the Republican party feeling thermometer, and the other partisan direction items have different signs lies in the way the partisan direction items are coded. In other words, *increasing* Republican thermometer ratings indicate greater affinity for the Republican party, whereas decreasing values for the other partisan direction measures represent this feeling. Hence, the findings concerning the partisan direction measures in the table are consistent. Though the correlations are small, blacks are more likely than whites to hold strong party attachments while whites are more likely than blacks to consider themselves independent from politics. In addition, the signs of the correlations between race and the indicators of partisan strength and independence are in the opposite direction and the correlations are about the same size. This implies that partisan strength and independence are unidimensional. Moreover, the absolute value of the correlation between race and the standard seven-point party identification scale is significantly higher (at the .001 level) than the correlation between race and the Republican feeling thermometer.[26] No other significant differences exist between the correlations for this variable and the standard and alternative party identification measures.

Since we also want to learn which of the two independence measures is the best indicator of political independence, we will report whether there is a significant disparity between the correlations for each criterion variable, the strength of independence scale, and the Independents thermometer. Our analysis reveals that race is more closely related to the strength of independence scale than to the Independents thermometer (significant at the .01 level). This finding shows that race is a better predictor of position on the strength of independence measure than of position on the Independents thermometer.

Age

Campbell and his colleagues found age had an important influence over party identification. Their analysis showed that the young were more likely than the old to call themselves Independents, and that the old were more likely than the young to be strong party identifiers.[27] Recent studies indicate this is even more true now than in the 1950s.[28]

There are two competing explanations which may account for this finding. Norval Glenn and Ted Hefner, and Paul Abramson argued that Americans' strength of party identification can be explained by the generation in which they first entered the electorate.[29] According to them, those who mature and begin to vote during a particular historical period undergo a unique experience that leaves an imprint on their attitudes and behaviors. Before and during the Depression, for example, the nature of the political world caused many to adopt strong party attachments. After the Depression the political climate stabilized, and there was no longer a reason for people to become strong partisans. (This situation changed in the 1960s.) Hence, those who entered the electorate prior to and during the 1930s are more likely to exhibit intense partisan feelings today than those who entered the electorate later. If present conditions change substantially in the future, the young could become more partisan than the old.

Other scholars believe that moving through successive phases of the life cycle naturally results in stronger party attachments; thus, the old will always be more partisan than the young. Perhaps as people age and inherit more responsibility, they begin to feel they have a greater stake in the way government is run. They soon choose a party to back, and as time goes by their loyalty is reinforced. This life-cycle change explanation was favored over the generational change explanation in *The American Voter*.[30] Philip Converse challenged the Glenn and Hefner, and Abramson findings and, based on his analysis, concluded that the life-cycle interpretation was more compelling.[31] According to Converse, the turbulent events or "period effects" of the 1960s could be confused with generation effects, something Glenn and Hefner, and Abramson failed to consider. Using a special merged data set of age cohorts—groups of people who were born at different points in time—he conducted separate analyses of the 1952–1964 "steady-state" period and the post–1964 period. While he found a distinct "aging" effect taking place during the steady-state period, he also discovered period effects overwhelmed all other changes in party identification during the post–1964 era. His results challenged the generational interpretation of partisan change beyond 1964.

Abramson later countered by introducing race as a control variable, something Converse was unable to do because of the nature of his data set.[32] He contended that Converse's inability to control for race led him to overestimate the impact of life-cycle effects. Abramson's analysis of the white electorate showed little gain in partisan strength among young whites during the 1952–1964 period. More importantly, his examination of whites' strength of identification between 1952 and 1976 revealed no gains in partisan strength as cohorts moved through the life cycle. His findings tended to dispute Converse's life-cycle thesis.

However, W. Phillips Shively analyzed the effect of life cycle on the percentage of partisans (strong and weak identifiers combined) and strong partisans in both the pre- and post–1964 periods.[33] This approach allowed him to control for period effects and compare directly the separate impact of life-cycle and generation effects on increased partisanship. He also controlled for race. In contrast to Abramson's findings, he discovered that aging influenced partisan strength about equally in both periods. Abramson attacked Shively's results because they were based on two questionable assumptions: (1) all whites who entered the electorate between 1940 and 1960 shared similar generational experiences, and (2) all voters reacted the same way to historical events (period effects) regardless of age.[34] Shively replied that Abramson's criticisms were also based on a problematic assumption; life-cycle effects did not influence the partisan strength of those who reached voting age between 1940 and 1960.

William Claggett's study shed additional light on the Shively-Abramson debate.[35] He postulated that partisan strength has two components, an acquisition component and an intensity component. This division is based on "the possibility that the processes regulating the initial acquisition of a party tie may be different from those governing the intensity of those attachments."[36] In attempting to offer evidence in support of his proposition, his findings confirmed Shively's contention that aging had an impact on the electorate in both the pre- and post–1964 periods. Additional inquiry is necessary, however, before we can be certain whether partisan strength contains more than one component.

All the studies discussed above employed age cohort analysis to test competing hypotheses. This technique allows one to use survey data to plot changes in party identification for specific age groups over time. A national panel study conducted over many years would yield the most interpretable results. Unfortunately, such a study has never been carried out, primarily because the large amount of funds required has never been made available. Researchers have therefore been forced to analyze data collected in separate surveys at different points in time.

Moreover, previous studies have only employed the standard party identification questions to measure partisan strength. Perhaps the employment of alternative partisan strength measures, like the ones described earlier in this chapter, would lead to different findings. In addition, the adoption of a multidimensional model of party identification would permit researchers to explore more fully the nature and degree to which life-cycle, generation, and period effects influence partisan direction and independence. We cannot pursue such an investigation here because several of the new party identification questions are only included in the 1980 election study. Yet, we can use the three dimensional model developed in this study to help us increase our knowledge about the relationship between age and party identification at this point in time and to compare the relationships between age and the various party identification measures.

Table 2-3 reports the Pearson correlations between age and party identification. There is only one weak relationship between age and partisan direction; it appears that older people are slightly more inclined to identify with the Democratic party than younger people. Also, as age increases, so does partisan strength. The reverse is true for the relationship between age and political independence; younger respondents are more likely to be independent than older ones. These findings are in line with those cited in the literature. Furthermore, the signs of the correlations between age and the partisan strength and independence measures are in the opposite direction and the correlations are similar in size. This supports the position long held that partisan strength and independence comprise the same dimension.

There are two significant differences between the correlations for age and the standard and alternative partisan direction measures. The correlations between age, the party closeness scale, and the Democrat thermometer are significantly higher (at the .05 and .001 levels, respectively) than the correlation between this variable and the traditional seven-point measure. In contrast, the correlations between age and the partisan strength and independence measures are approximately the same size.

Any study of the relationship between age and party identification should probably take race into account. There is a good chance that a higher percentage of older blacks than older whites feel they benefited from Roosevelt's New Deal programs and the Democratic party's effort to expand civil rights protection in the 1960s. If this is true, then a greater proportion of older blacks than older whites will align themselves with the Democratic party. Blacks (and even

Table 2-4
Pearson Correlations between Age and Party Identification for Blacks and Whites, Pre-Election Survey, 1980[a]

Items and Dimensions	Race Blacks	Whites
Partisan Direction		
Party Difference Index	.08 (164)	.02 (1205)
Party Closeness Scale	.24*** (174)	.06* (1364)
Party Support Scale	.27*** (177)	.06* (1357)
Democratic Party Feeling Thermometer	.27*** (172)	.14*** (1323)
Republican Party Feeling Thermometer	.01 (172)	.07** (1320)
Seven-Point Party Identification Scale	.11 (180)	.04 (1375)
Strength of Partisanship		
Folded Party Closeness Scale	.33*** (174)	.19*** (1364)
Folded Party Support Scale	.32*** (177)	.17*** (1357)
Four-Point Party Identification Scale	.31*** (180)	.22*** (1375)
Independence		
Strength of Independence Scale	-.22*** (183)	-.16*** (1361)
Independents Feeling Thermometer	-.13 (145)	-.11*** (1231)

a - Figures in parentheses are numbers of cases.

* Significant at the .05 level.
** Significant at the .01 level.
*** Significant at the .001 level.

whites) who entered the electorate after the 1960s are likely to have less reason to identify with either party.

Table 2-4 shows the Pearson correlations between age and party identification for blacks and whites. As one can see, the correlations between age and the partisan direction and partisan strength measures for blacks tend to be stronger than the correlations between age and these measures for whites. In other words, older blacks are more likely than older whites to prefer the Democratic party and be strong partisans. Younger blacks and whites are more inclined to say they are independent from politics than their elders. The data also suggest that partisan strength and independence fall along the same continuum.

There are a number of significant differences between the correlations in Table 2–4. For instance, the correlations between blacks' age, the party closeness scale, the party support scale, and the Democrat thermometer are significantly larger (at the .001, .001, and .05 levels, respectively) than the correlation between blacks' age and the standard seven-point measure. The relationship between whites' age and the Democrat thermometer ($r = .14$) is also significantly stronger (at the .001 level) than the relationship between whites' age and the standard seven-point measure ($r = .04$). Although the correlations between blacks' age and the three partisan strength measures are nearly equal in size, the correlation between whites' age and the traditional four-point partisan strength scale ($r = .22$) is significantly higher (at the .05 level) than the correlation between this variable and the folded party support scale ($r = .17$). Apparently, blacks' and whites' age is a better predictor of position on some of the alternative partisan direction measures than of position on the old seven-point measure. However, whites' age is a better predictor of position on the standard four-point scale than of position on the new folded party support scale. No significant differences exist between the correlations for blacks' and whites' age and the independence measures.

Region

To understand the relationship between region and party identification one must be familiar with the history of the United States during the last 120 years. The War between the States was considered by many to be Lincoln's war. After he was shot and the war ended, the Republican party imposed black enfranchisement upon the South under the Reconstruction Act of 1867. Led by white politicians, blacks threw their support behind the Republican party in state and local elections. Most native white southerners bitterly detested these actions. In 1877 Rutherford Hayes was elected president in return for withdrawal of federal troops from the South. Although the Fifteenth Amendment prohibited denial of the vote on the basis of race, southern state legislatures soon found ways to disenfranchise nearly all blacks (and even many whites). Poll taxes, literacy tests, "white primaries," and lengthy residence requirements were some of the strategies used to prevent blacks from voting. Personal threats and violence were also commonplace. David Knoke says that, "By 1908 all the states of the former Confederacy had adopted some form of legal or extralegal restriction on black voting," and for more than half a century conservative southern Democrats dominated the region and congressional politics.[37]

The outlawing of the "white primary" by the Supreme Court in 1944 only drew a small percentage of southern blacks to the polls in the 1950s, primarily because many families had not voted for over two generations and other obstacles to voting still existed. The Roosevelt legacy appeared to attract blacks to the Democrats, though their party attachments were weak at best. A national panel study conducted by the SRC from 1956 to 1960 revealed considerable instability in their party preferences between pre- and post-election interviews.[38] It was not until the civil rights movement in the 1960s that southern blacks were allowed unrestricted access to the polls, and that blacks all over the country swung toward the Democrats.

Southern white Democrats vehemently opposed the civil rights laws of the 1960s and blamed the national Democratic party for their passage. As a result, Richard Nixon was able to carry the entire region in the 1972 presidential election. Although Jimmy Carter did well in the South in 1976, Ronald Reagan won most of the region back in 1980. Recently, several southern states have elected Republican governors and U.S. Senators for the first time in this century, a sure sign that the Democratic party is losing its grip on the South.

The 1960s also marked the start of migration by many Northerners to the South and West. The South has become modernized and the population of the region has changed as a result of new people moving there. To what extent can migration explain partisan change in this part of the country? Norman Nie, Sidney Verba, and John Petrocik addressed this question in *The Changing American Voter*.[39] Their study suggested that migration into the South was a major cause of the decline in partisanship up to about 1964. There is no evidence, however, that the North-South population shift had much impact after 1964. Instead, their data showed a marked decline in Democratic affiliation among native Southerners after this date. The two trends together help explain the subsequent electoral volatility in this region in the 1970s and 1980s. Little research has been done on the political impact of migration from East to West.

Most political scientists have studied the relationship between region and party identification strictly from a North versus South perspective. There are two reasons why future analyses should focus instead on four regions—the Northeast, Midwest, South, and West. First, looking back at the last four presidential elections, it is clear that Nixon, Ford, and Reagan attempted to capture a coalition of southern and western states. Obviously, they felt they had the best chance of winning electoral votes in those two areas of the country and, judging by the outcome of the four elections, Nixon and Reagan were right. Ford won most of the western states, too. Kevin Phillips, in *The Emerging Republican Majority*, argued that Republicans should always pursue this strategy.[40] No doubt, future Republican presidential candidates will also adopt this formula, thus requiring students of politics to study party identification within each of the four regions.

Second, the population shift from East to West and North to South over the last three decades has given the sunbelt states a majority of the total U.S. population for the first time. The 1980 census added more congressional seats to the southern and western states at the expense of the northern and midwestern states. If the same migration pattern continues, the sunbelt states will gain ad-

Social Background and Party Identification 55

Table 2-5
Statistical Significance of Region by Party Identification, Pre-Election Survey, 1980[a]

Items and Dimensions	Region	Number of Cases
Partisan Direction		
Party Difference Index	NS	1389
Party Closeness Scale	.001	1559
Party Support Scale	NS	1555
Democratic Party Feeling Thermometer	.01	1517
Republican Party Feeling Thermometer	NS	1513
Seven-Point Party Identification Scale	.05	1577
Strength of Partisanship		
Folded Party Closeness Scale	.001	1559
Folded Party Support Scale	NS	1555
Four-Point Strength of Identification Scale	.05	1577
Independence		
Strength of Independence Scale	.05	1566
Independents Feeling Thermometer	NS	1397

a - Chi-square was used to determine significance levels.

ditional seats in the House of Representatives after the 1990 census, further increasing their influence in Congress and the federal government. Proper insight into the dynamics of such a power shift will require, among other things, a study of party orientation in all four regions.

A cross-tabular analysis between region and party identification was conducted. The chi-square statistic was used to indicate whether there was a statistically significant association between region and each party identification measure. Unlike the correlations we have examined thus far, this statistic only shows whether an association exists and cannot tell us the strength or direction of a relationship. According to Table 2–5, statistically significant associations exist between region and the party closeness scale, the Democrat feeling thermometer, the seven-point party identification scale, the folded party closeness measure, the four-point strength of identification measure, and the strength of independence scale.[41] Region is not significantly related to the other party identification measures.

The cross-tables for region, the party closeness measure, the Democrat thermometer, and the seven-point party identification scale merit some attention. All three tables reveal a high concentration of Democrats in the South, and an otherwise fairly equal distribution of Republicans and Democrats throughout the rest of the nation. However, the party closeness measure implies that Westerners are more likely to be partisans than voters living in other regions of the country (even the South) while the Democrat thermometer and the standard measure do not show this to be the case. Therefore, to a certain extent, these cross-tables present conflicting information about the relationship between region and partisan direction. No significant discrepancies exist between the cross-tables for region, the folded party closeness scale, and the traditional partisan strength measure. Finally, the cross-table for region and the strength of independence scale indicates that Southerners are least likely to be politically independent.

Place of Residence

Over the last three decades we have also witnessed population movements between different places of residence. During the 1950s large numbers of rural and farm dwellers moved to urban areas in search of better job opportunities, and many cities experienced rapid population growth as a result. In the 1960s and 1970s, however, a large number of people left the cities for the suburbs, and the urban population, particularly in the Northeast and Midwest, declined. These migrants tended to be white-collar, Republican voters. Today minorities, foreign immigrants, and semi- and unskilled workers, most of whom are Democratic voters, account for a large portion of the country's urban population. Election statistics from the 1970s and early 1980s demonstrate that these two streams of movement have given the Republican party considerable influence in the rural and suburban areas and the Democratic party control of the cities. In other words, as one moves from rural to urban areas, Democratic support at the ballot box increases. There is a conceptual difference, of course, between party identification and the vote. Still, place of residence might be related to party identification.

A correlation analysis was conducted between place of residence and the different party identification measures.[42] Although the data do reveal that increased urbanization is accompanied by Democratic party affiliation, the tau-c correlations are small and only vary between .08 and .12 among the six partisan direction items. Furthermore, the correlations between place of residence, the partisan strength measures, and the independence items are not significant. The correlations between where citizens live and the individual party identification measures do not differ significantly.

Religion

Religion has played an important role in American politics since the birth of the nation. The early colonial settlers were predominantly English-speaking people of dissenting religious faiths. The Protestants of these denominations exercised tremendous influence over the economic, political, and social institutions of the eastern seaboard states through the early 1800s.[43] The influx of a large number of Irish immigrants in the mid–1800s and eastern and southern European immigrants, such as Poles, Slavs, and Italians, in the late 1800s and early 1900s led to the establishment of a sizable Catholic block. Many Jews immigrated to the United States about this time, too.

Contrasting cultural backgrounds and differences over the role of government in religious and moral affairs in the 1800s spawned enduring social conflicts. The serious clashes between the "pietist" and "liturgical" ethno-religious subcultures resulted in the formation of well-organized and very active party coalitions.[44] Walter Dean Burnham wrote:

a visit to a Congregational or Methodist church on Sunday and a Republican rally on Monday in the Ohio Western Reserve a century or more ago would tend to produce cognitive consonance and partisan reinforcement. It would also be likely to produce intense party identification, highly stable party voting, and very high levels of political participation—at least so long as the military model of political campaigning was ascendant.[45]

In addition to an agrarian revolt and an economic depression, Democrat William Jennings Bryan's revivalist appeal to rural Protestants in the 1896 presidential election alienated many Catholics and forced the Democratic party into a secular decline. Religion played a smaller role in national politics for the next thirty years.

Disputes between religious groups in the late 1800s centered on temperance, prohibition, Sunday blue laws, government support of religious education, and restriction of immigration.[46] While northern Protestants believed that the Republican party endorsed their revivalist goals, Catholics viewed the Democratic party (outside the South) as a guardian of their civil liberties. Ethnicity also attracted many Catholics to the Democrats, particularly in large metropolitan areas. Although the candidacy of Catholic Democrat Al Smith in the 1928 presidential election revived dormant religious feelings, it was Roosevelt who solidified Catholic and Jewish support for the Democrats. The attachment of Protestants to the Republican party and religious minority groups to the Democratic party persisted well into the postwar era.

Religious identity has been treated as an important variable in previous empirical research on party identification. The Columbia voting studies conducted in the 1940s and early 1950s in Erie County, Ohio, and Elmira, New York, revealed that Catholics voted Democratic in greater proportion than did Protestants.[47] On the national level the authors of *The American Voter* found that Catholics were more likely to consider themselves Democrats than Republicans even though a substantial number voted for Eisenhower.[48] To some extent, religion was a factor in the 1960 presidential election. According to Converse, John Kennedy's Catholicism attracted the support of Republican Catholics but repelled Democratic Protestants.[49] Phillips' analysis of aggregate voting data for 1964 and 1968, however, suggested that these defections were only short-term.[50] More recently, Nie, Verba, and Petrocik's longitudinal study showed that Jews have become slightly less Democratic, Catholics have become more Democratic, and Protestants have become less Republican.[51]

Americans witnessed a unique blend of religious and political ideology in the 1980 election. The so-called "Moral Majority" was given credit for the defeat of several key liberal Democrats in Congress. Leaders of the Moral Majority, such as the Reverend Jerry Falwell, are ultraconservatives who believe that public policy goals should be consistent with traditional social values and strict moral codes. For instance, they tend to support "the right-to-life" movement (the outlawing of abortion) and prayer in the public schools. One could argue that the demands of the Moral Majority are not entirely new and actually have roots in early American Protestantism.

Most Moral Majority groups publicly backed Reagan's bid for the presidency and contributed large sums of money to his campaign, often through supposedly independent committees and organizations. The media attention the movement received during the campaign may have sensitized voters to their own religious beliefs and partisan attitudes and rekindled feelings about old religious group-party ties. Unfortunately, the data do not permit a direct test of this hypothesis. Nevertheless, the 1980 election provides an interesting setting for an analysis of religion and party identification.

Table 2–6 shows the relationship between religious preference and party identification. Respondents were categorized as either Protestants, Catholics, Jews, or members of other faiths. Overall, the chi-squares for the cross-tables between religion and the partisan direction and independence items are statistically significant. The folded party closeness scale is the only partisan strength measure which is significantly associated with religion. The percentages within the individual cross-tables for religious identification and the partisan direction items indicate that Jews are far more likely than Protestants or Catholics to consider themselves Democrats, and that about equal proportions of Protestants and Catholics are Democrats. The latter finding differs sharply from the results of previous research.[52] A slightly higher percentage of Protestants than Catholics call themselves Republicans as expected. Respondents belonging to other denominations equally prefer the Republicans and Democrats. The percentages in the cross-table for religious preference and the folded party closeness measure reveal that Protestants and Jews tend to hold stronger party attachments than Catholics and, in particular, people who are of other faiths. This is not at all evident in the cross-table for religion and the standard four-point strength of identification scale. The data also show that Catholics and members of other religious groups are more likely to place themselves higher (6 or 7) on the strength of independence scale than Protestants or Jews, and that a greater proportion of Protestants than Catholics, Jews, and those of other faiths score a zero on this measure.

Table 2-6
Statistical Significance of Religion and Opinion on the Bible by Party Identification, 1980[a]

Items and Dimensions	Religion	Opinion On Bible
Partisan Direction		
Party Difference Index	.01 (1282)	.05 (1177)
Party Closeness Scale	.001 (1431)	.001 (1304)
Party Support Scale	.05 (1429)	NS (1303)
Democratic Party Feeling Thermometer	.01 (1395)	.01 (1282)
Republican Party Feeling Thermometer	.001 (1392)	NS (1279)
Seven-Point Party Identification Scale	.001 (1452)	NS (1325)
Strength of Partisanship		
Folded Party Closeness Scale	.01 (1431)	.001 (1304)
Folded Party Support Scale	NS (1429)	.05 (1303)
Four-Point Strength of Identification Scale	NS (1452)	.05 (1325)
Independence		
Strength of Independence Scale	.001 (1441)	.001 (1312)
Independents Feeling Thermometer	.01 (1278)	.001 (1189)

a - Figures in parentheses are numbers of cases. Chi-square was used to determine significance levels.

Respondents reinterviewed in the post-election survey were asked the following question:

Here are four statements about the Bible, and I'd like you to tell me which is closest to your own view.

1. The Bible is God's work and all it says is true.
2. The Bible was written by men who were inspired by God but it contains some human errors.
3. The Bible is a good book because it was written by wise men, but God had nothing to do with it.
4. The Bible was written by men who lived so long ago that it is worth very little today.

Returning to Table 2-6, there is no significant relationship between respondents' beliefs about the Bible, the seven-point party identification measure, the party support scale, and the Republican thermometer. But there is a significant relationship between beliefs about the Bible, the party difference index, the party closeness scale, the Democrat thermometer, and the partisan strength and independence items. Unlike the cross-table between responses to this question and the standard seven-point measure, the cross-table between this item and the party closeness scale clearly shows that voters who feel "the Bible is God's work and all it says is true" are more likely to be Democrats than Republicans. Those who think "the Bible was written by men who were inspired by God but it contains some human errors" feel equally close to the Republican and Democratic parties. The data reveal that respondents who believe "the Bible is God's work and all it says is true" are most likely to be strong partisans and least likely to be independent from politics.

Since Protestants and Catholics have been the main protagonists throughout our country's history and are the two largest religious groups today, we analyzed the relationship between their opinions on this question and party identification. The analysis uncovered no major differences between the attitudes of these two groups and party identification. However, considerable differences were found between Protestants' and Catholics' reactions to other religious matters and party affiliation.

Those reinterviewed in the post-election survey were also asked, "Do you consider religion to be an important part of your life, or not?" Table 2-7 shows the Pearson correlations between responses to this question (coded zero for "no" and 1 for "yes") and party identification for Protestants and Catholics. The data show that Protestants and Catholics who consider religion to be an important part of their life rate the Democratic party high on the feeling thermometer. Moreover, Protestants who say religion is an important part of their life tend to be strong partisans. This does not appear to be true for Catholics. The data in the table provide conflicting evidence concerning the dimensionality of strength of identification and independence. In general, the correlations in the table are quite small.

In a few cases the relationships between importance of religion and the individual partisan direction measures for Protestants and Catholics differ significantly from one another. The correlations between importance of religion and the Democrat thermometer for both groups are significantly higher (at the .01 level) than the correlations between this attitude and the standard seven-point measure. In addition, the correlations between importance of religion, the party closeness scale, and the party support scale for Catholics are significantly greater (at the .01 and .05 levels, respectively) than the correlations between this question and the traditional seven-point measure. No significant differences exist between the correlations for importance of religion and the partisan strength and independence measures.

In contrast to importance of religion, which is an attitude, church attendance

Table 2-7
Pearson Correlations between Importance of Religion and Party Identification for Protestants and Catholics, 1980[a]

	Religious Group	
Items and Dimensions	Protestants	Catholics
Partisan Direction		
Party Difference Index	.00 (735)	.01 (275)
Party Closeness Scale	.01 (811)	.08 (308)
Party Support Scale	.04 (812)	.07 (306)
Democratic Party Feeling Thermometer	.09** (792)	.10* (302)
Republican Party Feeling Thermometer	.05 (792)	.02 (299)
Seven-Point Party Identification Scale	.00 (827)	-.03 (312)
Strength of Partisanship		
Folded Party Closeness Scale	.07* (811)	.06 (308)
Folded Party Support Scale	.12*** (812)	.08 (306)
Four-Point Strength of Identification Scale	.13*** (827)	.03 (312)
Independence		
Strength of Independence Scale	-.05 (815)	-.04 (311)
Independents Feeling Thermometer	-.01 (725)	-.02 (280)

a - Figures in parentheses are numbers of cases.
*   Significant at the .05 level.
**   Significant at the .01 level.
*** Significant at the .001 level.

measures religiosity in behavioral terms. Respondents interviewed in the pre-election survey were asked how often they attend church or synagogue.[53] An analysis between church attendance and party identification for Protestants and Catholics led to the same findings reported in Table 2–7.

There were two other items concerning religion in the post-election interview. The first question asked respondents whether religion provides some guidance in their daily life.[54] The second one sought to find out if people have had deep religious experiences which have changed their lives or, in other words, if they have been "born again."[55] The data showed no relationship between

Table 2-8
Pearson Correlations between Party Identification and Attitudes toward the Moral Majority, Post-Election Survey, 1980[a]

Items and Dimensions	Attitudes Toward the Moral Majority
Partisan Direction	
Party Difference Index	-.06* (1061)
Party Closeness Scale	-.05* (1169)
Party Support Scale	-.05* (1163)
Democratic Party Feeling Thermometer	.09** (1162)
Republican Party Feeling Thermometer	.18*** (1161)
Seven-Point Party Identification Scale	-.05 (1175)
Strength of Partisanship	
Folded Party Closeness Scale	.03 (1169)
Folded Party Support Scale	.03 (1163)
Four-Point Strength of Identification Scale	.06* (1175)
Independence	
Strength of Independence Scale	-.15*** (1173)
Independents Feeling Thermometer	-.01 (1099)

a - Figures in parentheses are numbers of cases.

*   Significant at the .05 level.
**   Significant at the .01 level.
***   Significant at the .001 level.

Protestants' and Catholics' responses to these two questions and their party orientation.

After the election respondents were asked to rate the Moral Majority on a feeling thermometer. Table 2–8 reports the Pearson correlations between party identification and respondents' ratings. The small but significant correlations between the partisan direction measures and the Moral Majority thermometer reveal that Republicans are somewhat more likely to have positive attitudes toward the movement than Democrats. However, the direction of the correlation between the Democrat thermometer and this item implies that some Democrats also hold positive attitudes toward the Moral Majority. While it is hard to say whether partisan strength is related to this question, the correlation between the strength of independence measure and this item suggests that Independents tend to have negative feelings about the Moral Majority. The large discrepancy between the correlations for the partisan strength measures, the strength of independence scale, and the Moral Majority thermometer indicates that strength of partisanship and independence are two separate components of party identification.

When the signs of the correlations are taken into account, the relationships between the two party thermometers and the Moral Majority thermometer are significantly stronger (at the .001 level) than the relationship between the standard seven-point scale and respondents' ratings. The correlations between the partisan strength measures and the Moral Majority thermometer do not differ significantly. Yet, the correlation between the strength of independence scale and attitudes toward the Moral Majority ($r = -.15$) is significantly higher (at the .001 level) than the correlation between the Independents thermometer and this question ($r = -.01$).

Table 2-9 shows the relationship between party identification and the Moral Majority thermometer for Protestants and Catholics. Based on the correlations involving both party thermometers, Protestant Democrats and Republicans and Catholic Republicans tend to support the Moral Majority. Furthermore, there is some evidence that Protestant strong party identifiers endorse the Moral Majority whereas Protestant Independents have reservations about the movement. The data on the two religious groups appear to support the view that partisan strength and independence represent one dimension.

When the direction of the correlations is considered, the relationships between the party thermometers and attitudes toward the movement are significantly closer (at least at the .01 level) than the relationship between the traditional seven-point measure and this question for Protestants. There are no other significant disparities between the correlations for the party identification measures and Protestants' and Catholics' ratings. Though the correlations in the table are small, they provide some interesting insights into the relationship between religion, party identification, and attitudes toward the Moral Majority.

Political Socialization

In the first chapter we discussed the relationship between parents' and children's party affiliation. Political socialization studies have demonstrated that offspring tend to share the party affiliation of their parents, but we still do not know the best explanation for this. Perhaps partisanship is directly transmitted

Table 2-9
Pearson Correlations between Party Identification and Attitudes toward the Moral Majority for Protestants and Catholics, Post-Election Survey, 1980[a]

	Religious Group	
Items and Dimensions	Protestants	Catholics
Partisan Direction		
Party Difference Index	-.02 (633)	-.07 (243)
Party Closeness Scale	-.04 (689)	-.04 (264)
Party Support Scale	-.02 (687)	-.04 (263)
Democratic Party Feeling Thermometer	.12*** (685)	.01 (264)
Republican Party Feeling Thermometer	.13*** (687)	.14* (262)
Seven-Point Party Identification Scale	-.03 (699)	-.08 (267)
Strength of Partisanship		
Folded Party Closeness Scale	.05 (689)	-.05 (264)
Folded Party Support Scale	.05 (687)	-.02 (263)
Four-Point Strength of Identification Scale	.09** (699)	-.06 (267)
Independence		
Strength of Independence Scale	-.13*** (693)	-.02 (267)
Independents Feeling Thermometer	.05 (645)	-.03 (251)

a - Figures in parentheses are numbers of cases.

*   Significant at the .05 level.
**   Significant at the .01 level.
***   Significant at the .001 level.

from parent to child, or it could be that children's party identification is shared along with their parents' social conditions and many of their parents' basic values. Because of the attention given to the relationship between parents' and children's party identification in the literature, we conducted an analysis of parents' and respondents' partisanship. The findings are presented in Table 2–10.

Clearly, a strong relationship exists between parents' and respondents' party identification in 1980.[56] As expected, respondents generally hold the same party attachments as their parents (Republican parents are coded zero and Democratic parents are coded 1). There is no association between parents' identification and

Table 2-10
Pearson Correlations between Parents' and Respondents' Party Identification, Pre-Election Survey, 1980[a]

Items and Dimensions	Parents' Party Identification
Partisan Direction	
Party Difference Index	.52*** (755)
Party Closeness Scale	.49*** (821)
Party Support Scale	.42*** (819)
Democratic Party Feeling Thermometer	.38*** (807)
Republican Party Feeling Thermometer	-.30*** (805)
Seven-Point Party Identification Scale	.61*** (832)
Strength of Partisanship	
Folded Party Closeness Scale	.01 (821)
Folded Party Support Scale	.03 (819)
Four-Point Strength of Identification Scale	.05 (832)
Independence	
Strength of Independence Scale	-.03 (822)
Independents Feeling Thermometer	-.09** (739)

a - Figures in parentheses are numbers of cases.

* Significant at the .05 level.
** Significant at the .01 level.
*** Significant at the .001 level.

children's partisan strength. The correlation between parents' affiliation and the Independents feeling thermometer indicates that Republican parents are more likely than Democratic parents to have politically independent offspring. On the whole, however, the data seem to imply that strength of partisanship and independence fall along a single continuum. The relationship between parents' affiliation and the Independents thermometer and the fact that the correlations between parents' party identification and the partisan direction measures are far from perfect ($r = 1.00$) suggest that political experiences outside the family environment influence partisan acquisition.

The same might be said for the strengthening of partisan attachments over time. Originally, M. Kent Jennings and Richard Niemi's analysis of panel data collected between 1965 and 1973 showed that the party identification of young adults was consistently less stable than the party identification of their parents.[57] They speculated that the intergenerational differences were due mainly to the lesser political experience of the offspring. Gregory Markus and M. Kent Jennings' analysis of panel data collected between 1973 and 1982 involving the same respondents reveals that the party identification of the offspring stabilizes over time to the point where the stability of their partisanship rivals that of their parents.[58] Electoral participation—an activity pursued outside the family environment—is found to be a major contributor to the increased durability of partisanship among the younger cohort.

The close relationship between parents' and respondents' partisanship depicted in Table 2–10 provides an excellent context in which to compare the various party identification measures. The correlation between parents' affiliation and the standard seven-point measure is significantly higher than the correlations between parents' identification and the alternative partisan direction measures (at the .001 level in all cases). In other words, parents' affiliation is a better estimate of respondents' position on the old seven-point scale than of respondents' position on the new partisan direction measures. The correlations between parents' partisanship and the partisan strength and independence items do not differ significantly.

Socioeconomic Status

Karl Marx was the first person to initiate serious study of the relationship between social class and political power.[59] His controversial theory of class and conflict, formulated during the Industrial Revolution in England, centered on the individual's position in the economic production system. He saw a class system evolving in which a small group of people controlled the means of production and a large number of workers (without property) sold their labor for wages at less than the value of the commodities they produced. The capitalists or bourgeoisie would reap huge profits through the exploitation of the rest of society and gain political power. The working class or proletariat would eventually develop a "class consciousness," organize, and revolt against the capitalists in the pursuit of better economic conditions and more political power. Max Weber, Ralf Dahrendorf, Seymour Martin Lipset, and others have offered varied interpretations and modifications of Marx's theory.[60]

The Marxist model of class conflict considered the owner-worker relationship to be the true cornerstone of politics. To the extent that "class consciousness" manifested itself among the workers, political parties would adopt positions favorable to class interests. Voters would respond by casting their ballots for the party which best represented their concerns, and eventually class and party would become one.[61]

Lipset, in *Political Man*, argued that this has occurred in economically developed countries. He observed:

More than anything else the party struggle is a conflict among classes, and the most impressive single fact about political party support is that in virtually every economically developed country the lower-income groups vote mainly for parties of the left, while the higher-income groups vote mainly for parties of the right.[62]

For example, there are fairly distinct class-party alignments in European countries. The frequent occurrence of severe economic and political crises, in addition to other factors, explains the presence of class based parties in these countries. The United States, however, has never experienced the same turmoil and class polarization as Europe and does not have sharp party cleavages along class lines.

Nonetheless, the United States has suffered two economic setbacks during the last one hundred years. The Depression of 1893 did not create class divisions within the electorate, primarily because it was relatively mild and lasted a short time. Yet the Great Depression, which began in 1929 and lasted for more than a decade, was serious enough to produce new and enduring class-party alignments. As we know, Roosevelt's New Deal programs appealed to the disadvantaged and brought them into the Democratic party. Although the Republicans initially criticized his policies, they later accepted his approach. But by then it was too late. The Democrats blamed Hoover and the Republicans for the economy's collapse, and the Republican party's base of support diminished to include only "big business" and small town residents. While the Republican party was tagged as "the party of the rich," the Democratic party became known as "the party of the workingperson." The Democrats' hold on "the Depression generation" lasted for a number of years; however, economic prosperity following World War II, the emergence of an affluent technological society, and greater interclass mobility have narrowed whatever gaps there were between the classes. Jimmy Carter's successful effort to mobilize the New Deal coalition in 1976 suggests that many people may still attach the Depression based labels to the parties.[63]

Critics of Marxist theory have introduced other notions of stratification with respect to the United States. They argue that our society is classless because no large cleavages can be identified which separate the population into homogeneous class groups.[64] To them, the prestige of an occupation, the esteem in which it is held by the society, is the best measure of a person's status. The Duncan Socioeconomic Index (SEI) is among the most commonly used measures of occupational status. Researchers also use income and education to measure socioeconomic status or class.

There has been considerable research on the relationship between socioeconomic status and party identification.[65] Employing the standard conceptualization of party identification, most investigators find that people of low status (the poor, minorities, and the elderly) tend to consider themselves Democrats, and

Table 2-11
Pearson Correlations between Family Income, the Duncan SEI, Education, and Party Identification, Pre-Election Survey, 1980[a]

Items and Dimensions	Family Income	Duncan SEI	Level of Education
Partisan Direction			
Party Difference Index	-.19*** (922)	-.12*** (850)	-.15*** (1384)
Party Closeness Scale	-.18*** (1023)	-.11*** (951)	-.14*** (1555)
Party Support Scale	-.19*** (1019)	-.08* (945)	-.13*** (1550)
Democratic Party Feeling Thermometer	-.23*** (1002)	-.16*** (926)	-.23*** (1512)
Republican Party Feeling Thermometer	.09*** (999)	.00 (927)	.02 (1508)
Seven-Point Party Identification Scale	-.20*** (1032)	-.13*** (950)	-.17*** (1572)
Strength of Partisanship			
Folded Party Closeness Scale	.05 (1023)	-.03 (951)	-.05* (1555)
Folded Party Support Scale	.01 (1019)	.00 (945)	-.03 (1550)
Four-Point Strength of Identification Scale	-.02 (1032)	.02 (950)	-.05 (1572)
Independence			
Strength of Independence Scale	.15*** (1023)	.14*** (950)	.22*** (1561)
Independents Feeling Thermometer	.07* (936)	.06* (889)	.14*** (1393)

a - Figures in parentheses are numbers of cases.
* Significant at the .05 level.
** Significant at the .01 level.
*** Significant at the .001 level.

people of high status (the wealthy, professionals, and businessmen and women) tend to call themselves Republicans. Longitudinal data show that the strength of this relationship has been slowly decreasing since the 1930s. From a theoretical standpoint, socioeconomic status remains an important concept in our understanding of political power in general, and party affiliation in particular. Therefore, we now turn to an analysis of socioeconomic status and party identification.

Table 2–11 reports the Pearson correlations between family income, the Duncan SEI, education, and party identification.[66] All three measures of socioeconomic status are significantly related to five of the six partisan direction items. Although family income is significantly related to the Republican feeling thermometer, education and the Duncan SEI are not. The correlations show that respondents with lower family incomes, Duncan SEI scores, and levels of education are more likely to be Democrats than Republicans. In contrast, nearly all the correlations between the status items and the partisan strength measures are close to zero and not significant. There is a positive relationship between status and party independence. More specifically, as family income, occupational prestige, and education rise, so does level of independence. The different findings involving status, partisan strength, and independence demonstrate that strength of partisanship and political independence represent two separate dimensions and not just one as many researchers assume. An analysis of other status indicators and party identification leads to the same results presented in Table 2–11.[67]

There are a number of significant differences between the correlations for the socioeconomic status and party identification measures. For example, the absolute values of the correlations between the three status indicators and the standard seven-point measure are significantly higher (at the .001 level in each case) than the correlations between the three status indicators and the Republican thermometer. Similarly, the relationships between the Duncan SEI, level of education, and the standard seven-point scale are significantly stronger (at the .05 level) than the relationships between these two status measures and the party support scale. However, the correlation between education and the Democrat thermometer ($r = -.23$) is significantly larger (at the .01 level) than the correlation between this status measure and the traditional seven-point measure ($r = -.17$). There is also a significant distance (at the .05 level) between the correlations for family income, the folded party closeness scale, and the standard four-point partisan strength scale. Finally, the relationships between the three status measures and the strength of independence scale are significantly closer (at least at the .05 level) than the relationships between the status measures and the Independents thermometer.

Class Self-Identification

The preceding analysis only examined the relationship between "objective" indicators of class or status and party identification. However, there are many researchers who conceptualize class in subjective or psychological terms. Their operationalization of the concept is based on people's self-classification into predetermined class groupings.

Richard Centers was among the first proponents of the subjective approach.[68] He defined classes as:

psycho-social groupings, something that is essentially subjective in character, dependent upon class consciousness (i.e., a feeling of group membership), and class lines of cleavage [which] may or may not conform to what seem to social scientists to be logical lines of cleavage in the objective or stratification sense.[69]

He believed that a person's class was part of his or her ego, "a feeling on his [or her] part of belongingness to something; one's identification with something larger than himself [or herself]."[70] Influenced by Marx, he apparently associated class identification with class consciousness and used people's self-identification as a reflection of their class consciousness. In 1945 he included the following question in a national survey: "If you were asked to use one of these four names for social class, which would you say you belonged in: the middle class, lower class, working class, or upper class?" Campbell, Converse, Miller, and Stokes modified Centers' class self-identification measure, and their version has been included in the National Election Studies since the 1950s.[71]

In the 1980 election study respondents were asked:

There's been some talk these days about different social classes. Most people say they belong either to the middle class or to the working class. Do you ever think of yourself as belonging to one of these classes? (If yes) which one? (If no) well if you had to make a choice, would you call yourself middle class or working class? (If working/middle class) would you say that you are about average working/middle class, or that you are in the upper part of the working/middle class?

Table 2–12 shows the tau-c correlations between class self-identification and party identification. Class self-identification is significantly related to all six partisan direction measures. The data indicate that respondents who place themselves in the "upper-middle class" tend to be Republicans and those who place themselves in the "average-working class" tend to be Democrats. Similar findings were reported in Table 2–11. In addition, an ascendance in class is accompanied by an increase in partisan strength and political independence, albeit the correlations are small. Moreover, the correlations between class self-identification and the partisan strength and independence measures are all positive, which suggests that partisan strength and independence represent two dimensions and not one as commonly thought. We will continue to address this question in subsequent chapters. No significant differences exist between the correlations for class and the separate party identification measures.[72]

A MULTIVARIATE ANALYSIS

Thus far we have confined our study to one-on-one relationships between social background variables and our party identification measures. Although such a bivariate analysis is helpful in discovering underlying patterns in the data, the results can sometimes be misleading, especially when the independent variables are empirically related to one another. The intercorrelations among the social background variables in the 1980 election study show that respondents who are well educated, for example, are also likely to be young, white, and upper-middle class. One then must ask, which social characteristic is really affecting party identification?

We have also been examining the relationships between social background

Table 2-12
TAU-C Correlations between Class Self-Identification and Party Identification, Pre-Election Survey, 1980[a]

Items and Dimensions	Class Self-Identification[b]
Partisan Direction	
Party Difference Index	-.13*** (1269)
Party Closeness Scale	-.07*** (1433)
Party Support Scale	-.05** (1426)
Democratic Party Feeling Thermometer	-.12*** (1385)
Republican Party Feeling Thermometer	.05* (1384)
Seven-Point Party Identification Scale	-.15*** (1440)
Strength of Partisanship	
Folded Party Closeness Scale	.07** (1433)
Folded Party Support Scale	.04* (1426)
Four-Point Strength of Identification Scale	.01 (1440)
Independence	
Strength of Independence Scale	.08*** (1434)
Independents Feeling Thermometer	.05** (1283)

a - Figures in parentheses are numbers of cases.
b - The coefficients to the right of the folded party closeness and four-point strength of identification scales are tau-b correlations.

* Significant at the .05 level.
** Significant at the .01 level.
*** Significant at the .001 level.

variables and different party identification measures to see whether the standard indicators of party identification should be replaced by new ones. Such an approach is valid if the criterion variables vary independently from one another. The fact that some overlapping association among the social background variables exists requires us to conduct a multivariate analysis of the data.

Multiple regression analysis, a sophisticated multivariate technique, was used to find out which social background variables have the greatest independent influence over party identification. This technique controls for interrelations among the independent variables and tells us the extent to which the independent variables account for the different scores in the dependent variable. The combined influence of the independent variables over the dependent variable is measured

Table 2-13
Multivariate Analysis between Social Background and Party Identification, Pre-Election Survey, 1980

Items and Dimensions	Proprotion of Explained Variance	Number of Cases
Partisan Direction		
Party Difference Index	.22135	787
Party Closeness Scale	.19989	886
Party Support Scale	.16630	879
Democratic Party Feeling Thermometer	.19020	857
Republican Party Feeling Thermometer	.07582	856
Seven-Point Party Identification Scale	.31436	884
Strength of Partisanship		
Folded Party Closeness Scale	.07650	886
Folded Party Support Scale	.06265	879
Four-Point Strength of Identification Scale	.14013	884
Independence		
Strength of Independence Scale	.06687	880
Independents Feeling Thermometer	.02706	799

in terms of "proportion of explained variance" (or R^2). Explained variance is usually reported in percent.

Table 2–13 shows the results of a multiple regression analysis between age, race, education, family income, religion, parents' party affiliation, and party identification.[73] The six social background variables explain more variance in the standard seven-point scale than in the alternative partisan direction measures. Parents' affiliation and, to a lesser extent, race account for more explained variance in all the partisan direction measures than the other social characteristics. Income and education also affect respondents' scores on the Democrat thermometer. Otherwise, age, income, education, and religion have less influence over partisan direction.

Additionally, the social background variables explain more variance in the standard four-point partisan strength scale than in the other two partisan strength measures. While race and parents' identification explain most of the variance in the traditional partisan strength measure, age and parents' identification explain most of the variance in the alternative partisan strength scales. In general, income, religion, and education have little influence over respondents' partisan strength.

The social characteristics included in the multiple regression analysis explain more variance in the strength of independence scale than in the Independents thermometer. Although age exerts some influence over respondents' scores on both independence measures, race, income, education, and parents' affiliation affect respondents' position only on the strength of independence scale. Finally, religion plays an insignificant role in determining independence.

Two conclusions can be drawn from the findings reported in Table 2–13. First, social background has a greater influence over partisan direction than over the other two dimensions of party identification. Second, the six social background variables account for more variance in the two standard measures of party identification than in the new measures. This finding implies that the traditional party identification scales measure partisan direction and partisan strength better than the alternative indicators. Of course, a final verdict cannot be reached until we complete our study.

SUMMARY

This chapter began with a detailed examination of the items and factors comprising Weisberg's four dimensional model of party identification. An attempt to replicate his study using data drawn from the 1980 SRC/CPS pre-election survey led to a reassessment of his model. Due to important empirical and theoretical concerns, the party systems support component was eliminated from the analysis and a modified three dimensional model was adopted. The new model was used in our investigation of the social environment and party identification.

The data have thrown considerable light on the relationships between social background and partisan direction, partisan strength, and political independence. We found that blacks, the old, Southerners, Jews, urban dwellers, those who believe "the Bible is God's work and all it says is true," respondents with Democratic parents, and people of low status or class were more likely to be Democrats than Republicans. There was also some evidence that Protestant Democrats and Republicans and Catholic Republicans tended to support the Moral Majority. In addition, blacks, the old, Protestants, Jews, and those who think the Bible contains no lies tended to be strong partisans. Whites, the young, and respondents of high status or class exhibited a propensity toward political independence. In contrast to previous findings, about an equal percentage of Catholics were Democrats and Republicans in 1980.

The data reported in this chapter provided some clues as to whether partisan strength and independence represent one or two dimensions. The direction and size of the correlations between race, age, the Moral Majority thermometer (when Protestants and Catholics were considered separately), parents' affiliation, and the indicators of partisan strength and independence tend to support the position that these two entities fall along a single continuum. However, the data reported on the Moral Majority (for the entire sample), socioeconomic status, class self-identification, and party identification indicate that partisan strength and independence are distinct. Further analysis involving a wider variety of criterion variables is necessary before we can draw any conclusions concerning this issue.

Whether social background was more closely related to either the standard or alternative partisan direction measures depended on the context. For example, we found that blacks' and whites' age and importance of religion for Protestants and Catholics were more highly correlated with the alternative partisan direction measures than with the standard seven-point scale. However, we also found that parents' party affiliation was a better predictor of position on the traditional seven-point scale than of position on the other partisan direction measures. With one or two exceptions, the correlations between the different social background variables and the old and new partisan strength items were similar in size. There were several cases where the strength of independence scale was more closely related to the criterion variable (e.g., race, the Moral Majority thermometer, and the three status measures) than was the Independents thermometer. Overall, the relationships between the social characteristics and individual party identification measures tended to be in the same direction.

A multivariate analysis revealed both the separate and combined influence of the social background variables over party identification. The findings of the multiple regression analysis indicated that the social environment was a better estimate of scores on the two standard measures and the strength of independence scale than of scores on the other measures. Further study is needed before we can draw any firm conclusions about the interchangeability of these items. Accordingly, the next chapter examines the relationship between party identification and orientations toward the political system.

NOTES

1. Herbert F. Weisberg, "A Multidimensional Conceptualization of Party Identification," *Political Behavior* Vol. 2 No. 1 (1980), pp. 33–60.

2. Ibid., pp. 36–38.

3. For a more elaborate explanation of factor analysis see: Richard A. Zeller and Edward G. Carmines, *Measurement in the Social Sciences: The Link between Theory and Data* (New York: Cambridge University Press, 1980), Chap. 2.

4. Weisberg's four principal components accounted for three-quarters of their total variance and were given a varimax rotation.

5. Respondents were asked:

In your own mind, do you think of yourself as a supporter of one of the political parties, or not? (If yes) which political party do you support? On this scale from 1 to 7 where 1 means "not very strongly" and 7 means "very strongly," please choose the number that describes how strongly you support the (Republican/Democratic) Party.

6. The question read:

(If no on the party support question) do you ever think of yourself as closer to one of the two major political parties, or not? (If a party supporter or if yes on the above closeness question) here is a scale from 1 to 7 where 1 means feeling very close to the Republican Party and 7 means feeling very close to the Democratic Party. Where would you place yourself on this scale?

7. Weisberg, "A Multidimensional Conceptualization of Party Identification," pp. 53–54.

8. Ibid., p. 53.

9. Clearly, some of the party identification measures are ordinal level variables (e.g., the seven-point party identification scale), and one could question the basis for their inclusion in a factor analysis. Weisberg also faced this problem in his study. It is thought that whatever measurement error might exist due to the ordinal nature of these items is not great enough to influence markedly the results of the factor analysis.

10. The data used in this study were made available by the Inter-University Consortium for Political and Social Research. The 1980 National Election Study was conducted under a grant from the National Science Foundation. Neither the original collectors of the data nor the Consortium bear any responsibility for the analyses or interpretations presented here.

11. A principal factoring method with iteration was used to generate the four components. The four factors accounted for 75 percent of their total variance and were given a varimax rotation.

12. The exact wording of the question was:

Next I will read some general statements about political parties. Please use the scale on this page to tell me how strongly you agree or disagree with each statement. The scale runs from "disagree very strongly" at point 1 to "agree very strongly" at point 7. After I read each statement, you can just give me the number from the scale that applies.

Responses to the following three statements were summed to form a "party system support scale":

The parties do more to confuse the issues than to provide a clear choice on issues.

It would be better if, in all elections, we put no party labels on the ballot.

The truth is we probably don't need political parties in America anymore.

The scale ranged from 3 to 21 (n = 1376) and was considered reliable (Cronbach's alpha = .71).

13. The exact wording of the question was:

Now we'd like to ask you how good a job you feel some of the parts of our government are doing. As I read, please give me the number that best describes how good a job you feel that part of government is doing for the country as a whole.

The political parties.

    0. very poor job
    1.
    2. poor job
    3.
    4. fair job
    5.
    6. good job

7.
8. very good job

14. Respondents were asked:

How much do you feel that political parties help to make the government pay attention to what the people think—a good deal, some, or not much?

15. The tau-c correlations between this item and the Democrat thermometer, the Republican thermometer, the political parties thermometer, and the maximum thermometer score were: .09 (n = 1304, significant at the .001 level), .05 (n = 1300, significant at the .05 level), .14 (n = 1244, significant at the .001 level), and .13 (n = 1297), significant at the .001 level), respectively.

16. The exact wording of the question was:

How much of the time do you think you can trust the government in Washington to do what is right—just about always, most of the time, or only some of the time (none of the time, if respondent volunteers)?

17. The tau-c correlations between these items are: .16 (n = 1496, significant at the .001 level), .00 (n = 1493, not significant), .13 (n = 1422, significant at the .001 level), and .11 (n = 1388, significant at the .001 level), respectively. The inclusion of four other questions concerning trust in government in the analysis led to the same findings.

18. Angus Campbell, Philip E. Converse, Warren E. Miller, and Donald E. Stokes, *The American Voter* (New York: John Wiley and Sons, 1960).

19. A principal factoring method with iteration was used to generate the three components. The three factors accounted for 71 percent of their total variance and were given a varimax rotation.

20. Admittedly, both ordinal (e.g., the seven-point party identification scale) and interval (e.g., the feeling thermometers) measures comprise our multidimensional model of party identification. In order to avoid having to compare ordinal and interval level correlations between a given criterion variable and the party identification items, I chose to report only tau or Pearson correlations depending on the criterion variable's level of measurement. Although the Pearson correlations between ordinal party identification items and interval external variables may contain some measurement error, it is thought that the amount of error involved is not great enough to alter radically the study's findings.

21. Campbell, Converse, Miller, and Stokes, *The American Voter*, Chap. 7.

22. For an excellent study of partisan shifts among social groups see: Norman Nie, Sidney Verba, and John R. Petrocik. *The Changing American Voter*, Enlarged Edition (Cambridge: Harvard University Press, 1979), Chap. 13.

23. Campbell, Converse, Miller, and Stokes, *The American Voter*, p. 160.

24. Ibid.

25. Robert S. Erikson, Norman R. Luttbeg, and Kent L. Tedin, *American Public Opinion: Its Origins, Content, and Impact*, Second Edition (New York: John Wiley and Sons, 1980), p. 170. In addition, refer to: William H. Flanigan and Nancy H. Zingale, *Political Behavior of the American Electorate*, Fourth Edition (Boston: Allyn and Bacon, 1979), pp. 78–80.

26. All significance tests between correlations are two-tailed. The formula used to compute the significance of the difference between Pearson correlations was:

$$t = \frac{(r_{xy} - r_{vy})\sqrt{(n-3)(1+r_{xv})}}{\sqrt{2(1 - r_{xy}^2 - r_{vy}^2 - r_{xv}^2 + 2r_{xy}r_{xv}r_{vy})}}$$

This formula was adopted from: Jacob Cohen and Patricia Cohen, *Applied Multiple Regression/Correlation Analysis for the Behavioral Sciences* (Hillsdale: Lawrence Erlbaum Associates, 1975), pp. 53–54.

27. Campbell, Converse, Miller, and Stokes, *The American Voter*, pp. 161–67.

28. For instance, see: Nie, Verba, and Petrocik, *The Changing American Voter*, pp. 59–65.

29. Norval D. Glenn and Ted Hefner, "Further Evidence on Aging and Party Identification," *Public Opinion Quarterly* Vol. 36 (Spring 1972), pp. 31–47; and Paul R. Abramson, "Generational Change in the American Electorate," *American Political Science Review* Vol. 68 (March 1974), pp. 93–105. Also, refer to footnote 25 in Chapter One for other works in this area.

30. Campbell, Converse, Miller, and Stokes, *The American Voter*, p. 161.

31. Philip E. Converse, *The Dynamics of Party Support* (Beverly Hills, Calif.: Sage Publications, 1976).

32. Paul R. Abramson, "Developing Party Identification: A Further Examination of Life-Cycle, Generational, and Period Effects," *American Journal of Political Science* Vol. 23 (February 1979), pp. 78–96.

33. W. Phillips Shively, "The Relationship between Age and Party Identification: A Cohort Analysis," *Political Methodology* Vol. 6 No. 4 (1979), pp. 437–46.

34. Paul R. Abramson, "Comment: On the Relationship between Age and Party Identification," *Political Methodology* Vol. 6 No. 4 (1979), pp. 447–55.

35. William Claggett, "Partisan Acquisition Versus Partisan Intensity: Life-Cycle, Generation, and Period Effects, 1952–1976," *American Journal of Political Science* Vol. 25 (May 1981), pp. 193–214.

36. Ibid., p. 198.

37. David Knoke, *Change and Continuity in American Politics: The Social Bases of Political Parties* (Baltimore: The Johns Hopkins University Press, 1976), p. 39.

38. Philip E. Converse, "A Major Political Realignment in the South?" in *Change in the Contemporary South*, ed. A.P. Sindler (Durham: Duke University Press, 1963), pp. 195–222.

39. Nie, Verba, and Petrocik, *The Changing American Voter*, pp. 219–21.

40. Kevin P. Phillips, *The Emerging Republican Majority* (New Rochelle: Arlington House, 1969).

41. The SRC/CPS region codes were used. The southern border states were combined with the states in the deep South.

42. Place of residence was coded according to the 1970 census with additions from census population reports. The belt code ranges from 1, "central cities," to 6, "outlying areas."

43. Robert A. Dahl, *Who Governs?* (New Haven: Yale University Press, 1961).

44. For an excellent discussion of this topic consult: Richard F. Jensen, *The Winning of the Midwest: Social and Political Conflict, 1888–1896* (Chicago: University of Chicago Press, 1971).

45. Walter Dean Burnham, "Theory and Voting Research: Some Reflections on Converse's 'Change in the American Electorate'," *American Political Science Review* Vol. 68 (September 1974), p. 1020.

46. Knoke, *Change and Continuity in American Politics*, p. 19. See Chapter Two in his book for an in-depth analysis of the relationship between religion and party identification. Also see: Seymour Martin Lipset, "Class, Politics, and Religion in Modern Society: The Dilemma of the Conservatives," in *Revolution and Counterrevolution*, ed. Seymour Martin Lipset (New York: Basic Books, 1968), pp. 246–303.

47. Paul F. Lazarsfeld, Bernard Berelson, and Hazel Gaudet, *The People's Choice* (New York: Columbia University Press, 1948); and Bernard Berelson, Paul F. Lazarsfeld, and William McPhee, *Voting: A Study of Opinion Formation in A Presidential Election* (Chicago: University of Chicago Press, 1954).

48. Campbell, Converse, Miller, and Stokes, *The American Voter*, p. 159.

49. Philip E. Converse, "Religion and Politics: The 1960 Election," in *Elections and the Political Order*, ed. Angus Campbell et al. (New York: John Wiley and Sons, 1966), pp. 96–124.

50. Phillips, *The Emerging Republican Majority*.

51. Nie, Verba, and Petrocik, *The Changing American Voter*, Chap. 13.

52. For example: Nie, Verba, and Petrocik, *The Changing American Voter*, pp. 229–32.

53. The exact wording of the question was: "(If any religious preference) would you say you go to church/synagogue every week, almost every week, once or twice a month, a few times a year, or never?"

54. The question read: "Would you say your religion provides some guidance in your day-to-day living, quite a bit of guidance, or a great deal of guidance in your day-to-day life?"

55. Respondents were asked:

Some people have had deep religious experiences which have transformed their lives. I'm thinking of experiences sometimes described as "being born again in one's life." There are deeply religious people who have not had an experience of this sort. How about you, have you had such an experience (yes or no)?

56. Respondents were simply asked: "Did your father/mother (or father/mother substitute) think of himself/herself mostly as a Democrat, as a Republican, as an Independent, or what?"

57. M. Kent Jennings and Richard G. Niemi, "The Persistence of Political Orientations: An Over-Time Analysis of Two Generations," *British Journal of Political Science* Vol. 8 (July 1978), pp. 333–63; and M. Kent Jennings and Richard G. Niemi, *Generations and Politics: A Panel Study of Young Adults and Their Parents* (Princeton: Princeton University Press, 1981).

58. Gregory B. Markus and M. Kent Jennings, "Partisan Orientations over the Long Haul: Results from the Three-Wave Political Socialization Panel Study," presented at the 1983 Annual Meeting of the American Political Science Association, Chicago, Illinois. In addition, see: Charles H. Franklin, "Issue Preferences, Socialization, and the Evolution of Party Identification," *American Journal of Political Science* Vol. 28 (August 1984), pp. 459–78.

59. Karl Marx, *Capital* Vols. 1–3 (Moscow: Foreign Languages Publishing House, 1962).

60. Ralf Dahrendorf, *Class and Class Conflict in Industrial Society* (Stanford: Stanford University Press, 1959); Max Weber, "Class, Status, Party," in *Class, Status, and Power*, Second Edition, ed. Reinhard Bendix and Seymour Martin Lipset (New York:

Free Press, 1966), pp. 21–28; and Seymour Martin Lipset, "Social Class," in *The International Encyclopedia of the Social Sciences*, Vol. 15, ed. D.L. Sills (New York: Macmillan, 1968), pp. 296–316. For a review of the literature in this area consult: Knoke, *Change and Continuity in American Politics*, pp. 59–65.

61. Knoke, *Change and Continuity in American Politics*, p. 60.

62. Seymour Martin Lipset, *Political Man: The Social Bases of Politics*, Expanded Edition (Baltimore: The Johns Hopkins University Press, 1981), p. 234.

63. Mary and Robert Jackman's study of class awareness showed that although class issues have played only a minor role in national elections, there is a marked awareness of social class at the grass roots level. Mary R. Jackman and Robert W. Jackman, *Class Awareness in the United States* (Berkeley: University of California Press, 1983).

64. Albert J. Reiss (ed.), *Occupations and Social Status* (New York: Free Press, 1961); Robert W. Hodge, Paul M. Siegel, and Peter H. Rossi, "Occupational Prestige in the United States, 1925–63," *American Journal of Sociology* Vol. 70 (November 1964), pp. 286–302; and Paul M. Siegel, "Prestige in the American Occupational Structure," unpublished Ph.D. dissertation, University of Chicago, 1971.

65. Campbell, Converse, Miller, and Stokes, *The American Voter*; Heinz Eulau, *Class and Party in the Eisenhower Years* (New York: Free Press, 1962); John C. Leggett, *Race, Class, and Political Consciousness* (Cambridge: Schenkman, 1972); Sidney Verba and Norman H. Nie, *Participation in America: Political Democracy and Social Equality* (New York: Harper and Row, 1972); Gerald M. Pomper, *Voters' Choice: Varieties of American Electoral Behavior* (New York: Dodd, Mead and Company, 1975); Richard Hamilton, *Restraining Myths: Critical Studies of U.S. Social Structure and Politics* (New York: John Wiley and Sons, 1975); Knoke, *Change and Continuity in American Politics*; Dennis S. Ippolito, Thomas G. Walker, and Kenneth L. Kolson, *Public Opinion and Responsible Democracy* (Englewood Cliffs: Prentice Hall, 1976); Flanigan and Zingale, *Political Behavior of the American Electorate*; Nie, Verba, and Petrocik, *The Changing American Voter*; William J. Crotty and Gary C. Jacobson, *American Parties in Decline* (Boston: Little, Brown, 1980); and Erikson, Luttbeg, and Tedin, *American Public Opinion*.

66. The family income categories were recoded to their midpoints to represent better equal intervals. The upper open-end interval ($50,000 and over) was recoded to its mean value using a Pareto curve:

$$\bar{x} = x \left(\frac{v}{v-1} \right)$$

where, x = lower limit of open-end interval and

$$V = \frac{c-d}{b-a}$$

where, a = Logarithm of lower limit of interval preceding open-end category
b = Logarithm of lower limit of open-end interval
c = Logarithm of the sum of the frequencies in the open-end interval and the one preceding it
d = Logarithm of the frequency in the open-end interval

The formula was adopted from: Henry S. Shyrock, Jacob S. Siegel, and Associates, *The Methods and Materials of Demography* (Washington, D.C.: U.S. Government Printing Office, 1975), pp. 365–67. Education was measured by number of years in school.

67. The other status indicators included personal income, the National Opinion Research Center (NORC) Prestige Scale, and a manual versus nonmanual occupation measure. The personal income categories were recoded using the same procedures outlined in footnote 66. David Knoke and David Long believe that the ambiguous nature of farming occupations in the class system (manual labor combined with capital ownership) makes their categorization problematic. Since they form such a small percentage of the work force (under 5 percent) they were excluded from the manual and nonmanual classifications. See: David Knoke and David E. Long, "The Economic Sensitivity of the American Farm Vote," *Rural Sociology* Vol. 40 (Spring 1975), pp. 7–17.

68. Richard Centers, *The Psychology of Social Classes* (Princeton: Princeton University Press, 1949).

69. Ibid., p. 27.

70. Ibid.

71. Campbell, Converse, Miller, and Stokes, *The American Voter*.

72. Approximate two-sided confidence intervals for tau-b or tau-c can be obtained from:

$$\text{tau} - b/c \pm \text{psd}$$

where, p = the appropriate percentile of the unit normal distribution
sd = the standard deviation

where for tau-b,

$$sd \leq \sqrt{n \frac{2}{(1 - \text{tau} - b^2)}}$$

and for tau − c,

$$sd \leq \sqrt{\frac{2}{n}\left[\left(\frac{m}{m-1}\right)^2 - \text{tau} - c\right]^2}$$

where m represents the number of rows or columns, whichever is smaller. This is a conservative procedure for obtaining the approximate upper bound for the estimated standard deviation of tau-b or tau-c. For more information refer to: Alan Stuart, "The Estimation and Comparison of Strengths of Association in Contingency Tables," *Biometrika* Vol. 40 Parts 1 and 2 (June 1953), pp. 105–10; Maurice G. Kendall, *Rank Correlation Methods*, Fourth Edition (New York: Hafner, 1970); H.T. Reynolds, *The Analysis of Cross-Classifications* (New York: Free Press, 1977).

73. Earlier regression models contained region, personal income, opinion on the Bible, place of residence, the Duncan SEI, the NORC Prestige Scale, class self-identification, and the manual-nonmanual measure. These variables were excluded from the final model for empirical and theoretical reasons. Religion and parents' party affiliation were transformed into dummy variables, and the independent variables were not entered into the regression equation in a predetermined order. An analysis of the missing data did not reveal any significant biases. Multicolinearity does not appear to be a major problem in the final regression model.

3
PARTY IDENTIFICATION AND ORIENTATION TOWARD THE POLITICAL SYSTEM

A substantial segment of the population feel the American political system is extremely complicated and have difficulty learning about the way government is run. This confusion is most apparent at election time when voters have to arrive at decisions about complex issues and candidates they know little about. Those who lack the necessary time, skill, or motivation to develop a good understanding of politics probably use familiar cues and symbols to help them formulate views on issues, candidates, and the political system. Party identification, no doubt, is an important cue for many Americans.

This chapter analyzes the relationship between party identification and orientation toward the political system. Specifically, this chapter examines the relationships between party identification and psychological involvement in politics, media attentiveness to politics, knowledge about the candidates, whether people watched the Carter-Reagan debate, perceived outcome of the debate, party system support, political trust, and political efficacy. As the reader will soon see, researchers have studied these associations for quite some time. This investigation will not only reveal partisans' and nonpartisans' attitudes toward and degree of involvement in the political system, but it will also increase our knowledge about the dimensionality of partisan strength and political independence as well as the various measures of party identification.

PSYCHOLOGICAL INVOLVEMENT

One would expect to find partisanship and level of psychological involvement in politics to be related. The authors of *The American Voter* found that as people's sense of attachment to one of the parties increases, so does their involvement in political affairs.[1] Common sense, more than anything else, explains this finding. What remains unclear, however, is the direction of causation. Researchers have yet to agree on whether one first develops an affinity for a party and then becomes involved in politics, or whether the opposite occurs. Perhaps a reciprocal relationship exists between the two variables.

The degree to which Independents are psychologically involved in politics has long been a topic of discussion. Prior to the publication of *The American Voter*, Independents were thought of as concerned citizens who carefully reviewed the issue positions of parties and candidates before deciding how to vote. Yet, Angus Campbell and his colleagues found that Independents in the 1950s cared much less about politics than partisans.[2] Voting studies conducted in the 1960s and 1970s indicated that this was an overstatement. What Independents' attitude is towards politics in 1980 will be explored shortly.

Interest in Politics

Norman Nie, Sidney Verba, and John Petrocik examined the level of interest in presidential campaigns, a measure of psychological involvement, between 1952 and 1972.[3] In addition to finding a relatively low level of campaign interest among Americans over the twenty year span (only 36 percent on the average were "very interested"), they reported that level of interest is quite variable and has little to do with educational attainment. Instead, their data showed that there might be a connection between interest in politics and political trust. The post-1968 period is marked by a decline in interest and a concomitant rise in distrust in government, possibly due to the turmoil of the late 1960s and early 1970s. According to them, "the decline in interest appears to represent more a conscious rejection of politics than a withdrawal into more neutral apathy."[4] Such a decline, they speculated, led to increased partisan infidelity and a rise in political independence in the 1970s. They therefore hypothesized that interest in politics, political trust, and party identification are interrelated.

John Pierce, Kathleen Beatty, and Paul Hagner's analysis of the 1976 SRC/CPS National Election Study showed that leaning Independents were just as likely to be "very interested" in the campaign as were weak party identifiers.[5] While strong party identifiers were the most likely to be "very interested" in the campaign, pure Independents were the least likely to feel this way. They, of course, used the standard seven-point party identification scale in their investigation.

Based on the results of previous research, we expect to find a positive correlation between interest in the 1980 political campaign and strength of partisanship, and a negative correlation between campaign interest and political independence. In other words, increased interest should coincide with increased partisan strength and decreased political independence.

Those interviewed in the post-election survey were asked the following question:

Table 3-1
TAU-C Correlations between Party Identification and Interest in Political Campaign, Post-Election Survey, 1980[a]

Items and Dimensions	Interest in Political Campaign
Partisan Direction	
Party Difference Index	-.11*** (1217)
Party Closeness Scale	-.08*** (1358)
Party Support Scale	-.03 (1355)
Democratic Party Feeling Thermometer	-.05* (1331)
Republican Party Feeling Thermometer	.10*** (1327)
Seven-Point Party Identification Scale	-.08** (1376)
Strength of Partisanship	
Folded Party Closeness Scale	.21*** (1358)
Folded Party Support Scale	.22*** (1355)
Four-Point Strength of Identification Scale	.17*** (1376)
Independence	
Strength of Independence Scale	.07*** (1366)
Independents Feeling Thermometer	.02 (1231)

a - Figures in parentheses are numbers of cases.

*   Significant at the .05 level.
**   Significant at the .01 level.
***   Significant at the .001 level.

Some people don't pay much attention to campaigns. How about you? Would you say that you were very much interested, somewhat interested, or not much interested in following the political campaigns this year?

Table 3-1 shows the tau-c correlations between party identification and responses to this question (coded 1 to 3, "not much interested" to "very much interested"). Excluding the party support scale, the correlations between the partisan direction measures and campaign interest reveal that Republicans were somewhat more psychologically involved in the election than were Democrats. Also, there is a positive correlation between strength of partisanship and campaign interest as we expected. That is, as partisan strength rises, so does interest in politics. However, contrary to what we anticipated, there is a weak but significant relationship between the strength of independence scale and campaign interest. In other words, the more detached people were from politics, the more interested they were in the 1980 election. This conflicts with findings reported in *The American Voter* and challenges the assertion by the authors that Independents are largely uninterested and uninvolved in politics. In addition, the date in Table 3–1 support the premise that partisan strength and political independence are not the same thing and rather are two separate components of party identification. There are no significant differences between the correlations for the various party identification measures and interest in politics.

Concern over Election Outcome

Concern over the outcome of an election is another measure of psychological involvement in politics. Campbell, Converse, Miller, and Stokes examined the relationship between party identification and concern over the outcome of the 1956 election and found that partisans, particularly strong partisans, were more likely to care about who won the election than Independents. Just before the 1980 election respondents were asked, "Generally speaking, would you say that you personally care a good deal which party wins the presidential election this fall, or that you don't care very much which party wins?" Those who responded "no" were coded zero and those who said "yes" were coded 1. Table 3–2 shows the results of an analysis between party identification and answers to this question.

As the reader can see, there are weak but significant relationships between the party support scale, the two party thermometers, and concern over the outcome of the 1980 election. Based on the direction of the correlations, it appears that both Republicans and Democrats were concerned about the election's result. The correlations between partisan strength and this question are noticeably stronger, and the data show that strong partisans cared more about who won the election than did weak partisans. There are also weak but significant relationships between the independence measures and this item, indicating that Independents tended to be unconcerned about the election's outcome. On the surface, this finding seems to be inconsistent with the positive relationship between independence and level of political interest reported in Table 3–1. However, it may reflect a basic dissatisfaction with both parties and their candidates by Independents rather than a low level of psychological involvement in the election. The large disparity between the size of the correlations for the partisan strength and independence measures and concern over the outcome of the election sug-

Table 3-2
Pearson Correlations between Party Identification and Concern over Election Outcome, Pre-Election Survey, 1980[a]

Items and Dimensions	Concern over Election Outcome
Partisan Direction	
Party Difference Index	-.01 (1309)
Party Closeness Scale	.03 (1471)
Party Support Scale	.06* (1463)
Democratic Party Feeling Thermometer	.08** (1430)
Republican Party Feeling Thermometer	.07** (1426)
Seven-Point Party Identification Scale	.00 (1485)
Strength of Partisanship	
Folded Party Closeness Scale	.36*** (1471)
Folded Party Support Scale	.38*** (1463)
Four-Point Strength of Identification Scale	.35*** (1485)
Independence	
Strength of Independence Scale	-.07** (1471)
Independents Feeling Thermometer	-.05* (1319)

a - Figures in parentheses are numbers of cases.

* Significant at the .05 level.
** Significant at the .01 level.
*** Significant at the .001 level.

gests that partisan strength and independence are two different components of party identification.

In a few cases there are significant differences between the correlations for the standard and alternative partisan direction measures and concern over the election's outcome. The correlations between the Democratic and Republican party thermometers and concern over the election's outcome are significantly higher (at the .001 and .01 levels, respectively) than the correlation between the standard seven-point measure and this item. Also, the relationship between the party support scale and whether respondents care about the election's result is significantly stronger (at the .01 level) than the relationship between the traditional seven-point measure and this question. The correlations between the partisan strength and independence measures and concern over the election's outcome are about the same size.

MEDIA ATTENTIVENESS

Presidential candidates try to reach as many voters as possible during an election campaign. Before the election is over they will meet and speak to hundreds of citizens' groups and organizations with the obvious intent of persuading voters to support them on election day. Although they will travel thousands of miles and visit many towns and cities during the campaign, the fact remains that few people will experience the campaign first-hand. Instead, most Americans will follow the election through the media—magazines, newspapers, radio, and television.

The media are an important source of political information for voters.[6] This is clearly demonstrated in studies by Philip Converse, Edward Dreyer, Doris Graber, and C. Richard Hofstetter and Terry Buss.[7] Reporters and their staffs work around the clock to gather, assimilate, and transmit news and information about the issues, the candidates, and the campaign. A lack of time, money, and education, along with other factors, prevent citizens from doing such a thorough job.

The media's role in American politics has increased dramatically over the last three decades. Television, of course, has become *the* medium through which campaigns are conducted and followed. Herbert Asher's analysis of the frequency of media usage between 1952 and 1976 revealed that while 51 percent reported using television as a source of campaign information in 1952, 89 percent relied on this medium in 1976.[8] Moreover, television has become the most trusted source of information.[9] A majority of the public have also relied on newspapers for information over the years. Since 1956, however, less than half of the electorate have used radio and magazines to follow campaigns. Data collected in the 1980 election study show that these figures remain relatively unchanged.

Increased reliance on television has had a significant impact on campaign expenditures and the role of political parties in the electoral process. Although a thirty-second spot during prime time can cost tens of thousands of dollars, millions of people can be reached. Consequently, candidates have been forced to raise large sums of money so that they can appear on television as frequently as possible. The result has been larger campaign budgets and more personalized campaigns emphasizing candidates over parties.[10] There is also a fear that television is setting the issue agenda by increasing the flow of information about political issues and the candidates' stands on those issues. This encourages voters to rely on issue and candidate cues (rather than on party cues) in elections, thereby diminishing the influence of the parties. Clearly, individuals running for office no longer rely heavily on party workers and party support as they once did, and strong dependence on television is likely to continue in the future.[11]

Several researchers have studied the effects of the media on the public's level of information, attitudes, and behavior. Robert Erikson's investigation of the impact of newspaper endorsements in 233 northern counties during the 1964 presidential campaign revealed that a Democratic endorsement from the local newspaper added about five percentage points to the 1960–1964 Democratic gain.[12] However, since Republicans have a monopoly on newspaper endorsements (1964 was a rare exception), their candidates will usually benefit, especially in areas where there are no rival newspapers. Upon repeating this analysis on a smaller scale in the 1968 and 1972 elections he found that "a newspaper effect similar to that of 1964 was also present in the 1972 election, but probably not in 1968."[13] Hence, "newspapers may be more powerful forces in highly ideological contests, such as 1964 and 1972, than in more 'normal' elections such as 1968."[14]

Michael Robinson's study of the influence of television on the 1968 presidential election showed that Independents and Democrats who were more reliant on television for information were more likely to vote for George Wallace or Richard Nixon, even when income and education were controlled.[15] This was particularly true for Democrats within the lower and middle socioeconomic strata. No relationship was found between television dependency and the vote for Republicans. According to him, the medium helped to produce votes for Wallace and probably hurt Hubert Humphrey.[16]

Peter Clarke and Eric Fredin's analysis of the effect of newspapers and television on political reasoning in 1974 revealed that news markets with competition among daily newspapers exhibit greater levels of information than monopoly areas, even after controlling for education and interest in politics.[17] Surprisingly, television was found to have a suppressing effect on political reasoning. Their findings suggested that a decline in newspaper penetration, lessened competition, and a shift toward television usage for news weakens people's understanding about partisan candidates.

Arthur Miller, Edie Goldenberg, and Lutz Erbring analyzed data from the 1974 SRC/CPS National Election Study along with the front-page content of ninety-four newspapers to see whether there was a relationship between the degree of negative political criticism found in newspapers and their readers' feelings of political trust and efficacy.[18] They found that negative newspaper criticism increased distrust more than inefficacy, even when education and media exposure were controlled. This was especially evident among those with only a grade school education, probably because "their attitudes are more sensitive to media differences . . . and that media impact is more likely heightened for them by the interaction of exposure and negative content."[19]

Unlike the studies reviewed above, the authors of *The Changing American Voter* considered campaign attentiveness in the media to be a measure of political involvement.[20] They assumed that voters who follow a campaign through the media are involved in it. This approach can be adopted in our analysis of party identification. Using media attentiveness as an indicator of involvement, one would expect to find increased partisan strength to be accompanied by greater attentiveness to campaigns in the various media. We begin by examining the printed media.

The Printed Media

In the 1980 post-election survey respondents were asked whether they read about the campaign in any magazines or newspapers and, if they had, how many articles they read in each medium.[21] Possible responses to these questions were "just one or two," "several," and "a good many," coded 1, 2, and 3, respectively. A code of zero was assigned to those who did not read any articles in either medium. Table 3-3 shows the relationship between party identification and level of attentiveness to the campaign in the printed media. The data reveal that Republicans are more likely to pay greater attention to the campaign in magazines and, to a lesser extent, newspapers than are Democrats. However, this relation disappears when education is controlled.

Partisan strength is not associated with the degree to which respondents follow the campaign in magazines. There is a weak but significant relationship between partisan strength and attentiveness to newspapers. In other words, as partisan strength increases, so does the regularity with which voters pay attention to the election in this medium. Increased independence from politics is also accompanied by a rise in the number of magazine and newspaper articles read. These findings hold even after controlling for education.

Even though the correlations are small in Table 3-3, the results are interesting. Perhaps strong party identifiers and Independents follow the campaign in magazines and newspapers closely for different reasons. While party loyalists probably want to track the progress of their party's candidates, Independents may desire additional information about the race before voting. Of course, further study is needed to verify this. This finding offers support for the view that partisan strength and independence are two dimensions. Overall, there are no significant differences between the correlations for the individual party identification measures and attentiveness to the campaign in the printed media.

The Electronic Media

Identical questions concerning the extent to which people used the radio and television to follow the 1980 campaign were included in the post-election survey. Table 3-4 reports the relationship between party identification and level of attentiveness to the campaign in the electronic media. Although the correlations in the table seem to suggest that Republicans follow the campaign on ra-

Table 3-3
TAU-C Correlations between Party Identification and Attentiveness to Printed Media, Post-Election Survey, 1980[a]

Items and Dimensions	Attention to Magazines[b]	Attention to Newspapers[b]
Partisan Direction		
Party Difference Index	-.08*** (1215)	-.05* (1212)
Party Closeness Scale	-.07*** (1355)	-.03 (1351)
Party Support Scale	-.05** (1352)	-.02 (1348)
Democratic Party Feeling Thermometer	-.09*** (1328)	-.02 (1324)
Republican Party Feeling Thermometer	.04* (1324)	.03 (1321)
Seven-Point Party Identification Scale	-.09*** (1373)	-.05* (1368)
Strength of Partisanship		
Folded Party Closeness Scale	.02 (1355)	.09*** (1351)
Folded Party Support Scale	.02 (1352)	.11*** (1348)
Four-Point Strength of Identification Scale	-.03 (1373)	.08*** (1368)
Independence		
Strength of Independence Scale	.11*** (1363)	.12*** (1359)
Independents Feeling Thermometer	.09*** (1229)	.03 (1228)

a - Figures in parentheses are numbers of cases.

b - The coefficients to the right of the folded party closeness and four-point strength of identification scales are tau-b correlations.

* Significant at the .05 level.

** Significant at the .01 level.

*** Significant at the .001 level.

dio and television with greater regularity than do Democrats, the relationship disappears after controlling for education. The already small but significant correlations between the independence measures and attentiveness to the campaign in the two media also move closer to zero when education is held constant. The data do show that as strength of partisanship increases, so does the degree to which respondents paid attention to the campaign on radio and television, regardless of education. Here again, there are no significant differences between the correlations for the separate party identification measures and usage of the electronic media.

Table 3-4
TAU-C Correlations between Party Identification and Attentiveness to Electronic Media, Post-Election Survey, 1980[a]

Items and Dimensions	Attention to Radio[b]	Attention to Television[b]
Partisan Direction		
Party Difference Index	-.04* (1216)	-.06** (1214)
Party Closeness Scale	-.02 (1357)	-.04* (1354)
Party Support Scale	-.02 (1354)	.00 (1351)
Democratic Party Feeling Thermometer	-.02 (1330)	.01 (1327)
Republican Party Feeling Thermometer	.04 (1326)	.09*** (1323)
Seven-Point Party Identification Scale	-.04* (1375)	-.04 (1372)
Strength of Partisanship		
Folded Party Closeness Scale	.07*** (1357)	.13*** (1354)
Folded Party Support Scale	.08*** (1354)	.16*** (1351)
Four-Point Strength of Identification Scale	.08*** (1375)	.11*** (1372)
Independence		
Strength of Independence Scale	.05** (1365)	.08*** (1362)
Independents Feeling Thermometer	.04* (1230)	.02 (1228)

a - Figures in parentheses are numbers of cases.
b - The coefficients to the right of the folded party closeness and four-point strength of identification scales are tau-b correlations.
* Significant at the .05 level.
** Significant at the .01 level.
*** Significant at the .001 level.

KNOWLEDGE ABOUT THE PRESIDENTIAL CANDIDATES

During the course of a campaign, Americans are exposed to various sources of information about the candidates. As discussed in the previous section, a large segment of the public use the media to follow the election. But the media are not the only source of information. Voters also learn about the issues and candidates through the mail, visits to their home by party workers, rallies, and conversations with co-workers, friends, and relatives.

Exactly how much information about the candidates voters retain is another question. Education, interest in the campaign, and party identification are among the major factors which affect level of knowledge about a race. With respect to the latter factor, one would think that strong partisans would follow the election closely enough to learn something about the candidates. Like basketball fans who make an effort to familiarize themselves with the teams and the players, party loyalists probably try to learn about the parties and the candidates.[22]

Those interviewed in the pre-election survey were asked the following question:

I am going to hand you a list of persons who have been presidential candidates this year. Many people tell us they have not heard much about some of the persons on this list. Would you please read over the list and, in the box provided, put a zero over the name of any candidate you have heard of.

After the respondents carried out this instruction they were asked:

Many people also tell us there are candidates they feel they don't know much about, even though they have heard their names before. Would you please go down the list of candidates again and, in the box, put an "X" by the name of any candidate you have heard of but feel you don't know much about.

If respondents had heard of a candidate and knew something about him they left the box blank. Respondents who had not heard of a candidate were coded zero, those who recognized a candidate's name but did not know much about him were coded 1, and those who recognized a candidate's name and knew something about him were coded 2. Reactions to the names of thirteen presidential candidates were summed to form a "level of knowledge about the presidential candidates index."[23]

Table 3–5 reports the Pearson correlations between party identification and the level of knowledge about the presidential candidates index. The data show that Republicans were more familiar with the major candidates running for the presidency in 1980 than were Democrats. There is a weak but significant relationship between partisan strength and level of knowledge. That is, as partisan strength increases, so does knowledge. In addition, Table 3–5 indicates that greater independence from politics is accompanied by greater familiarity with the candidates. Controlling for education does not change these findings. Republicans, Independents, and strong partisans are probably more knowledgeable about the presidential candidates than their counterparts in the electorate because they are also more interested in politics (as we saw in Table 3–1). The data in the table provide additional evidence that partisan strength and independence are distinct entities.

There are two significant differences between the correlations for the standard and alternative partisan direction measures and level of knowledge about the presidential candidates. There is a significant disparity (at the .05 level) between the correlations for the seven-point party identification scale, the party

Table 3-5
Pearson Correlations between Party Identification and Knowledge about Presidential Candidates, Pre-Election Survey, 1980[a]

Items and Dimensions	Knowledge About Presidential Candidates
Partisan Direction	
Party Difference Index	-.17*** (1330)
Party Closeness Scale	-.12*** (1497)
Party Support Scale	-.10*** (1493)
Democratic Party Feeling Thermometer	-.15*** (1452)
Republican Party Feeling Thermometer	.10*** (1449)
Seven-Point Party Identification Scale	-.15*** (1511)
Strength of Partisanship	
Folded Party Closeness Scale	.07** (1497)
Folded Party Support Scale	.09*** (1493)
Four-Point Strength of Identification Scale	.07** (1511)
Independence	
Strength of Independence Scale	.19*** (1500)
Independents Feeling Thermometer	.05* (1336)

a - Figures in parentheses are numbers of cases.

* Significant at the .05 level.
** Significant at the .01 level.
*** Significant at the .001 level.

support scale, and level of knowledge. More specifically, the traditional seven-point measure is more closely related to the criterion variable ($r = -.15$) than is the alternative party support measure ($r = -.10$). Also, the absolute value of the correlation between the seven-point measure and level of information about the candidates is significantly higher (at the .05 level) than the correlation between the Republican thermometer and this variable. No significant differences exist between the correlations for the standard and alternative partisan strength measures and knowledge. The correlation between the strength of independence scale and how familiar respondents are with the presidential candidates ($r = .19$)

is significantly greater (at the .001 level) than the correlation between the Independents thermometer and this question (r = .05).[24]

THE 1980 PRESIDENTIAL DEBATE

Given the potential impact of television on public opinion, presidential candidates carefully weigh the possible benefits and costs of engaging in televised debates before deciding whether to do so. Generally speaking, candidates who are far ahead in the polls avoid appearing in televised debates, primarily because they do not want to risk a poor performance. There is always the chance that the stressful conditions which normally accompany such events will cause a participant to make a controversial statement. For example, few will forget President Ford's faux pas concerning Poland's relationship with the Soviet Union during his debate with Carter. In response to a question from the panel, Ford said that Poland was completely free from the influence of the Soviet Union. Several weeks passed before he retracted his statement but by then the damage had been done.

Usually, those behind in the polls will try to persuade their opponents to debate them. For example, Gore Vidal, running far behind Governor Jerry Brown in the 1982 Democratic primary race for United States Senator from California, tried to persuade Brown to debate him by offering to contribute $25,000 to his opponent's favorite charity. Vidal obviously felt he had little to lose and everything to win. Brown, however, rejected the offer.[25]

Debates are most likely to take place in close races, such as the 1960, 1976, and 1980 presidential elections.[26] Exactly how much impact a televised debate has on the outcome of an election is unclear since other factors also affect the vote. The research design problems inherent in such investigations have limited the number of studies conducted on this question.

A few studies have been done on party identification, whether people watch debates, and perceived candidate performance. Based on analyses using the standard party identification questions, Roberta Sigel found that partisanship tends to color voters' perceptions of the candidates in general.[27] Arthur Miller and Michael MacKuen, in their study on the Carter-Ford debates, reported that party affiliation reinforces partisans' positive attitudes toward their candidate and heightens their distaste for the opposition in a debate.[28] As far as the 1980 Carter-Reagan debate is concerned, we would expect to find partisans, particularly strong partisans, to most likely have watched the confrontation on television and concluded that their party's candidate had won.

Respondents were queried about the Carter-Reagan debate in the post-election survey. In response to the question, "Did you watch the televised debate between Carter and Reagan?" approximately 70 percent (n = 974) of the sample said they had. Those who did not see the contest on television were coded zero while those who watched it were coded 1.[29]

Table 3-6
Pearson Correlations between Party Identification and Whether People Watched the Carter-Reagan Debate, Post-Election Survey, 1980[a]

Items and Dimensions	Did Respondent Watch the Debate
Partisan Direction	
Party Difference Index	-.09*** (1200)
Party Closeness Scale	-.07** (1341)
Party Support Scale	-.06* (1338)
Democratic Party Feeling Thermometer	-.04 (1313)
Republican Party Feeling Thermometer	.06* (1309)
Seven-Point Party Identification Scale	-.09*** (1358)
Strength of Partisanship	
Folded Party Closeness Scale	.08** (1341)
Folded Party Support Scale	.13*** (1338)
Four-Point Strength of Identification Scale	.07** (1358)
Independence	
Strength of Independence Scale	.07** (1349)
Independents Feeling Thermometer	.00 (1216)

a - Figures in parentheses are numbers of cases.

* Significant at the .05 level.
** Significant at the .01 level.
*** Significant at the .001 level.

Table 3-6 shows the relationship between party identification and whether respondents saw the Carter-Reagan debate. For the most part, the correlations between the partisan direction measures and whether people watched the debate indicate that Republicans were somewhat more likely to have seen the event than were Democrats. Strong party identifiers were also more likely to have viewed the debate than were weak party identifiers. There is some evidence that Independents saw the confrontation, too, suggesting that partisan strength and independence are two different components of party identification. Admittedly, the correlations in Table 3-6 tend to be quite small.

There are a few significant discrepancies between the correlations for the individual party identification measures and whether respondents watched the Carter-Reagan debate. The relationship between the standard seven-point measure and whether voters saw the debate ($r = -.09$) is significantly stronger (at the .05 level) than the relationship between the Democrat thermometer and this question ($r = -.04$). Furthermore, the correlation between the folded party support scale and whether people watched the debate ($r = .13$) is significantly higher (at the .05 level) than the correlation between the standard four-point strength of identification scale and this behavior ($r = .07$). Finally, the correlation between the strength of independence scale and whether respondents witnessed the debate ($r = .07$) is significantly larger (at the .05 level) than the correlation between the Independents thermometer and engagement in this activity ($r = .00$). Based on these findings, the traditional seven-point measure is a better predictor of whether voters saw the debate than is the Democrat thermometer, whereas the folded party support scale is a better estimate of participation in this activity than is the traditional four-point partisan strength measure. Moreover, the strength of independence scale is a more accurate determinant of this behavior than is the Independents thermometer.

Respondents who witnessed the debate were asked which candidate had impressed them the most. The exact wording of the question was:

Now, thinking just about the debate and not the rest of the campaign, which of the two candidates impressed you as being more qualified to be President?

The data clearly show that Reagan impressed more viewers than did Carter. While 49 percent of those interviewed said Reagan performed better than Carter, only 30 percent said the reverse. Another 14 percent thought "neither" man came out ahead and the remaining 7 percent felt that "both" were equally qualified to be President based on their performance.[30] Although Democrats outnumber Republicans in general, a higher percentage of Republicans than Democrats in the electorate witnessed the event.[31]

Table 3–7 reports the association between party identification and perceived outcome of the Carter-Reagan debate. The table shows that there is a significant relationship between partisan direction, partisan strength, and perceived outcome. No relationship exists, however, between independence from politics and how people responded to the question.

A close examination of the cross-tables between party identification and perceived outcome of the debate reveals that Democrats were most likely to say Carter, "neither" candidate, or "both" candidates (in that order) performed well in the debate. Republicans, on the other hand, were far more impressed with Reagan than with Carter. On the whole, partisan direction had more influence over the public's assessment of the two candidates' performance than partisan strength. Still, those with loose party attachments were somewhat more likely to say that Reagan performed better than Carter.

Table 3-7
Statistical Significance of Party Identification by Perceived Outcome of the Carter-Reagan Debate, Post-Election Survey, 1980[a]

Items and Dimensions	Perceived Outcome of the Carter-Reagan Debate
Partisan Direction	
Party Difference Index	.001 (839)
Party Closeness Scale	.001 (920)
Party Support Scale	.001 (920)
Democratic Party Feeling Thermometer	.001 (911)
Republican Party Feeling Thermometer	.001 (909)
Seven-Point Party Identification Scale	.001 (939)
Strength of Partisanship	
Folded Party Closeness Scale	NS (920)
Folded Party Support Scale	.01 (920)
Four-Point Strength of Identification Scale	.001 (939)
Independence	
Strength of Independence Scale	NS (924)
Independents Feeling Thermometer	NS (850)

a - Figures in parentheses are numbers of cases. Chi-square was used to determine significance levels.

Judging from our analysis of the cross-tables, party affiliation appears to have a strong effect on the electorate's perception of candidate behavior. A more revealing exercise would be to exclude those respondents who thought "neither" candidate or "both" candidates did well, and conduct a correlation analysis between party identification and only whether Carter or Reagan was more impressive. Such an analysis would allow us to draw more meaningful comparisons between the individual party identification measures.

Table 3–8 reports the Pearson correlations between party identification and respondents' evaluations of the candidates' performance (Carter was coded zero and Reagan was coded 1). Not surprisingly, there is a strong relationship between partisan direction and perceived outcome of the debate. While Republicans were more impressed with Reagan's performance, Democrats believed that Carter had done better. A weak relationship also exists between partisan strength and perceived outcome. Specifically, an increase in partisan strength is associated with a tendency to say that Carter was more impressive than Reagan. The

Table 3-8
Pearson Correlations between Party Identification and Whether Carter or Reagan Won the Debate, Post-Election Survey, 1980[a]

Items and Dimensions	Did Carter or Reagan Win
Partisan Direction	
Party Difference Index	-.57*** (671)
Party Closeness Scale	-.47*** (723)
Party Support Scale	-.47*** (722)
Democratic Party Feeling Thermometer	-.43*** (721)
Republican Party Feeling Thermometer	.38*** (720)
Seven-Point Party Identification Scale	-.48*** (743)
Strength of Partisanship	
Folded Party Closeness Scale	-.09** (723)
Folded Party Support Scale	-.07* (722)
Four-Point Strength of Identification Scale	-.13*** (743)
Independence	
Strength of Independence Scale	.06 (727)
Independents Feeling Thermometer	.06 (667)

a - Figures in parentheses are numbers of cases.

* Significant at the .05 level.
** Significant at the .01 level.
*** Significant at the .001 level.

numerical advantage of Democrats over Republicans among strong partisans explains this finding. No relationship exists between independence from politics and whether Carter or Reagan performed better in their meeting.

There are two significant differences between the correlations for the partisan direction measures and public opinion on the debate. The data show that the absolute value of the correlation between the standard seven-point measure and perceived candidate performance is significantly higher (at the .01 level) than the correlation between the Republican thermometer and this variable. In addition, the relationship between the party difference index and perceived outcome (r = −.57) is significantly closer (at the .001 level) than the relationship between the traditional seven-point measure and perceived outcome (r = −.48). The correlations between the partisan strength and independence measures and views on candidate performance do not vary significantly.

PARTY SYSTEM SUPPORT

The notion of party system support was introduced in the last chapter during our discussion of Herbert Weisberg's model of party identification.[32] Party system support, you will recall, refers to the public's endorsement of America's party system and is therefore a much broader concept than party identification. In fact, Jack Dennis considered party affiliation to be an indicator of party system support.[33] Pierce, Beatty, and Hagner went a step further when they said, "The best-known aspect of party support is party identification."[34] They assumed that voters who align themselves with a particular party also approve of the party system as a whole. In order to gain a clearer understanding of the relationship between party identification and party system support, it would be useful to discuss briefly how parties differ from other political groups, their role in a functioning democracy such as ours, and the possible consequences of a weakening party institution.[35]

Party versus Other Political Groups

Frank Sorauf believes there are five characteristics of American political parties which set them apart from other political organizations.[36] First, parties are involved in the contesting of elections in a manner and to a degree that other political organizations are not. Although interest groups attempt to influence candidates and voters during elections, too, they also devote a considerable amount of time lobbying federal and state legislators, influencing rule making in administrative agencies, and pursuing other activities. Second, unlike most other political organizations, parties try to make appeals that are broad and inclusive. Since their goal is to attract diverse segments in the electorate and win elections, they cannot afford to articulate views on a narrow range of concerns. Third, major American parties and similar parties elsewhere are fully committed to political activity. Other political organizations almost always maintain some sphere of nonpolitical action. Fourth, while parties tend to exist for a relatively long period of time, many single-issue groups and ad hoc organizations disappear as quickly as they appear. Lastly, in contrast to other groups, parties serve as cues and reference symbols for a large portion of the population. Their label allows individuals to make choices despite campaign rhetoric and the confusion of American politics.

The Functions of Parties

Political scientists often explain the important role parties play in America by pointing to the specific functions they perform.[37] Parties have been said to simplify issues and alternatives, produce automatic majorities, recruit leaders and personnel, and nominate candidates. They also encourage public participation and promote adherence to the basic democratic rules of the game, such as abiding by the outcome of elections. Moreover, they organize minority interests, facilitate moderation and compromise, further political consensus and legitimacy, and bridge the gap between the three branches of government. In essence, American political parties serve democracy by reaffirming and promoting its fundamental values and by sustaining a workable system of representation.[38]

A Weakening of Party System Support

Many students of parties argue that the recent emergence of single-issue groups, increased reliance on the electronic media, the adoption of nonpartisan elections and the direct primary, and reforms in campaign financing laws have led to a weakening of the party system.[39] One way to verify this is to study public support—or "diffuse support" according to David Easton—for the party institution over a period of time.[40] After analyzing party system support among Wisconsin adults from 1964 to 1974, Dennis concluded:

public support for the parties, both in historical and cross-institutional perspective, is relatively weak. Attitudes toward the parties and the evaluations of the importance of the party institution show, with few exceptions, a general state of low public regard and legitimation.[41]

One cannot be certain whether and, if so, to what extent these trends will continue in the future.

According to Robert Blank, a continued weakening of public approval for the party system can lead to three major consequences.[42] First, a decline in support can increase further the importance of interest groups and other political organizations at the expense of the parties. Second, decreased support can lead to the election of more nonpoliticians with little government experience. We might see, for example, a larger number of movie stars, sports figures, and television personalities running for office than before. Finally, a further weakening of the party structure may result in a greater shift toward policy advocacy by the parties. Instead of promoting mediation and consensus, party activists might only back those candidates who espouse particular policy stands.[43] Such a situation could lead to serious rifts and diminish the possibility of compromise.[44]

Party Identification and Party System Support

In Dennis' Wisconsin study he analyzed the relationship between party identification and party system support.[45] Using the standard party identification questions, he examined the relationship between the seven-point party identification scale, the four-point strength of identification scale, and party system support. Although he did not find a significant association between the standard seven-point measure and public support for the party system, he did find a positive association between partisan strength and perceived importance of party. In other words, as partisan strength increased, so did approval of the party system.

Items similar to those used by Dennis as indicators of party system support were included in the 1980 election study. As reported in Chapter Two, respondents were read a list of five statements and asked how strongly they agreed or disagreed with each one on a scale from 1, "disagree very strongly," to 7, "agree very strongly." Responses to the following three statements were found to be unidimensional and were summed to form a "party system support scale":[46]

The parties do more to confuse the issues than to provide a clear choice on issues.

It would be better if, in all elections, we put no party labels on the ballot.

The truth is we probably don't need political parties in America.

Table 3–9 reports the Pearson correlations between the various party identification measures and the party system support scale. As one can see, there is a positive relationship between the party support scale, the two party feeling thermometers, and the party system support scale. The correlations between the party difference index, the party closeness scale, the seven-point party identification measure, and party endorsement are not significant. Even though the questions used to construct the party support scale specifically referred to only *one* party, it appears that individual party endorsements spill over into the general realm of support for the *entire* party system. This can also be inferred from the positive correlations between the two party thermometer items and the party system support measure, albeit the correlations are low. The main point is this: Had Dennis adopted either the party support scale or the two feeling thermometer measures in his study, he might have reached a different conclusion about the link between partisan direction and approval of the party institution.

Furthermore, Table 3–9 reveals that significant correlations exist between the partisan strength and independence measures and the party system support scale. As previous research has shown, increasing partisan strength is associated with greater support for the party system. Independents, however, are less likely to endorse the institution. The correlations between the partisan strength measures and the party system support scale are noticeably higher than the correlations between the independence measures and this variable, indicating that partisan strength and independence do not fall along the same continuum.

Significant differences exist between the correlations for the separate party identification measures and the party system support scale. The correlations between the party support scale, the Democrat thermometer, and the party system support measure are significantly higher (at the .001 level) than the correlation between the standard seven-point scale and this measure. The split between the correlations for the Republican thermometer, the traditional seven-point mea-

Table 3-9
Pearson Correlations between Party Identification and Party System Support, Pre-Election Survey, 1980[a]

Items and Dimensions	Party System Support Scale
Partisan Direction	
Party Difference Index	.01 (1233)
Party Closeness Scale	.04 (1345)
Party Support Scale	.10*** (1336)
Democratic Party Feeling Thermometer	.09*** (1336)
Republican Party Feeling Thermometer	.05* (1336)
Seven-Point Party Identification Scale	.01 (1358)
Strength of Partisanship	
Folded Party Closeness Scale	.23*** (1345)
Folded Party Support Scale	.30*** (1336)
Four-Point Strength of Identification Scale	.29*** (1358)
Independence	
Strength of Independence Scale	-.17*** (1352)
Independents Feeling Thermometer	-.09*** (1264)

a - Figures in parentheses are numbers of cases.

* Significant at the .05 level.
** Significant at the .01 level.
*** Significant at the .001 level.

sure, and party endorsement is not significant. Yet, there is a stronger relationship (significant at the .05 level) between the standard four-point partisan strength measure and party support (r = .29) than between the folded party closeness scale and this attitude (r = .23). Finally, the correlation between the strength of independence measure and party support (r = −.17) is significantly larger (at the

.05 level) than the correlation between the Independents thermometer and this predisposition (r = −.09).

Respondents were also questioned about the party system at other points in the election study. As mentioned in Chapter Two, those interviewed were asked a feeling thermometer question on "the political parties, in general," and to rate the performance of the political parties on a scale ranging from zero, "very poor job," to 8, "very good job."[47] Later in the survey respondents were asked, "How much do you feel that political parties help to make the government pay attention to what the people think—a good deal, some, or not much?" A correlation analysis between party identification and these three questions led to virtually the same findings reported in Table 3–9.

In addition to the three items which comprise the party system support scale, respondents were given two other statements about the party institution. The statements read:

The best rule in voting is to pick a candidate regardless of party label.

It is better to be a firm party supporter than to be a political independent.

Again, respondents were requested to say how strongly they agreed or disagreed with each statement on a seven-point scale.

Table 3–10 shows the relationship between party identification and the public's reaction to these two statements. As the size and direction of the correlations indicate, Democrats are more likely than Republicans to hold positive feelings about the parties. There is an even stronger relationship between partisan strength and attitudes toward the party system. More specifically, an ascendance in partisan strength is associated with increased disagreement that "the best rule in voting is to pick a candidate regardless of party label" and increased agreement that "it is better to be a firm party supporter than to be a political independent." The correlations between the partisan strength measures and responses to the latter statement are nearly double those between the partisan strength measures and responses to the former statement, probably because the latter statement addresses party support more directly.

This can also be seen by examining the correlations between the political independence measures and attitudes toward the party system. The data show that as independence from politics increases, so does agreement on "the best rule in voting is to pick a candidate regardless of party label" and disagreement on "it is better to be a firm party supporter than to be a political independent." The correlations between the independence measures and reactions to the latter statement are twice the size of those between the independence measures and reactions to the former statement. Also, the correlations between the partisan strength and independence measures and these two variables are in the opposite direction and are about the same size, suggesting that partisan strength and independence are unidimensional.

Several significant differences exist between the correlations for the various

Table 3-10
Pearson Correlations between Party Identification and Attitudes toward the Parties, Pre-Election Survey, 1980[a]

Items and Dimensions	Candidate Versus Party Label	Party Support Versus Independence
Partisan Direction		
Party Difference Index	.11*** (1352)	.14*** (1325)
Party Closeness Scale	.12*** (1504)	.15*** (1463)
Party Support Scale	.11*** (1499)	.14*** (1456)
Democratic Party Feeling Thermometer	.12*** (1477)	.27*** (1444)
Republican Party Feeling Thermometer	-.04 (1474)	.02 (1442)
Seven-Point Party Identification Scale	.13*** (1520)	.15*** (1478)
Strength of Partisanship		
Folded Party Closeness Scale	.20*** (1504)	.39*** (1463)
Folded Party Support Scale	.24*** (1499)	.39*** (1456)
Four-Point Strength of Identification Scale	.25*** (1520)	.46*** (1478)
Independence		
Strength of Independence Scale	-.24*** (1507)	-.49*** (1468)
Independents Feeling Thermometer	-.12*** (1367)	-.29*** (1356)

a - Figures in parentheses are numbers of cases.

* Significant at the .05 level.
** Significant at the .01 level.
*** Significant at the .001 level.

party identification measures and attitudes toward the party system. Ignoring the direction of the correlations for the moment, the relationships between the standard seven-point measure and the two questions involving the party system are significantly stronger (at the .001 level) than the relationships between the Republican thermometer and these two items. In contrast, the correlation between the Democrat thermometer and public opinion on whether "it is better to be a firm party supporter than to be a political independent" ($r = .27$) is significantly greater (at the .001 level) than the correlation between the standard seven-point measure and responses to this question ($r = .15$). In addition, the relationship between the traditional four-point partisan strength measure and views on whether "the best rule in voting is to pick a candidate regardless of party label" is significantly stronger (at the .05 level) than the relationship between the folded party closeness scale and views on this issue. The same holds true (significant at the .05 level) regarding the correlations between the old four-point partisan strength scale, the two alternative partisan strength measures, and opinion on whether "it is better to be a firm party supporter than to be a political independent." Furthermore, the correlations between the strength of independence scale, whether "the best rule in voting is to pick a candidate regardless of party label," and whether "it is better to be a firm party supporter than to be a political independent" are significantly larger (at the .001 level) than the correlations between the Independents thermometer and these two items. The analysis demonstrates that the standard partisan strength scale and the strength of independence scale are more accurate measures of feelings on both party support questions than are the other partisan strength and independence indicators, respectively.

POLITICAL TRUST AND EFFICACY

Most students of politics consider political distrust and inefficacy to be major components of political alienation.[48] Political trust refers "to the public's basic evaluative orientation toward the government in Washington," and it is usually measured in terms of high trust or "confidence" in government to distrust or "cynicism."[49] Distrust or cynicism often represents "a negative evaluation of government and reflects the belief that government is not functioning in accordance with individual expectations of efficiency, honesty, competence and equity."[50] Efficacy, on the other hand, concerns the degree to which people feel their actions will bring about a desired change in the affairs of government. Stated another way, "The lack of efficacy or the feeling of inefficacy indicates the belief that the public cannot influence political outcomes because government leaders and institutions are unresponsive to their needs."[51]

The authors of *The American Voter* paid little attention to political trust and efficacy, probably because the electorate felt reasonably satisfied with the government and efficacious in the 1950s.[52] Since the publication of *The American Voter*, however, there has been a marked decline in trust and efficacy.[53] This weakened support for the regime has caught the attention of political observers. President Carter's "crisis of confidence" speech in July 1979 brought the problem to the public's attention.

The decline in trust has triggered a lively debate among political scientists. The controversy centers on whether the decline represents weakened support for the political system as a whole, or whether it represents public disaffection with particular leaders in office. The significance of this question was discussed by Paul Abramson and Ada Finifter:

> The decline in political trust may have far greater implications if it reflects a withdrawal of support for the political community or the regime, and is not merely a rejection of the incumbents. Disaffection with incumbents can, in principle at least, be remedied

through the electoral process. The behavioral implications of more widespread discontent could be far greater.[54]

The two major protagonists in this debate are Arthur Miller and Jack Citrin.[55] After analyzing the decline in political trust from 1964 to 1972, Miller concluded that the decline can partially be tied to changing views on racial integration and America's involvement in the Vietnam War. He implied that the perceived failure of political leaders to implement more acceptable public policies can be translated into a broader dissatisfaction with the regime as a whole. Citrin, on the other hand, disagreed with Miller's interpretation of the data and argued that the electorate's increased cynicism probably represents opposition to incumbents which cannot be readily generalized to the regime. According to him, this trend is considerably less threatening than Miller thinks because both trusting and distrusting respondents exhibit similar behavior patterns. Moreover, people tend to give cynical answers because they are "fashionable." Miller and his two colleagues addressed this issue in their study on the impact of newspapers on public trust and concluded that, "Cynicism evidently reflects general dissatisfaction with government performance and not simply a lack of support for specific incumbents and is at the same time a direct cause of disillusionment with broader regime norms regarding institutional evaluations."[56]

The dispute between Miller and Citrin touches upon the precise referents of the SRC/CPS trust in government questions which have been included in the National Election Studies for over two decades. At issue is whether the standard trust in government questions measure attitudes toward public officeholders specifically, or whether they measure attitudes toward the political system as a whole. In the past, researchers have combined these items to form a "political trust index."[57] Abramson and Finifter recently attempted to address this problem by comparing four new political trust questions included in the 1978 SRC/CPS election study with the standard trust index.[58] The new questions specifically referred to President Carter, the Carter Administration, and the United States Congress (two questions addressed the latter object). The similarity in the wording of the old and new items, however, prevented them from reaching any final judgments about the interpretation of the standard trust items. They concluded that their "analysis strongly suggests the need to develop new measures that more clearly separate evaluations of incumbents from those of the political system more generally in order to resolve this question definitively."[59]

Similarly, previous research on political efficacy has focused on the conceptual-operational coordination problem. As with the trust items, several questions concerning efficacy have been included in the SRC/CPS National Election Studies for a number of years, and respondents' answers to these questions have been used to construct a "sense of political efficacy scale." George Balch's extensive analysis of the internal and external consistency of the items comprising this measure led him to conclude that the scale represented two different dimensions and not one as originally thought.[60] More precisely, the items appeared to measure personal competence (people's evaluations of their own political abilities) and institutional responsiveness.[61] Most researchers now use only those items which represent institutional responsiveness as indicators of political efficacy.[62] Studies comparing efficacy and political trust have shown efficacy to be more stable than political trust.[63]

Several investigations have included brief examinations of party identification, political trust, and efficacy. Robert Agger, Marshall Goldstein, and Stanley Pearl's 1961 analysis of two major cities in Oregon revealed similar levels of cynicism among Republicans, Democrats, and Independents after controlling for education.[64] As part of a more general analysis of the association between a large number of theoretically related outside variables and dimensions of political alienation, Ada Finifter found significant correlations between partisan direction, partisan strength, "normlessness" (distrust), and "powerlessness" (inefficacy). That is, Democrats and those with loose party attachments tended to be slightly more distrustful and inefficacious than Republicans and strong partisans.[65] More recently, Miller and his colleagues found that "efficacy, unlike trust, is relatively independent of the influence of partisan loyalty."[66] Pierce and his associates' presentation of survey data collected in 1976, however, showed that Republicans tended to feel somewhat more efficacious than Democrats, although controlling for education could erase this association.[67]

There are two reasons why we should study the relationships between the different party identification measures, political trust, and efficacy. As one might expect, only the standard partisan direction and partisan strength measures have been used in analyses of trust and efficacy, and, as Weisberg suggested, the alternative measures of party identification may be related differently to these two concepts.[68] Secondly, trust and efficacy have received considerable attention in the literature and are considered important concepts in our understanding of support for the political system. For these reasons we now turn to an analysis of party identification, political trust, and efficacy.

Party Identification and Political Trust

An attempt was made to construct a "trust in government scale" using the standard SRC/CPS political trust items included in the 1980 election study. Responses to the five questions, however, did not exhibit the statistical properties required to form a scale and the effort was abandoned.[69] Instead, the political trust items were correlated separately with the different party identification measures.

Of the five items, trust in government is probably most clearly addressed in the question, "How much of the time do you think you can trust the government in Washington to do what is right—just about always, most of the time, or only some of the time?" Responses were scored from 1, "none of the time (if respondents volunteered)," to 4, "just about always." Table 3–11 reports the tau-c correlations between party identification and responses to this question. With the exception of the Republican feeling thermometer, there is a significant relationship between partisan direction and political trust; Democrats expressed more confidence in the federal government than did Republicans in 1980. The data also show that as partisan strength increases, so does trust in government. The reverse is true for party independence and trust. More specifically, increased independence is accompanied by increased cynicism. The data imply that strength of partisanship and independence represent one dimension. In general, the correlations in Table 3–11 are small, and no significant differences exist between the correlations for the individual party identification measures and the political trust item.

The following two questions relating to public confidence were also included in the survey:

Would you say the government is pretty much run by a few big interests looking out for themselves or that it is run for the benefit of all the people?
Do you feel that almost all of the people running the government are smart people, or do you think that quite a few of them don't seem to know what they are doing?

The more cynical responses, "the government is pretty much run by a few big interests looking out for themselves" and "quite a few of the people running the government don't seem to know what they are doing," were coded zero whereas the most trusting responses, "the government is run for the benefit of all the people" and "almost all of the people running the government are smart people," were coded 1. The Pearson correlations between party identification and these questions appear in Table 3–12. Excluding the Republican thermometer and the seven-point party identification scale, Democrats are more likely to say that "the government is run for the benefit of all the people" and that "almost all of the people running the government are smart people" than are Republicans. Respondents with strong party attachments are more likely to say that "the government is run for the benefit of all the people" than those with loose party attachments. Based on the correlation between the strength of independence scale and the question concerning for whom is government run, Independents tend to feel that "the government is pretty much run by a few big interests looking out for themselves." Partisan strength and political independence are not related to whether "almost all of the people running the government are smart people." The correlations in the table suggest that strength of identification and independence are the same thing.

The data show that significant disparities exist between the correlations for the party identification measures and the two political trust items in Table 3–12. The correlations between the party closeness scale, the Democrat thermometer, for whom is government run, and whether government is run by mostly smart people are significantly higher (at least at the .05 level) than the correlations between the standard seven-point measure and responses to these two questions. Similarly, the relationship between the party difference index and

Table 3-11
TAU-C Correlations between Party Identification and How Often People Can Trust Government in Washington to Do What Is Right, Pre-Election Survey, 1980[a]

Items and Dimensions	Trust in Government in Washington[b]
Partisan Direction	
Party Difference Index	.11*** (1373)
Party Closeness Scale	.08*** (1525)
Party Support Scale	.08*** (1521)
Democratic Party Feeling Thermometer	.16*** (1496)
Republican Party Feeling Thermometer	.00 (1493)
Seven-Point Party Identification Scale	.08*** (1544)
Strength of Partisanship	
Folded Party Closeness Scale	.06** (1525)
Folded Party Support Scale	.04* (1521)
Four-Point Strength of Identification Scale	.09*** (1544)
Independence	
Strength of Independence Scale	-.06*** (1535)
Independents Feeling Thermometer	-.02 (1383)

a - Figures in parentheses are numbers of cases.

b - The coefficients to the right of the folded party closeness and four-point strength of identification scales are tau-b correlations.

* Significant at the .05 level.

** Significant at the .01 level.

*** Significant at the .001 level.

whether government is run by mostly smart people ($r = .10$) is significantly stronger (at the .001 level) than the relationship between the standard seven-point measure and this item ($r = .04$). In contrast, the correlation between the traditional seven-point measure and for whom is government run ($r = .07$) is significantly larger (at the .01 level) than the correlation between the Republican thermometer and views on this matter ($r = .00$). The correlations between the partisan strength and independence measures and opinions on these two questions do not differ significantly.[70]

Table 3-12
Pearson Correlations between Party Identification, for Whom Is Government Run, and Whether Government Is Run by Mostly Smart People, Pre-Election Survey, 1980[a]

Items and Dimensions	For Whom Is Government Run	Is Government Run By Mostly Smart People
Partisan Direction		
Party Difference Index	.09*** (1276)	.10*** (1343)
Party Closeness Scale	.12*** (1415)	.08** (1485)
Party Support Scale	.10*** (1409)	.06** (1480)
Democratic Party Feeling Thermometer	.16*** (1388)	.12*** (1460)
Republican Party Feeling Thermometer	.00 (1386)	-.06* (1458)
Seven-Point Party Identification Scale	.07** (1433)	.04 (1507)
Strength of Partisanship		
Folded Party Closeness Scale	.07** (1415)	.01 (1485)
Folded Party Support Scale	.11*** (1409)	-.01 (1480)
Four-Point Strength of Identification Scale	.08*** (1433)	.01 (1507)
Independence		
Strength of Independence Scale	-.07** (1418)	-.03 (1497)
Independents Feeling Thermometer	.04 (1284)	.02 (1349)

a - Figures in parentheses are numbers of cases.

* Significant at the .05 level.
** Significant at the .01 level.
*** Significant at the .001 level.

Party Identification and Political Efficacy

Respondents were asked a series of questions in the post-election study about their own sense of political efficacy. Three items were found to be unidimensional and were summed to form a "sense of political efficacy scale."[71] The three items are indicators of institutional responsiveness rather than personal competence.

Table 3–13 reports the Pearson correlations between party identification and respondents' scores on the political efficacy scale. Those who feel "warmly" toward the Republican and Democratic parties also tend to be efficacious. The correlation between the seven-point party identification measure and the effi-

Table 3-13
Pearson Correlations between Party Identification and Political Efficacy, Post-Election Survey, 1980[a]

Items and Dimensions	Sense of Political Efficacy Scale
Partisan Direction	
Party Difference Index	-.01 (1074)
Party Closeness Scale	-.03 (1177)
Party Support Scale	-.01 (1173)
Democratic Party Feeling Thermometer	.05* (1172)
Republican Party Feeling Thermometer	.06* (1171)
Seven-Point Party Identification Scale	-.05* (1196)
Strength of Partisanship	
Folded Party Closeness Scale	.05* (1177)
Folded Party Support Scale	.10*** (1173)
Four-Point Strength of Identification Scale	.11*** (1196)
Independence	
Strength of Independence Scale	.02 (1186)
Independents Feeling Thermometer	.04 (1091)

a - Figures in parentheses are numbers of cases.

* Significant at the .05 level.
** Significant at the .01 level.
*** Significant at the .001 level.

cacy scale indicates that Republicans are slightly more efficacious than Democrats. In addition, as strength of partisanship increases, so does sense of effectiveness. No relationship exists between political independence and position on the efficacy scale.[72] The noticeable difference in the size of the correlations for two of the three partisan strength measures, both independence measures, and the political efficacy scale supports the belief that partisan strength and independence are unique elements. Overall, the correlations in Table 3–13 are weak at best.

There are a couple of significant discrepancies between the correlations for the partisan direction measures and the sense of political efficacy scale. The correlation between the standard seven-point measure and political efficacy is significantly higher (at the .05 level) than the correlations between the party difference index, the party support scale, and this predisposition. The relationships between the partisan direction and independence measures and efficacy are similar in strength.

We also analyzed the relationship between party identification and the political efficacy scale after controlling for education. While the Democrat and Republican feeling thermometer items remain significantly correlated with efficacy after controlling for education, the seven-point party identification measure does not. At the same time, the three partisan strength measures are still related to effectiveness when education is held constant. No association still exists between independence and efficacy. Thus, controlling for education only affects the relationship between the seven-point measure and efficacy.

SUMMARY

This chapter examined the relationship between party identification and orientation toward the political system. An analysis of party identification and interest in the 1980 campaign revealed that Republicans, Independents, and strong partisans tended to be more interested in politics than their counterparts in the electorate. Partisans and intense party loyalists exhibited concern over the outcome of the 1980 election whereas Independents were less concerned about who won. While Independents were most likely to follow the election through magazines and newspapers, strong partisans were most likely to use newspapers and the electronic media. In addition, Republicans, Independents, and strong partisans possessed some knowledge about the presidential candidates and reported seeing the Carter-Reagan debate on television. The data showed that Republicans were more impressed with Reagan's performance in the debate than Democrats were with Carter's performance. Furthermore, respondents who tended to support one party also tended to support the whole party system. Although our analysis indicated that Democrats were more supportive of the party system than were Republicans, increased partisan strength was clearly accompanied by increased approval of the party institution. At the same time, Independents were less likely to endorse the party system. While Democrats and strong partisans tended to trust the regime, Independents tended to be somewhat cynical. Finally, after controlling for education, Democrats, Republicans, and strong partisans were found to be efficacious.

The data analyzed in this chapter provided some hints about whether partisan strength and political independence represent two dimensions or one dimension. In general, we found the correlations between the partisan strength and independence items and the criterion variables to either be in the same direction (e.g., knowledge about the presidential candidates, Table 3–5) or the opposite direction but vary in size (e.g., concern over the outcome of the 1980 election,

Table 3–2). These findings suggest that partisan strength and independence are two separate components of party identification. However, we did find the correlations between the partisan strength and independence items and views on two questions concerning party system support (Table 3–10) to be in the opposite direction and about the same size. One could interpret this result as support for the position that the two elements fall along a single continuum. We will continue to address this question in other instances.

Whether the standard or alternative partisan direction measures were superior predictors of orientations toward the political system depended on the context. For example, the standard seven-point measure was a better estimate of respondents' level of knowledge about the presidential candidates in 1980 than were the party support scale and the Republican thermometer. However, the party difference index was a more accurate determinant of whether Carter or Reagan won the debate than was the traditional seven-point measure. Moreover, there was a stronger relationship between the Democrat thermometer and two of the three trust in government questions than there was between the seven-point measure and these same questions. The findings reported in this chapter raise serious doubts about the interchangeability of the old and new partisan direction measures in specific situations.

In nearly every case, the correlations between the standard four-point partisan strength measure and the criterion variables were equal to or greater than the correlations between the alternative partisan strength measures and these variables. For instance, the standard four-point partisan strength measure was more closely related to whether "it is better to be a firm party supporter than to be a political independent" than were the other two partisan strength scales. At one point we did find that the folded party support scale was a better predictor of whether respondents had watched the Carter-Reagan debate than was the traditional four-point partisan strength measure. But on the whole, the correlations between the old and new partisan strength measures and attitudes toward the political system were at least similar in strength.

There were several instances where the relationships between the strength of independence scale and predispositions toward the political system were significantly closer than the relationships between the Independents feeling thermometer and these predispositions. For example, the strength of independence measure was a better estimate of responses on all the party system support questions than was the Independents thermometer. It was also a superior determinant of knowledge about the presidential candidates. These findings indicate that the two independence measures may not be interchangeable in certain important contexts.

In the next chapter we will continue to study whether and, if so, to what extent the different party identification measures are equivalent. Chapter Four examines the relationships between party identification and opinions on groups and issues.

NOTES

1. Angus Campbell, Philip E. Converse, Warren E. Miller, and Donald E. Stokes, *The American Voter* (New York: John Wiley and Sons, 1960), pp. 142–45.
2. Ibid., p. 143.
3. Norman H. Nie, Sidney Verba, and John R. Petrocik, *The Changing American Voter*, Enlarged Edition (Cambridge: Harvard University Press, 1979), pp. 272–84.
4. Ibid., p. 280.
5. John C. Pierce, Kathleen M. Beatty, Paul R. Hagner, *The Dynamics of American Public Opinion: Patterns and Processes* (Glenview: Scott, Foresman and Company, 1982), pp. 252–53.
6. An extensive analysis of media usage and level of information about presidential politics appears in: John H. Kessel, *Presidential Campaign Politics: Coalition Strategies and Citizen Response* (Homewood, Ill.: The Dorsey Press, 1980), Chap. 7.
7. Philip E. Converse, "Information Flow and the Stability of Partisan Attitudes," in *Elections and the Political Order*, ed. Angus Campbell et al. (New York: John Wiley and Sons, 1966), pp. 136–57; Edward C. Dreyer, "Media Use and Electoral Choices: Some Political Consequences of Information Exposure," *Public Opinion Quarterly* Vol. 35 (Winter 1971–72), pp. 544–53; Doris Graber, *Mass Media and American Politics* (Washington, D.C.: Congressional Quarterly Press, 1980); and C. Richard Hofstetter and Terry F. Buss, "Politics and Last Minute Political Television," *Western Political Quarterly* Vol. 33 (March 1980), pp. 24–37.
8. Herbert B. Asher, *Presidential Elections and American Politics: Voters, Candidates and Campaigns Since 1952*, Revised Edition (Homewood, Ill.: The Dorsey Press, 1980), pp. 229–32.
9. Ibid., p. 232.
10. Pierce, Beatty, and Hagner, *The Dynamics of American Public Opinion*, p. 243.
11. Also see: Bernard Hennessy, *Public Opinion*, Fourth Edition (Monterey: Brooks/Cole Publishing Company, 1981), Chap. 16.
12. Robert S. Erikson, "The Influence of Newspaper Endorsements in Presidential Elections: The Case of 1964," *American Journal of Political Science* Vol. 20 (May 1976), pp. 207–33.
13. Ibid., p. 220.
14. Ibid.
15. Michael J. Robinson, "Public Affairs Television and the Growth of Political Malaise: The Case of 'The Selling of the Pentagon'," *American Political Science Review* Vol. 70 (June 1976), pp. 409–32.
16. Ibid., p. 409, footnote 5 contains a long list of studies which conclude that television campaigns seldom affect voting choice (and voting turnout) directly. Robinson's findings obviously challenged the results of these studies.
17. Peter Clarke and Eric Fredin, "Newspapers, Television and Political Reasoning," *Public Opinion Quarterly* Vol. 42 (Summer 1978), pp. 143–60.
18. Arthur H. Miller, Edie N. Goldenberg, and Lutz Erbring, "Type-Set Politics: Impact of Newspapers on Public Confidence," *American Political Science Review* Vol. 73 (March 1979), pp. 67–84. Also refer to: Lutz Erbring, Edie Goldenberg, and Arthur H. Miller, "Front-Page News and Real-World Cues: A New Look at Agenda-Setting by the Media," *American Journal of Political Science* Vol. 24 (February 1980), pp. 16–49.

19. Miller, Goldenberg, and Erbring, "Type-Set Politics," p. 76.
20. Nie, Verba, and Petrocik, *The Changing American Voter*, pp. 272–75.
21. Respondents were asked:

Did you read about the campaign in any newspapers (magazines)? (If yes) how many newspaper (magazine) articles did you read about the campaign? Would you say you read a good many, several, or just one or two?

22. Keep in mind that political information can also influence party identification. Kessel, *Presidential Campaign Politics*, pp. 239–40.
23. The thirteen presidential candidates included in the list were: Jimmy Carter, Ronald Reagan, Ted Kennedy, John Connally, Gerald Ford, Jerry Brown, Howard Baker, Walter Mondale, George Bush, Philip Crane, Robert Dole, John Anderson, and Patrick Lucey.
24. In a similar analysis, only strength of partisanship was found related to knowledge about the candidates for the House of Representatives after controlling for education. There were no significant differences between the correlations for the various measures of party identification and familiarity with candidates for the House.
25. *The Los Angeles Times*, June 5, 1982, p. 29. Of course, candidates who decline to debate run the risk of appearing to sidestep discussion of important issues.
26. Sidney Kraus (ed.), *The Great Debates* (Bloomington: Indiana University Press, 1962); John W. Ellsworth, "Rationality and Campaigning: A Content Analysis of the 1960 Presidential Campaign Debates," *Western Political Quarterly* Vol. 18 (December 1965), pp. 794–802; Alan Abramowitz, "The Impact of a Presidential Debate on Voter Rationality," *American Journal of Political Science* Vol. 22 (August 1978), pp. 680–90; Kenneth D. Wald and Michael B. Lupfer, "The Presidential Debate As a Civics Lesson," *Public Opinion Quarterly* Vol. 42 (Fall 1978), pp. 342–59; Douglas D. Rose, "Citizen Users of the Ford-Carter Debates," *Journal of Politics* Vol. 41 (February 1979), pp. 214–21; Arthur H. Miller and Michael MacKuen, "Learning About the Candidates: The 1976 Presidential Debates," *Public Opinion Quarterly* Vol. 43 (Fall 1979), pp. 326–46; and Sidney Kraus (ed.), *The Great Debates, 1976: Ford Versus Carter* (Bloomington: Indiana University Press, 1979).
27. Roberta S. Sigel, "Effect of Partisanship on the Perception of Political Candidates," *Public Opinion Quarterly* Vol. 28 (Fall 1964), pp. 483–96.
28. Miller and MacKuen, "Learning About the Candidates," pp. 340–41.
29. Thirteen respondents who said they had listened to the debate on radio were excluded from the analysis.
30. Despite the careful wording of the question, the outcome of the election may have influenced public recall of the two candidates' performance.
31. This is true regardless of what partisan direction measure is considered.
32. Herbert F. Weisberg, "A Multidimensional Conceptualization of Party Identification," *Political Behavior* Vol. 2 No. 1 (1980), pp. 33–60.
33. Jack Dennis, "Support for the Party System by the Mass Public," *American Political Science Review* Vol. 60 (September 1966), p. 601.
34. Pierce, Beatty, and Hagner, *The Dynamics of American Public Opinion*, p. 230.
35. A comprehensive review of these factors would go beyond the focus of this study. Students who desire additional information should consult an introductory text on political parties.

36. Frank J. Sorauf, *Party Politics in America*, Fourth Edition (Boston: Little, Brown and Company, 1980), pp. 15–18.

37. E.E. Schattschneider, *Party Government* (New York: Rinehart, 1942); and Theodore Lowi, "Toward Functionalism in Political Science: The Case of Innovation in Party Systems," *American Political Science Review*, Vol. 57 (September 1963), pp. 570–83. Also see: Austin Ranney, *The Doctrine of Responsible Party Government: Its Origins and Present State* (Urbana: University of Illinois Press, 1962).

38. Moisei Ostrogorski, however, argued that the parties should be curbed because they have become too powerful. Moisei Ostrogorski, *Democracy and the Organization of Political Parties*, Volume Two (New York: Anchor, 1964). Also consult: Robert Michels, *Political Parties* (Glencoe: Free Press, 1949).

39. For a comprehensive discussion of these factors see: Walter Dean Burnham, *Critical Elections and the Mainsprings of American Politics* (New York: Norton, 1970); David S. Broder, *The Party's Over: The Failure of Party Politics in America* (New York: Harper, 1971); and John G. Steward, *One Last Chance: The Democratic Party, 1974–1976* (New York: Praeger, 1974).

40. David Easton, *A Systems Analysis of Political Life* (New York: John Wiley and Sons, 1965), pp. 273–74.

41. Jack Dennis, "Trends in Public Support for the American Party System," *British Journal of Political Science* Vol. 5 Part 2 (April 1975), p. 218.

42. Robert Blank, *Political Parties* (Englewood Cliffs: Prentice-Hall, 1980), pp. 455–60.

43. Nelson W. Polsby and Aaron Wildavsky, *Presidential Elections: Strategies of American Electoral Politics*, Fifth Edition (New York: Charles Scribner's Sons, 1980), pp. 255–56.

44. Some do not believe such dire consequences will result if the party system disappears. For instance, see: Leon D. Epstein, *Political Parties in Western Democracies* (New York: Praeger, 1967), pp. 7–8; and Anthony King, "Political Parties in Western Democracies: Some Skeptical Reflections," *Polity* Vol. 2 (Winter 1969), pp. 111–41.

45. Dennis, "Trends in Public Support for the American Party System." Also see his earlier article, Dennis, "Support for the Party System by the Mass Public," pp. 600–15.

46. Refer to footnote 12 in Chapter Two for information about question wording, scale construction, and reliability.

47. The precise wording of the question appears in footnote 13 in Chapter Two.

48. Joel Aberbach, "Alienation and Political Behavior," *American Political Science Review* Vol. 63 (March 1969), pp. 86–99; Ada W. Finifter, "Dimensions of Political Alienation," *American Political Science Review* Vol. 64 (June 1970), pp. 389–410; and David B. Hill and Norman R. Luttbeg, *Trends in American Electoral Behavior*, Second Edition (Itasca, Ill.: F.E. Peacock Publishers, 1983), pp. 114–15.

49. Miller, Goldenberg, and Erbring, "Type-Set Politics," p. 67.

50. Ibid.

51. Ibid.

52. Campbell, Converse, Miller, and Stokes, *The American Voter*.

53. The decline has been well documented. Consult, for example: Philip E. Converse, "Change in the American Electorate," in *The Human Meaning of Social Change*, ed. Angus Campbell and Philip E. Converse (New York: Russell Sage Foundation, 1972),

pp. 263–337; and Arthur H. Miller, "Political Issues and Trust in Government: 1964–1970," *American Political Science Review* Vol. 68 (September 1974), pp. 951–72.

54. Paul R. Abramson and Ada W. Finifter, "On the Meaning of Political Trust: New Evidence from Items Introduced in 1978," *American Journal of Political Science* Vol. 25 (May 1981), p. 298.

55. Miller, "Political Issues and Trust in Government"; Jack Citrin, "Comment: The Political Relevance of Trust in Government," *American Political Science Review* Vol. 68 (September 1974), pp. 973–88; and Arthur H. Miller, "Rejoinder to 'Comment' by Jack Citrin: Political Discontent or Ritualism?" *American Political Science Review* Vol. 68 (September 1974), pp. 989–1001.

56. Miller, Goldenberg, and Erbring, "Type-Set Politics," p. 79.

57. Ibid., p. 82.

58. Abramson and Finifter, "On the Meaning of Political Trust."

59. Ibid., p. 306.

60. George I. Balch, "Multiple Indicators in Survey Research: The Concept 'Sense of Political Efficacy'," *Political Methodology* Vol. 1 (Spring 1974), pp. 1–43.

61. Philip Converse, too, has reached the same conclusion. Converse, "Change in the American Electorate."

62. For example: Miller, Goldenberg, and Erbring, "Type-Set Politics," p. 82.

63. Converse, "Change in the American Electorate"; Miller, "Political Issues and Trust in Government"; and ibid.

64. Robert E. Agger, Marshall N. Goldstein, and Stanley A. Pearl, "Political Cynicism: Measurement and Meaning," *Journal of Politics* Vol. 23 (August 1961), pp. 477–506.

65. Finifter, "Dimensions of Political Alienation," p. 398. Joel Aberbach also found Democrats to be slightly more distrustful than Republicans in 1958. Joel Aberbach, "Alienation and Political Behavior," p. 94.

66. Miller, Goldenberg, and Erbring, "Type-Set Politics," p. 76. Warren Miller takes this position in: Warren E. Miller, "Misreading the Public Pulse," *Public Opinion* Vol. 2 (October/November 1979), pp. 9–15, 60.

67. Pierce, Beatty, and Hagner, *The Dynamics of American Public Opinion*, pp. 252–53.

68. Weisberg, "A Multidimensional Conceptualization of Party Identification," p. 53.

69. In sharp contrast to Miller, Goldenberg, and Erbring's findings, the five political trust items in the 1980 election study *do not* form a Guttman scale. Every attempt to form a Guttman scale resulted in unacceptable levels of scalability and reproducibility. David Valentine and John Van Wingen reached the same conclusion in their analysis of the 1952, 1968, 1972, and 1976 election studies. David C. Valentine and John R. Van Wingen, "Partisanship, Independence, and the Partisan Identification Question," *American Politics Quarterly* Vol. 8 (April 1980), pp. 165–86.

70. Controlling for education did not substantially alter the relationships in Tables 3–11 and 3–12. An analysis of party identification and the two remaining political trust questions: ("How much tax money do people in government waste" and "how many people running the government are crooked?") led to findings similar to those reported in Table 3–11.

71. Respondents were asked whether they "agree" or "disagree" with the following three statements:

I don't think public officials care much what people like me think.

Generally speaking, those we elect to Congress in Washington lose touch with the people pretty quickly.

Parties are only interested in people's votes but not in their opinions.

Responses to these statements were found to be unidimensional and were summed to form a "sense of political efficacy scale." The scale ranged from zero, "low efficacy," to 3, "high efficacy" (n = 1215) and was considered reliable (Cronbach's alpha = .70).

72. Identical results were obtained in an analysis of party identification and the items which reflected personal competence.

4
VIEWS ON GROUPS AND ISSUES

Chapter Three examined the relationship between party identification and orientations toward the political system. How voters align themselves, or fail to align themselves as the case may be, with a party tended to affect their perspective on the political world. It appears that many Americans, particularly those who find politics difficult to understand, use party identification as a guide in their formulation of attitudes toward the political system.

Whether party affiliation also acts as a cue in the development of views on groups and issues is examined in this chapter.[1] We begin with an analysis of party identification and attitudes toward minority groups, labor unions, "big" business, the elderly, people on welfare, and civil rights leaders. We then investigate the relationship between party identification and opinions on diverse issues. The next section analyzes the relationship between party orientation and political ideology. A summary of the findings is presented at the end of the chapter. The criterion variables introduced in this chapter (and subsequent chapters) are thought to be more directly related to party identification than others examined thus far. Together they provide an excellent context in which to study the dimensionality of partisan strength and political independence and the interchangeability of the various party identification measures.

ATTITUDES TOWARD GROUPS

In Chapter Two we analyzed the party attachments of different social groups in the electorate. Although the Democratic party traditionally has been viewed as the champion of the disadvantaged and the Republican party has been characterized as a supporter of the wealthy and "big" business, for the most part only weak relationships were found between social group membership and party identification. Apparently, the new deal coalition formed in the 1930s has steadily eroded over time.

In order to study this phenomenon further, we analyzed the relation between party identification and attitudes toward certain groups in the society. While particular groups may no longer align themselves with the parties as closely as they once did, it is still possible that Republicans and Democrats have an affinity for specific segments of the population. In other words, even though lower class or status people, for example, do not affiliate themselves with the Democratic party in such large numbers as before, Democratic party identifiers as a whole may still feel considerable sympathy for this sector of society. Data collected in the 1980 election study allow us to address this question.

Hispanics and Blacks

During the post-election survey, respondents were asked to assign feeling thermometer scores (ranging from zero to 100 degrees) to a host of social and political groups and government institutions. Respondents' party identification was correlated with their ratings of these groups and institutions, and only those findings which are considered theoretically and empirically revealing are reported in this chapter.

The extension of voting rights and changes in the composition of the electorate have placed minority groups in a more prominent position in American politics. Increased voter turnout by blacks and hispanics, especially in the South and Southwest, has made a difference in some key races at the state and local level. The hispanic population, in particular, is growing rapidly in the United States, and it may become the largest minority group in the country before the turn of the century. How Republicans and Democrats presently view blacks and hispanics may eventually affect the formulation of legislation involving these groups. In turn, these minority groups will probably support the party that appears to be championing their causes. An examination of the relationship between party identification and views on blacks and hispanics in 1980 might therefore prove fruitful.

Table 4–1 shows the Pearson correlations between party identification and attitudes toward "hispanics" and "blacks." The data indicate that Democrats feel more "warmly" toward these individuals than do Republicans, albeit the correlations are small. Blacks, in particular, are relatively well liked by Democrats. Strong partisans, too, feel positively toward the two groups. The relationship between level of political independence and attitudes toward the two groups is less clear. When race is controlled the correlations between partisan direction, partisan strength, and feelings about "blacks" decrease only slightly and remain significant. In addition, the weak but significant negative relationship between the strength of independence scale and dispositions toward blacks disappears while the correlation between the Independents feeling thermometer

Table 4-1
Pearson Correlations between Party Identification and Attitudes toward Hispanics and Blacks, Post-Election Survey, 1980[a]

Items and Dimensions	Hispanics	Blacks
Partisan Direction		
Party Difference Index	.14***	.27***
	(1069)	(1184)
Party Closeness Scale	.12***	.24***
	(1180)	(1314)
Party Support Scale	.13***	.24***
	(1173)	(1310)
Democratic Party Feeling Thermometer	.18***	.33***
	(1174)	(1294)
Republican Party Feeling Thermometer	-.01	-.07**
	(1171)	(1292)
Seven-Point Party Identification Scale	.12***	.22***
	(1194)	(1327)
Strength of Partisanship		
Folded Party Closeness Scale	.05	.13***
	(1180)	(1314)
Folded Party Support Scale	.07**	.15***
	(1173)	(1310)
Four-Point Strength of Identification Scale	.05*	.15***
	(1194)	(1327)
Independence		
Strength of Independence Scale	.02	-.07**
	(1190)	(1325)
Independents Feeling Thermometer	.13***	.06*
	(1111)	(1201)

a - Figures in parentheses are numbers of cases.

* Significant at the .05 level.
** Significant at the .01 level.
*** Significant at the .001 level.

and this question increases somewhat. Although the findings reported in Table 4–1 suggest that Democrats and strong partisans feel more positively toward minorities than their counterparts in the electorate, the relationships are weaker than one might expect. The positive direction of the correlations between the strength of identification measures, the Independents thermometer, and attitudes toward ''hispanics'' support the position that partisan strength and independence comprise two dimensions of party identification.

There are a number of significant differences between the correlations for the individual party identification measures and feelings about "hispanics" and "blacks." To begin, the correlations between the Democratic party feeling thermometer and attitudes toward "hispanics" and "blacks" are significantly higher (at the .05 and .001 levels, respectively) than the correlations between the seven-point party identification scale and attitudes toward these two groups. In other words, the Democrat thermometer tends to be a better predictor of dispositions toward these citizens than the standard seven-point measure. The relationships between the party difference index and feelings about "blacks" ($r=.27$) is also significantly stronger (at the .01 level) than the relationship between the standard seven-point measure and feelings about "blacks" ($r=.22$). However, the relationships between the traditional seven-point measure and respondents' thermometer ratings of "hispanics" and "blacks" are significantly closer (at the .001 level) than the relationships between the Republican thermometer and respondents' ratings of these minorities. Also, the Independents thermometer is a more precise estimate of views on "hispanics" than is the strength of independence scale (significant at the .01 level). The differences between the correlations remain virtually unchanged after race is controlled. No significant disparities exist between the correlations for the partisan strength measures and support for the two groups.

Labor Unions and Big Business

The media often identify labor unions and "big" business as two important voting blocks in elections. Because of the political events that took place in the 1930s involving these groups, most observers believe the Republicans tend to support "big" business (and vice versa) and Democrats tend to support labor (and vice versa). Whether Republicans and Democrats are as sympathetic toward these groups as they once were is questionable. Nevertheless, an analysis of partisans' and nonpartisans' attitudes toward these sectors of society might provide additional clues concerning the different party identification measures.

Respondents were asked to rate "labor unions" and "big business" on a feeling thermometer. The Pearson correlations between party identification and reactions to these groups appear in Table 4–2. The data show that Democrats and strong partisans are more likely than Republicans and those with loose partisan ties to feel "warm" toward "labor unions." Republicans and strong partisans tend to feel slightly more positive toward "big business" than Democrats and weak partisans. The correlations between the partisan strength measures and feelings about "labor unions" and "big business" are stronger than those between the independence measures and feelings about these two groups, which suggests that partisan strength and independence are two different entities. According to the findings in Tables 4–1 and 4–2, Democrats do tend to feel more sympathy for labor and minorities than Republicans, and Republicans do tend to be more supportive of "big business" than Democrats. Yet, the relatively

Table 4-2
Pearson Correlations between Party Identification and Attitudes toward Labor Unions and Big Business, Post-Election Survey, 1980[a]

Items and Dimensions	Labor Unions	Big Business
Partisan Direction		
Party Difference Index	.26***	-.13***
	(1168)	(1150)
Party Closeness Scale	.21***	-.09***
	(1283)	(1264)
Party Support Scale	.22***	-.07**
	(1280)	(1259)
Democratic Party Feeling Thermometer	.36***	.06*
	(1277)	(1255)
Republican Party Feeling Thermometer	-.05*	.25***
	(1274)	(1254)
Seven-Point Party Identification Scale	.23***	-.12***
	(1299)	(1283)
Strength of Partisanship		
Folded Party Closeness Scale	.09***	.10***
	(1283)	(1264)
Folded Party Support Scale	.14***	.12***
	(1280)	(1259)
Four-Point Strength of Identification Scale	.13***	.10***
	(1299)	(1283)
Independence		
Strength of Independence Scale	-.07**	-.05
	(1295)	(1272)
Independents Feeling Thermometer	.01	.05*
	(1194)	(1171)

a - Figures in parentheses are numbers of cases.

* Significant at the .05 level.
** Significant at the .01 level
*** Significant at the .001 level.

low correlations suggest that political commentators run the risk of overstating these relationships in the 1980s.[2]

As in Table 4–1, several significant differences exist between the correlations for the separate party identification measures and attitudes toward "labor unions" and "big business." For instance, there are significant differences between the correlations for the Democrat thermometer, the standard seven-point measure, and feelings about "labor unions." Stated another way, the correlation between the Democrat thermometer and dispositions toward this group ($r = .36$) is significantly higher (at the .001 level) than the correlation between the standard seven-point measure and dispositions toward this segment of the electorate ($r = .23$). In addition, the relationship between the traditional seven-point measure and views on "big business" (r = −.12) is significantly closer (at the .05 level) than the relationship between the party support scale and views on this sector of society (r = −.07). Ignoring the direction of the relationships for the moment, the correlation between the seven-point measure and respondents' ratings of "labor unions" is significantly greater (at the .001 level) than the correlation between the Republican thermometer and respondents' ratings of this group. In contrast, the correlation between the Republican thermometer and attitudes toward "big business" is significantly higher (at the .001 level) than the correlation between the old seven-point measure and attitudes toward "big business." Furthermore, the correlations between the independence measures and opinions on "labor unions" and "big business" vary significantly (at least at the .05 level). No significant differences exist between the correlations for the standard and alternative partisan strength measures and attitudes toward these segments of the population.

The Elderly and People on Welfare

The poor and the elderly are among a large number of Americans who heavily depend on social programs, specifically welfare and social security, to maintain an adequate quality of life. In the past, the Democrats have supported the continued funding of these programs while the Republicans have recommended cutbacks in these areas. The changing state of the economy and the rising cost to administer these programs have accented the differences between the parties on these issues. Perhaps Republicans and Democrats take the stands they do because of their different attitudes toward the elderly and citizens on welfare. If this is true, then one would expect Democrats to hold more positive attitudes toward these two groups than Republicans.

Table 4–3 reports the Pearson correlations between party identification and respondents' feeling thermometer ratings of "older people" and "people on welfare." The data show that Democrats feel more "warmly" toward the elderly and especially citizens on welfare than Republicans. Strong partisans are also more likely to feel positively toward these two groups than weak partisans. There is evidence that increased independence from politics is accompanied by negative views on these sectors of society, however, the correlations are quite small. As in Table 4–2, the difference in size of the correlations between the partisan strength and independence measures and feelings about "older people" and "people on welfare" implies that partisan strength and independence are two different things. Controlling for age has no effect on the association between party identification and attitudes toward "older people."

There are several significant gaps between the correlations for the party identification measures and feelings about "older people" and "people on welfare." The correlations between the Democrat thermometer and attitudes toward the elderly and those on welfare are significantly larger (at the .001 and .01 levels, respectively) than the correlations between the seven-point party

Table 4-3
Pearson Correlations between Party Identification and Attitudes toward Older People and People on Welfare, Post-Election Survey, 1980[a]

Items and Dimensions	Older People	People on Welfare
Partisan Direction		
Party Difference Index	.07**	.29***
	(1204)	(1138)
Party Closeness Scale	.06*	.25***
	(1341)	(1262)
Party Support Scale	.07**	.26***
	(1338)	(1259)
Democratic Party Feeling Thermometer	.15***	.32***
	(1316)	(1248)
Republican Party Feeling Thermometer	.06*	-.11***
	(1312)	(1244)
Seven-Point Party Identification Scale	.07**	.25***
	(1356)	(1280)
Strength of Partisanship		
Folded Party Closeness Scale	.15***	.14***
	(1341)	(1262)
Folded Party Support Scale	.12***	.12***
	(1338)	(1259)
Four-Point Strength of Identification Scale	.12***	.14***
	(1356)	(1280)
Independence		
Strength of Independence Scale	-.06*	-.09***
	(1350)	(1273)
Independents Feeling Thermometer	.01	.02
	(1218)	(1160)

a - Figures in parentheses are numbers of cases.

* Significant at the .05 level.
** Significant at the .01 level.
*** Significant at the .001 level.

identification scale and attitudes toward these two groups. Moreover, the relationship between the party difference index and feelings about "people on welfare" ($r = .29$) is significantly stronger (at the .05 level) than the relationship between the standard seven-point scale and feelings about these citizens ($r = .25$). The party difference index is therefore a better predictor of reactions to this segment of the electorate than the traditional seven-point scale. In contrast, the correlation between the seven-point measure and respondents' ratings of "people on welfare" is significantly greater (at the .001 level) than the absolute value of the correlation between the Republican thermometer and respondents' ratings of this group. The data also show that the strength of independence scale is a more accurate determinant of views on "older people" and "people on welfare" (significant at least at the .05 level) than the Independents thermometer. The correlations between the partisan strength measures and the two thermometer items in Table 4–3 are similar in size.

Civil Rights Leaders

In the 1960s, a number of individuals—including Whitney Young of the National Urban League, Roy Wilkins of the National Association for the Advancement of Colored People (NAACP), and the Reverend Martin Luther King, Jr., of the Southern Christian Leadership Conference—played an important role in the civil rights movement. Their ability to organize and lead large but peaceful demonstrations increased their political influence. Eventually, Congress was forced to enact major civil rights legislation over the strong objections of powerful southern Democratic and conservative Republican legislators. Democrats outside the South, as previously discussed, tended to be more receptive to the demands of civil rights leaders than southern Democrats and conservative Republicans. Since the tumultuous 1960s, news reporters have paid less attention to the activities of civil rights leaders. Though less prominent, activists such as Benjamin Hooks (Executive Director of the NAACP) and John E. Jacob (head of the National Urban League) occasionally appear in the media. While their tactics have obviously changed, their goals have not. Consequently, Americans may still hold perceptions of civil rights leaders which differ along traditional partisan lines.[3]

Table 4–4 shows the relationship between party identification and respondents' thermometer ratings of "civil rights leaders." Clearly, Democrats feel more "warmly" toward "civil rights leaders" than Republicans. In addition, as partisan strength and political independence increase, so does support for these individuals. Controlling for race tends to depress slightly the correlations between partisan direction, partisan strength, and feelings about "civil rights leaders" and increase slightly the correlations between political independence and feelings about this group. As one can see, the correlations between the partisan strength measures, the Independents thermometer, and attitudes toward these leaders are in the same direction, which suggests that partisan strength and independence are two separate dimensions.

There are significant differences between the correlations for the party identification measures and attitudes toward these individuals. The correlations between the party difference index, the Democrat thermometer, and support for "civil rights leaders" ($r = .34$ and .35, respectively) are significantly higher (at the .001 and .01 levels, respectively) than the correlation between the standard seven-point measure and support for this group ($r = .28$). *Again, the party difference index and the Democrat thermometer provide better estimates of attitudes toward a given group.* On the other hand, the correlation between the

Table 4-4
Pearson Correlations between Party Identification and Attitudes toward Civil Rights Leaders, Post-Election Survey, 1980[a]

Items and Dimensions	Civil Rights Leaders
Partisan Direction	
Party Difference Index	.34*** (1161)
Party Closeness Scale	.28*** (1280)
Party Support Scale	.31*** (1276)
Democratic Party Feeling Thermometer	.35*** (1269)
Republican Party Feeling Thermometer	-.18*** (1268)
Seven-Point Party Identification Scale	.28*** (1294)
Strength of Partisanship	
Folded Party Closeness Scale	.09*** (1280)
Folded Party Support Scale	.12*** (1276)
Four-Point Strength of Identification Scale	.13*** (1294)
Independence	
Strength of Independence Scale	.03 (1288)
Independents Feeling Thermometer	.13*** (1187)

a - Figures in parentheses are numbers of cases.

* Significant at the .05 level.
** Significant at the .01 level.
*** Significant at the .001 level.

traditional seven-point measure and views on "civil rights leaders" is significantly higher (at the .01 level) than the absolute value of the correlation between the Republican thermometer and views on these leaders. Also, the relationship between the Independents thermometer and respondents' ratings of "civil rights leaders" ($r = .13$) is significantly stronger (at the .01 level) than the relationship between the strength of independence scale and ratings of these activists ($r = .03$). Finally, no significant discrepancies exist between the correlations for the partisan strength measures and feelings about these individuals.[4]

VIEWS ON ISSUES

Prior to the development of sophisticated survey research methods and scientific sampling techniques, students of politics assumed that citizens paid careful attention to the issues and voted in line with their attitudes on the issues. However, Angus Campbell, Philip Converse, Warren Miller, and Donald Stokes found that Americans in the 1950s were unfamiliar with seemingly important domestic and foreign policy questions and inconsistent in their issue positions.[5] Generally speaking, the public demonstrated an inability to sort out personal and candidate issue positions, and the idea of the responsible citizen carefully weighing the issues before casting his or her ballot appeared to be a myth. Instead, psychological characteristics such as party identification and partisan attitudes were the best determinants of the vote.

Studies conducted on the electorate of the 1960s and early 1970s painted a radically different picture. John Pierce, David RePass, Gerald Pomper, and Norman Nie and Kristi Andersen, along with others, found the electorate after 1960 to be more aware of and better able to conceptualize policy issues, especially those pertaining to race and the economy, and to vote accordingly.[6] Pomper, in particular, dispelled suspicions that social and demographic changes were responsible for the sudden rise in issue awareness and consistency.[7] His investigation showed that increases in issue awareness and consistency cut across differences in age, race, education, and region. A concomitant decline in partisanship was also noted in these studies. While the events of the 1950s failed to provide voters with sufficient stimulus to become conscious of the issues, the problems and incidents of the 1960s and early 1970s penetrated people's daily lives and forced them to take stands on policy concerns before voting. These findings led to accusations that *The American Voter* was time bound and raised doubts about other parts of the study.[8]

Issue Voting Reconsidered

Edward Carmines and James Stimson classified issues into two types, "easy" issues and "hard" issues.[9] "Easy" issues are more symbolic than technical, tend to deal with policy ends and not means, and have been on the political agenda a long time. "Hard" issues, in contrast, are multifaceted and complex, tend to address policy means rather than ends, and have existed only a short time. "Easy" issues require little sophistication to be understood while "hard" issues are more difficult to comprehend. In 1972, according to Carmines and Stimson, racial desegregation was an "easy issue" and the pace of withdrawal from Vietnam was a "hard issue." Their analysis of survey data collected during the 1972 election showed that "easy-issue" voters were no more sophisticated than "non-issue" voters. This finding implies that "issue voting, as it has been traditionally conceptualized and measured, overestimates the amount of sophisticated policy calculation going on in the electorate."[10] Issue voting probably occurs in waves or surges, only in those rare cases where the parties and the candidates are sharply divided over the issues in the voters' minds. They therefore concluded that "increased issue voting . . . says little about the political sophistication of the American electorate."[11]

Petrocik's study of the 1976 presidential election tended to support these assertions.[12] His analysis revealed that "party identification was more important and issues less important than in any election since 1960. . . ."[13] According to him, the percentage voting their party identification in 1976 was nearly identical to the rates of party voting in the 1952, 1956, and 1960 elections.[14] The 1976 election, similar to the Eisenhower and Kennedy elections, presented few burning issues to the electorate, and, as a result, people used party as a cue in deciding for whom to vote. Thus, voters are not more or less consistent in their issue positions than in the past, rather the political context has changed.[15] Based on his findings, voters are strongly influenced by the prevailing political environment and are likely to change as it changes.

What about the 1980 election? Preliminary analyses indicate that voters in 1980 tended to focus on the personality of the candidates and Carter's performance as President instead of party or issues.[16] The election of a conservative Republican President, the capture of the Senate by the Republican party, and the substantial Republican gains in the House do not represent an enduring move to the right by the electorate but rather an outright rejection of Carter the man and his record.[17] These findings, in addition to others, have prompted Jack Dennis to speculate that we may "have entered a new period in which 'personalismo' in races for the president—and thus pure candidate-centered voting—has replaced both party voting and issue voting."[18]

As one can see, most researchers have examined issues and party identification with respect to the vote. Yet, there is considerable interplay between party identification and opinions on policies, too, though the direction of causation is often unclear. Since many adopt an identification with a party at an early age, there is a good chance that their affiliation influences their issue positions as they grow older. It is also conceivable that changes in political conditions and life circumstances cause shifts in policy positions which, in turn, affect partisan direction, partisan strength, and independence. Carmines and Stimson, for example, showed how the evolution of the race issue over the last twenty years has had a profound effect on the recruitment of new party identifiers.[19] Whatever the case may be, one would expect to find a relationship between party identification and attitudes on issues. This section of the chapter will analyze the association between party identification and issue stands.

DEFENSE AND PUBLIC SERVICES SPENDING

Reagan and Carter touched upon defense and government services spending frequently during the campaign. Reagan, in particular, voiced concern over the Soviet Union's huge military buildup and America's "widening window of vulnerability." Carter, on the other hand, staunchly defended his efforts to reach a second Strategic Arms Limitation Treaty (SALT II) with the Soviet Union and hoped that the public would view Reagan as a "war monger." Furthermore, Reagan promised to cut government services sharply, trim the bureaucracy, and balance the budget if elected. Carter argued that such a feat could not be accomplished in four years without placing undue hardship on the American people, especially the poor.

These exchanges over defense and government services spending prompted the designers of the 1980 election study to include items on both issues in the pre-election questionnaire. On a scale ranging from 1 to 7 respondents were asked whether "we should spend much less money for defense" (coded 1) or "greatly increase defense spending" (coded 7).[20] Also, on a seven-point scale, respondents were asked whether "the government should provide fewer services in order to reduce spending" (scored 1) or "continue the services it now provides even if it means no reduction in spending" (scored 7).[21]

Table 4–5 reports the correlations between party identification and opinions on defense and government services spending. As one can see, Republicans are more likely than Democrats to favor increased defense spending and decreased public services spending. Strong partisans tend to prefer more appropriations for defense and continued government support for services. Independents, however, believe cutbacks are necessary in both areas. The correlations between the partisan strength and independence measures and these two items are in the opposite direction and are similar in size. This implies that partisan strength and independence fall along a single continuum. The data in Table 4–5 show that Republicans, Democrats, strong partisans, and Independents hold different views on these two issues.

Comparisons can also be made between the correlations for the separate party identification measures and positions on defense and government services spending. Significant differences exist between the correlations for the party difference index, the seven-point measure, and public opinion on the two issues. More specifically, the correlations between the party difference index and attitudes on defense and government services spending ($r = -.21$ and $.39$, respectively) are significantly higher (at the .05 and .001 levels, respectively) than the correlations between the standard seven-point measure and views on these two questions ($r = -.17$ and $.34$, respectively). Moreover, there are significant differences between the absolute values of the correlations for the Democrat and Republican thermometer items, the seven-point measure, and support for increased defense expenditures. Disregarding the direction of the correlations for the moment, the relationship between the traditional seven-point scale and position on defense spending is significantly stronger (at the .05 level) than the relationship between the Democrat thermometer and attitudes on this issue, and is significantly weaker (at the .001 level) than the association between the Republican thermometer and attitudes on this question. Although the correlation between the seven-point measure and opinion on appropriations for public services is significantly higher (at the .001 level) than the absolute value of the correlation between the Republican thermometer and support for this issue, the

Table 4-5
Pearson Correlations between Party Identification and Government Spending, Pre-Election Survey, 1980[a]

Items and Dimensions	Defense	Government Services
Partisan Direction		
Party Difference Index	-.21*** (1207)	.39*** (1156)
Party Closeness Scale	-.16*** (1338)	.32*** (1277)
Party Support Scale	-.16*** (1334)	.33*** (1273)
Democratic Party Feeling Thermometer	-.11*** (1313)	.37*** (1258)
Republican Party Feeling Thermometer	.26*** (1313)	-.19*** (1261)
Seven-Point Party Identification Scale	-.17*** (1346)	.34*** (1287)
Strength of Partisanship		
Folded Party Closeness Scale	.06* (1338)	.08** (1277)
Folded Party Support Scale	.06* (1334)	.09*** (1273)
Four-Point Strength of Identification Scale	.03 (1346)	.09*** (1287)
Independence		
Strength of Independence Scale	-.06* (1340)	-.12*** (1282)
Independents Feeling Thermometer	-.11*** (1236)	.05 (1181)

a - Figures in parentheses are number of cases.

*   Significant at the .05 level.
**   Significant at the .01 level.
*** Significant at the .001 level.

correlations between the Democrat thermometer, the seven-point measure, and views on this policy are about the same size. Finally, there is a significant distance (at the .001 level) between the correlations for the two independence measures and views on government services spending. The relationships between the partisan strength measures and attitudes on public services procurements are similar in strength.

Aid to Minorities and Government Power

The issue of continued government aid to minority groups was also addressed in the 1980 election survey. Changing priorities (e.g., a desire to improve the nation's defense) and burgeoning budget deficits have forced policy makers to rethink well-intended but expensive social programs designed to help blacks and other minorities. A large number of these programs were enacted in the 1960s and have grown rapidly in size. The question of whether and, if so, how much these programs should be cut has sparked heated debates between lawmakers on Capitol Hill. Unless priorities change or sizeable reductions in the budget deficit are achieved, the controversy surrounding this issue is likely to persist.

Another issue addressed in the election study was increased government power. Citing a growing bureaucracy and the passage of many rules and regulations directly affecting citizens' lives, Reagan repeatedly stated during the campaign that the federal government has become too powerful. He promised that, if elected President, he would "get the federal government off the public's back" by transferring control over social welfare and health care programs to state and local governments. His "new federalism" program is supposed to do just that.

After the election respondents were asked to place themselves on a seven-point scale ranging from "the government in Washington should help minority groups," coded 1, to "minority groups should help themselves," coded 7.[22] Later in the survey they were asked whether "the government in Washington is not getting too strong" (coded zero) or "the government in Washington is getting too powerful for the good of the country and the individual person" (coded 1).[23] Table 4–6 indicates the degree to which Republicans and Democrats differ on these two issues. The data show that Republicans are more likely than Democrats to oppose continued government aid to minorities and to agree that the federal government has become "too powerful." Weaker relationships exist between partisan strength, political independence, and attitudes on these two problems. Based on the results of the analysis, the correlations between the standard four-point partisan strength measure, the Independents thermometer, and opinions on aid to minorities are in the same direction, and the correlations between the partisan strength and independence measures and opinions on government power differ in magnitude. These patterns in the data suggest that partisan strength and independence are two dimensions.

The findings reported in Table 4–6 concerning the relationships between the standard and alternative partisan direction measures and views on aid to minorities and government power are, to some extent, similar to those presented in Table 4–5. For example, the correlations between the party difference index and feelings about aid to minorities and government power ($r = -.29$ and $-.32$, respectively) are significantly higher (at the .05 and .01 levels, respectively) than the correlations between the standard seven-point measure and feelings about the same two issues ($r = -.25$ and $-.27$, respectively). *Thus, the data indicate that position on the party difference index is a better predictor of attitudes on both issues than position on the traditional seven-point scale.* But, in contrast to the results in Table 4–5, the absolute values of the correlations between the party thermometers, the seven-point measure, and opinions on aid to minorities

Table 4-6
Pearson Correlations between Party Identification, Aid to Minorities, and Government Power, Post-Election Survey, 1980[a]

Items and Dimensions	Aid to Minorities	Government Power
Partisan Direction		
Party Difference Index	-.29*** (1062)	-.32*** (792)
Party Closeness Scale	-.25*** (1166)	-.29*** (876)
Party Support Scale	-.25*** (1164)	-.27*** (871)
Democratic Party Feeling Thermometer	-.23*** (1158)	-.28*** (871)
Republican Party Feeling Thermometer	.22*** (1158)	.21*** (872)
Seven-Point Party Identification Scale	-.25*** (1185)	-.27*** (887)
Strength of Partisanship		
Folded Party Closeness Scale	-.05 (1166)	-.13*** (876)
Folded Party Support Scale	-.03 (1164)	-.09** (871)
Four-Point Strength of Identification Scale	-.05* (1185)	-.13*** (887)
Independence		
Strength of Independence Scale	-.01 (1179)	.06* (871)
Independents Feeling Thermometer	-.09*** (1088)	.06* (817)

a - Figures in parentheses are numbers of cases.

* Significant at the .05 level.
** Significant at the .01 level.
*** Significant at the .001 level.

and government power are nearly equal. In addition, the relationship between the Independents thermometer and aid to minorities ($r = -.09$) is significantly stronger (at the .05 level) than the relationship between the strength of independence measure and views on this matter ($r = -.01$). The correlations between the old and new partisan strength measures and responses to these questions do not differ significantly.

The Economy

The nation's economy proved to be a focal point of attention for the media, the parties, and the candidates in 1980. Double-digit inflation and moderately high unemployment in 1979 and 1980 prompted Reagan to invent a "misery-index"—the sum of the inflation and unemployment rates—to portray the plight of the economy under the Carter Administration. He contended that a substantial tax cut (about 30 percent) and less government intervention in the marketplace would reduce inflation and create jobs. Carter felt Reagan's proposals would actually fuel inflation, keep interest rates high, and add to the already large federal budget deficit. He also argued that it would be difficult to increase employment under these conditions.

As we discussed before, the two parties have often taken divergent stands on economic policy. While Republicans have traditionally been characterized as supporters of "big" business and laissez-faire, Democrats have been viewed as supporters of the poor and the workingperson. Although these lines are not as sharply drawn as they were during the New Deal period, the economic philosophy of many party followers probably still reflects the division created at the time. Therefore, on the question of employment, we would expect Democrats to be more supportive of direct federal government involvement in the creation of more jobs.

Prior to the election, respondents were asked how willing they would be to trade off inflation against unemployment. Specifically, respondents were requested to place themselves on a seven-point scale ranging from "reduce inflation even if unemployment goes up a lot" (coded 1) to "reduce unemployment even if inflation goes up a lot" (coded 7).[24] Those interviewed after the election were asked the extent to which people should be guaranteed a job and a good standard of living by the federal government. Using a seven-point scale again, respondents were asked whether "the government in Washington should see to it that every person has a job and a good standard of living" (scored 1) or "the government should just let each person get ahead on his own" (scored 7).[25] Based on the data in Table 4–7, the relationship between party identity and public opinion on these two issues is in the expected direction. Democrats are more likely to favor "reducing unemployment even if inflation goes up a lot" and believe "the government in Washington should see to it that every person has a job and a good standard of living," while Republicans tend to favor "reducing inflation even if unemployment goes up a lot" and think "the government should just let each person get ahead on his own." Judging by the size of the correlations, the two parties are more divided over government job and standard of living guarantees than over the tradeoff between inflation and unemployment. In addition, strong partisans show an inclination to side with the Democrats while Independents tend to agree with the Republicans on both issues. The correlations between partisan strength, political independence, and these two issues are smaller than those between partisan direction and these two questions. The correlations between the partisan strength measures, the strength of independence scale, and these two items are in the opposite direction and are similar in size. This finding supports the position that partisan strength and independence fall along a single continuum.

Table 4-7
Pearson Correlations between Party Identification and Public Opinion on Employment, 1980[a]

Items and Dimensions	Inflation Versus Unemployment	Guaranteed Jobs and Standard of Living
Partisan Direction		
Party Difference Index	.21*** (840)	-.38*** (1033)
Party Closeness Scale	.19*** (917)	-.33*** (1143)
Party Support Scale	.19*** (911)	-.31*** (1139)
Democratic Party Feeling Thermometer	.21*** (916)	-.34*** (1127)
Republican Party Feeling Thermometer	-.10*** (915)	.23*** (1127)
Seven-Point Party Identification Scale	.20*** (921)	-.32*** (1161)
Strength of Partisanship		
Folded Party Closeness Scale	.09** (917)	-.06* (1143)
Folded Party Support Scale	.14*** (911)	-.07* (1139)
Four-Point Strength of Identification Scale	.09** (921)	-.12*** (1161)
Independence		
Strength of Independence Scale	-.07* (919)	.09** (1153)
Independents Feeling Thermometer	-.02 (870)	-.03 (1048)

a - Figures in parentheses are numbers of cases.

* Significant at the .05 level.
** Significant at the .01 level.
*** Significant at the .001 level.

The data in Table 4–7 also provide a meaningful context in which to compare the various party identification measures. Based on our analysis, there are significant differences between the absolute values of the correlations for the Republican thermometer, the seven-point measure, and attitudes on inflation versus unemployment and whether the federal government should provide job and standard of living guarantees for everyone. Ignoring the direction of the relationships for the moment, the correlations between the standard seven-point measure and views on inflation versus unemployment and government job and standard of living guarantees are significantly higher (at the .01 level) than the correlations between the Republican thermometer and views on these two questions. Moreover, the correlation between the party difference index and support for government job and standard of living guarantees (r = −.38) is significantly greater (at the .001 level) than the correlation between the traditional seven-point scale and support for this issue (r = −.32). Also, the relationship between the standard four-point strength of identification measure and opinion on government job and standard of living guarantees (r = −.12) is stronger (significant at the .05 level) than the relationship between the folded party closeness scale and opinion on this issue (r = −.06). Lastly, there is a significant disparity (at the .001 level) between the correlations for the independence measures and responses to the guaranteed job and standard of living question.

Civil Rights

The two parties have also clashed over social issues. As previously noted, the Democratic party (excluding southern Democrats) has been viewed as a promoter of minority civil rights since the 1960s, while the Republican party has shown less sympathy toward efforts to expand such rights. Although the salience of the civil rights issue has decreased over the years, one would think that traditional partisan cleavages over the issue still exist.

Respondents were asked whether they felt civil rights leaders were moving either "too fast" (coded 1), "just about the right speed" (coded 2), or "too slow" (coded 3).[26] Table 4–8 shows the relationship between party identification and Americans' views on this issue. The direction of the tau-c correlations indicates that Democrats are more likely than Republicans to say that civil rights leaders are moving "too slow."[27] Furthermore, a weak but significant relationship exists between political independence and attitudes on this issue. That is, increased independence tends to be accompanied by increased endorsement for the civil rights movement. Partisan strength, on the other hand, is not related to public opinion on civil rights. These data support the view that partisan strength and independence are two components of party identification and not one as commonly assumed. No significant differences were found between the correlations for the individual party identification measures and views on this question.

Equal Rights Amendment

Leaders of the women's rights movement (such as Gloria Steinem) and opponents of the movement (such as Phyllis Schlafly) made the proposed Equal Rights Amendment (ERA) to the United States Constitution a major social issue in the 1970s. Even the two presidential candidates were divided over the question: while Carter supported the passage of the ERA, Reagan opposed its enactment. Reagan contended that the ERA was unnecessary since a large number of state and federal laws designed to protect the rights of women already exist. But Carter argued that most of these laws have been ineffective in pro-

Table 4-8
TAU-C Correlations between Party Identification and Civil Rights, Post-Election Survey, 1980[a]

Items and Dimensions	Civil Rights
Partisan Direction	
Party Difference Index	.17***
	(1138)
Party Closeness Scale	.11***
	(1251)
Party Support Scale	.12***
	(1248)
Democratic Party Feeling Thermometer	.11***
	(1239)
Republican Party Feeling Thermometer	-.13***
	(1238)
Seven-Point Party Identification Scale	.13***
	(1277)
Strength of Partisanship	
Folded Party Closeness Scale	.04
	(1251)
Folded Party Support Scale	.01
	(1248)
Four-Point Strength of Identification Scale	.03
	(1277)
Independence	
Strength of Independence Scale	.05*
	(1263)
Independents Feeling Thermometer	.12***
	(1152)

a - Figures in parentheses are numbers of cases.

* Significant at the .05 level.

** Significant at the .01 level.

*** Significant at the .001 level.

viding women equal rights. The Amendment legally died on June 30, 1982, only three states short of the thirty-eight needed for its enactment. Women rights leaders vow to reintroduce the measure in Congress and fight again for its passage.

Table 4-9
Tau-C Correlations between Party Identification and the Equal Rights Amendment, Post-Election Survey, 1980[a]

Measures and Dimensions	ERA[b]
Partisan Direction	
Party Difference Index	.31***
	(1061)
Party Closeness Scale	.24***
	(1171)
Party Support Scale	.22***
	(1164)
Democratic Party Feeling Thermometer	.21***
	(1154)
Republican Party Feeling Thermometer	-.22***
	(1154)
Seven-Point Party Identification Scale	.24***
	(1186)
Strength of Partisanship	
Folded Party Closeness Scale	.00
	(1171)
Folded Party Support Scale	.03
	(1164)
Four-Point Strength of Identification Scale	.00
	(1186)
Independence	
Strength of Independence Scale	.05*
	(1173)
Independents Feeling Thermometer	.05*
	(1089)

[a] Figures in parentheses are numbers of cases.

[b] The coefficients to the right of the folded party closeness and four-point strength of identification scales are tau-b correlations.

* Significant at the .05 level.

** Significant at the .01 level.

*** Significant at the .001 level.

Those interviewed were asked how much they approve or disapprove of the ERA.[28] Responses ranged from "strongly disapprove," coded 1, to "strongly approve," coded 4. The tau-c correlations between party identification and views on the ERA appear in Table 4–9. The data show that Democrats are more supportive of the ERA than Republicans. In addition, there is a weak but significant relationship between independence and attitudes on this issue; as independence rises, so does support for this issue. Partisan strength, however, is not related to opinion on this question. As in the previous table, this finding endorses the position that partisan strength and independence are two separate dimensions. No significant differences were found between the correlations for the party identification measures and views on the ERA. The next section analyzes the relationship between political ideology and party orientation.[29]

IDEOLOGY

Campbell, Converse, Miller, and Stokes define an ideology as a "particularly elaborate, close-woven, and far-reaching structure of attitudes."[30] Although an ideology "is a highly differentiated attitude structure, . . . its parts are organized in a coherent fashion."[31] Liberalism and conservatism are examples of political ideologies.

As we mentioned earlier, Campbell and his colleagues found only a small percentage of the electorate took consistent stands on the issues in the 1950s. In addition to this finding, they discovered that only 11 1/2 percent of the respondents in the 1956 election study were able to evaluate the parties and the presidential candidates in ideological terms.[32] These results challenged the popular notion that voters have well-developed belief systems, weigh the parties' and candidates' issue positions in a sophisticated manner, and cast their ballots accordingly.

Philip Converse, in his seminal article entitled "The Nature of Belief Systems in Mass Publics," elaborated further on the concepts and findings concerning ideology and political belief systems that were first discussed in *The American Voter*.[33] He defined a belief system as a "configuration of ideas and attitudes in which the elements are bound together by some form of constraint or functional interdependence."[34] Moreover, a belief system should contain abstract "objects of centrality" and have a wide scope. He explained that constraint represents internal consistency of attitudes on issues and implied that such consistency generally falls along a single underlying dimension (whether it be left to right or some other continuum). One's ideology therefore reflects one's belief system structure. His analysis of the 1952, 1956, and 1960 elections again showed that a large segment of the electorate were unable to order their attitudes in a systematic fashion.

James Stimson, in his excellent article "Belief Systems: Constraint, Complexity, and the 1972 Election," reexamined the electorate's ability to conceptualize issues.[35] Unlike Converse, he found that a significant portion of the electorate, particularly those with high levels of "cognitive ability" (i.e., education and political information), tended to take consistent positions on issues along the traditional liberal-conservative dimension. Earlier we identified other researchers who also reported finding high levels of issue awareness and consistency within the electorate in 1964 and 1968. Stimson concluded that although "Converse's approach to measuring belief structure has been fundamentally correct all along . . . the presidential elections which were the subject of Converse's analysis were vastly less ideological in the minds of the voters than all those which have occurred since then."[36]

Generally speaking, students of politics consider the Democratic party to be more "liberal" or "progressive" than the Republican party. By more liberal we mean that Democrats often support government involvement in the public's social, political, and economic life. Conservative Republicans, however, oppose such efforts unless law and order issues are involved. Thus, for example, liberals are more likely to see the advantages of government attempts to help minorities and the disadvantaged, whereas conservatives will tend to dwell on the harmful consequences of such actions. While liberals believe people are equal and should be treated equally, conservatives feel people are inherently unequal and are due unequal rewards. Liberals also think planned change brings the possibility of improvement, while conservatives exalt tradition, order, and authority. In foreign policy, conservatives are more fearful of communism and are more supportive of a strong national defense than liberals.

It would be incorrect to infer from our discussion that all Democrats are more liberal than all Republicans on every issue, or that there are no conservatives in the Democratic party and no liberals in the Republican party. Conservative Democrats in the South and liberal Republicans in the Northeast have often disagreed with their party's position on certain issues (e.g., civil rights). Yet, based on our knowledge of American politics, we would speculate that more Democrats call themselves liberals than Republicans.

Respondents were asked to place themselves on a seven-point liberal-conservative scale in the pre-election wave. The scale ranged from "extremely liberal" (scored 1) to "extremely conservative" (scored 7). An examination of the item's frequency distribution reveals that about one-third of the sample were unable to locate themselves on the scale. This result is in line with the findings reported in *The American Voter* and in Converse's follow-up study on belief systems.[37] More recent studies also show that the liberal-conservative dimension is not common to everyone in the electorate, and that many order their thoughts along other dimensions.[38] Stimson demonstrated, you will recall, that only those with high levels of cognitive ability order their issue positions along a liberal-conservative continuum.[39] He therefore concluded:

When we examine the ideology of the mass public, we are quite likely to overstate its impact because the evidence of impact is most slight for that part of the electorate that systematically selects itself out of such analyses by . . . not responding to measures of ideology.[40]

This should be kept in mind as we move through the analysis.

Table 4–10 contains the Pearson correlations between party identification and ideological self-classification. The data show that Democrats are indeed more likely than Republicans to consider themselves liberal. There is also a weak but significant relationship between political independence and ideology. That is, as independence increases, so does liberalism. No significant relationship exists between partisan strength and ideology. *Once again, the results of our analysis*

Table 4-10
Pearson Correlations between Party Identification and Ideology, Pre-Election Survey, 1980[a]

Items and Dimensions	Ideological Self-Identification
Partisan Direction	
Party Difference Index	-.41***
	(898)
Party Closeness Scale	-.37***
	(983)
Party Support Scale	-.36***
	(974)
Democratic Party Feeling Thermometer	-.30***
	(975)
Republican Party Feeling Thermometer	.32***
	(978)
Seven-Point Party Identification Scale	-.39***
	(995)
Strength of Partisanship	
Folded Party Closeness Scale	.05
	(983)
Folded Party Support Scale	.05
	(974)
Four-Point Strength of Identification Scale	.03
	(995)
Independence	
Strength of Independence Scale	-.10***
	(981)
Independents Feeling Thermometer	-.12***
	(920)

a - Figures in parentheses are numbers of cases.

* Significant at the .05 level.
** Significant at the .01 level.
*** Significant at the .001 level.

appear to challenge the popular assumption that partisan strength and independence occupy the same dimension.

There are a few significant differences between the correlations for the standard and alternative partisan direction measures and ideological self-classification. Specifically, significant differences exist between the absolute values of the correlations for the two party thermometers, the seven-point measure, and location on the liberal-conservative scale. Disregarding the direction of the relationships, the correlation between the standard seven-point measure and ideology is significantly higher than the correlations between the Democrat and Republican thermometers and ideology (at the .001 and .05 levels, respectively). The relationships between the other party identification measures and ideological self-classification are similar in strength.

SUMMARY

This chapter analyzed the relationships between party identification, attitudes toward groups and issues, and ideological self-identification. With respect to partisan direction, we found that Democrats felt "warmer" than Republicans toward hispanics, blacks, the elderly, "people on welfare," labor unions, and civil rights leaders. Republicans, on the other hand, were more supportive of "big" business. In addition, the two parties took different issue positions. For instance, Republicans were more likely than Democrats to favor a reduction in public services spending. While Democrats tended to identify themselves as liberals, Republicans tended to classify themselves as conservatives.

To a lesser extent, partisan strength was related to attitudes toward groups and issues. We found that increased partisan strength was accompanied by increased support for different segments of the electorate. With the exception of civil rights, aid to minorities, and the ERA, there was a weak but significant relationship between degree of party loyalty and the issues we studied. Strength of identification, however, was not associated with ideology.

We also found weak but significant relationships between political independence and many of the items. Independents' views on different groups tended to be mixed. Furthermore, they were most likely to favor a reduction in spending for defense and government services, feel that the federal government had become "too strong," and support civil rights and the ERA. They also characterized themselves as being more conservative than liberal.

The data permitted us to examine whether partisan strength and political independence comprise the same dimension as commonly assumed, or whether they are two separate components of party identification. In several instances we found the correlations between the partisan strength and independence measures and the criterion variables to be in the opposite direction and similar in size (e.g., views on defense and public services spending, the supposed trade-off between inflation and unemployment, and job and standard of living guarantees). These results, of course, suggest that partisan strength and independence are the same thing. There were more occasions, however, where the correlations between these measures and the criterion variables were in the opposite direction but differed noticeably in size (e.g., attitudes toward labor unions, "big" business, the elderly, citizens on welfare, government power, the civil rights movement, and the ERA, and respondents' ideology). And in three cases the correlations between the partisan strength and independence measures and the outside variables (feelings about "hispanics," civil rights leaders, and aid to minorities) were in the *same* direction. *These findings seriously challenge the long-held belief that strength of identification and independence are unidimensional.*

Our analysis uncovered a large number of significant differences between the correlations for the various party identification measures and the criterion variables examined in this chapter. Although these differences are too numerous to review, some general patterns in the data can be gleaned. Most importantly, the correlations (that were significant) between the party identification measures and the criterion variables were always in the same direction. But on the basis of our study's findings, the party difference index often provides a more accurate estimate of views on political groups and issues than does the standard seven-point measure. *Overall, the party difference index was more closely related to over half the criterion variables analyzed in this chapter.* These findings suggest that the two partisan direction measures are not equivalent in many instances. The remaining relationships between the party difference measure, the traditional seven-point measure, and the outside variables are similar in strength. In contrast, the old four-point partisan strength measure performed well throughout most of the analysis. The results concerning the strength of independence scale and the Independents thermometer tended to be mixed, and it appears that the independence measures are not interchangeable in certain situations. Whether these findings can be generalized to the sphere of party and candidate evaluations will be examined in the next chapter.

NOTES

1. As discussed in Chapter One, there will be times when the reverse is true (i.e., views on groups and issues will influence the development of party identification).

2. There is some evidence that the public is becoming increasingly resentful of labor unions. For instance, see: Seymour Martin Lipset, "Labor, Democrats Are Hurting Themselves," *Los Angeles Times* October 7, 1983, Part II, p. 13.

3. An excellent history of the civil rights movement is offered in: James Q. Wilson, *American Government: Institutions and Policies* (Lexington: D.C. Heath, 1980), Chap. 19.

4. In addition to the groups appearing in Tables 4–1 through 4–4, feeling thermometer ratings were also obtained for "poor people," "liberals," "southerners," "radical students," "the U.S. Supreme Court," "environmentalists," "the federal government," "the military," "young people," "conservatives," "the women's liberation movement," "people working for the federal government," "black militants," "workingmen and workingwomen," "Congress," "farmers," "whites," "middle class people," and "businessmen and businesswomen." However, analysis of party identification and attitudes toward these objects yielded either no meaningful findings or results similar to those reported in Tables 4–1 through 4–4.

5. Angus Campbell, Philip E. Converse, Warren E. Miller, and Donald E. Stokes, *The American Voter* (New York: John Wiley and Sons, 1960), Chaps. 8–9.

6. John C. Pierce, "Party Identification and the Changing Role of Ideology in American Politics," *Midwest Journal of Political Science* Vol. 14 (February 1970), pp. 25–42; David E. RePass, "Issue Salience and Party Choice," *American Political Science Review* Vol. 65 (June 1971), pp. 389–400; Gerald M. Pomper, "From Confusion to Clarity: Issues and American Voters, 1956–1968," *American Political Science Review* Vol. 66 (June 1972), pp. 415–28; and Norman H. Nie and Kristi Andersen, "Mass Belief Systems Revisited: Political Change and Attitude Structure," *Journal of Politics* Vol. 36 (August 1974), pp. 540–91. Other works in the area include: John O. Field and

Ronald E. Anderson, "Ideology in the Public's Conceptualization of the 1964 Election," *Public Opinion Quarterly* Vol. 33 (Fall 1969), pp. 380–98; the entire June 1972 issue of the *American Political Science Review*; Benjamin I. Page and Richard A. Brody, "Policy Voting and the Electoral Process: The Vietnam War Issue," *American Political Science Review* Vol. 66 (September 1972), pp. 979–95; Arthur H. Miller, Warren E. Miller, Alden S. Raine, and Thad A. Brown, "A Majority Party in Disarray: Policy Polarization in the 1972 Election," *American Political Science Review* Vol. 70 (September 1976), pp. 753–78; Michael Margolis, "From Confusion to Confusion: Issues and the American Voter (1956–1972)," *American Political Science Review* Vol. 71 (March 1977), pp. 31–43; Benjamin I. Page, *Choices and Echoes in Presidential Elections: Rational Man and Electoral Democracy* (Chicago: Chicago University Press, 1978); Norman H. Nie, Sidney Verba, and John R. Petrocik, *The Changing American Voter*, Enlarged Edition (Cambridge: Harvard University Press, 1979); Edward G. Carmines and James A. Stimson, "The Two Faces of Issue Voting," *American Political Science Review* Vol. 74 (March 1980), pp. 78–91; and Edward G. Carmines and James A. Stimson, "Issue Evolution, Population Replacement, and Normal Partisan Change," *American Political Science Review* Vol. 75 (March 1981), pp. 107–18.

7. Pomper, "From Confusion to Clarity."

8. Other scholars, however, argued that the reported increase in the public's issue consistency was the result of better attitude questions asked by survey researchers beginning in the mid-1960s. Provocative works on this topic include: Hugh L. LeBlanc and Mary B. Merrin, "Mass Belief Systems Revisited," *Journal of Politics* Vol. 39 (November 1977), pp. 1082–87; John L. Sullivan, James E. Piereson, and George E. Marcus, "Ideological Constraint in the Mass Public: A Methodological Critique and Some New Findings," *American Journal of Political Science* Vol. 22 (May 1978), pp. 233–49; George F. Bishop, Alfred J. Tuchfarber, and Robert W. Oldendick, "Change in the Structure of American Political Attitudes: The Nagging Question of Question Wording," *American Journal of Political Science* Vol. 22 (May 1978), pp. 250–69; George F. Bishop, Robert W. Oldendick, and Alfred J. Tuchfarber, "Effects of Question Wording and Format on Political Attitude Consistency," *Public Opinion Quarterly* Vol. 42 (Spring 1978), pp. 81–92; George F. Bishop, Robert W. Oldendick, Alfred J. Tuchfarber, and Stephen E. Bennett, "The Changing Structure of Mass Belief Systems: Fact or Artifact?" *Journal of Politics* Vol. 40 (August 1978), pp. 781–87; Gregory G. Brunk, "The 1964 Attitude Consistency Leap Reconsidered," *Political Methodology* Vol. 5 No. 3 (1978), pp. 347–59; and George F. Bishop, Alfred J. Tuchfarber, Robert W. Oldendick, and Stephen E. Bennett, "Questions About Question Wording: A Rejoinder to Revisiting Mass Belief Systems Revisited," *American Journal of Political Science* Vol. 23 (February 1979), pp. 187–92. Answers to these criticisms can be found in: John R. Petrocik, "Comment: Reconsidering the Reconsiderations of the 1964 Change in Attitude Consistency," *Political Methodology* Vol. 5 No. 3 (1978), pp. 361–68; Norman H. Nie and James N. Rabjohn, "Revisiting Mass Belief Systems Revisited: Or, Why Doing Research Is Like Watching A Tennis Match," *American Journal of Political Science* Vol. 23 (February 1979), pp. 139–75; Nie, Verba, and Petrocik, *The Changing American Voter*, pp. 367–70; and John R. Petrocik, "Contextual Sources of Voting Behavior: The Changeable American Voter," in *The Electorate Reconsidered*, ed. John C. Pierce and John L. Sullivan (Beverly Hills, Calif.: Sage Publications, 1980), pp. 257–77.

9. Carmines and Stimson, "The Two Faces of Issue Voting."

10. Ibid., p. 88.

11. Ibid.

12. Petrocik, "Contextual Sources of Voting Behavior." Also refer to: Arthur H. Miller, "Partisanship Reinstated?: A Comparison of the 1972 and 1976 U.S. Presidential Elections," *British Journal of Political Science* Vol. 8 (April 1978), pp. 129–52.

13. Petrocik, "Contextual Sources of Voting Behavior," p. 268.

14. Ibid.

15. Ibid., p. 276.

16. Paul R. Abramson, John H. Aldrich, and David W. Rhode, *Change and Continuity in the 1980 Elections* (Washington, D.C.: Congressional Quarterly Press, 1982).

17. Austin Ranney (ed.), *The American Elections of 1980* (Washington, D.C.: American Enterprise Institute, 1981); Ellis Sandoz and Cecil V. Crabb, Jr. (eds.), *A Tide of Discontent: The 1980 Elections and Their Meaning* (Washington, D.C.: Congressional Quarterly Press, 1981); and Everett C. Ladd, "The Brittle Mandate: Electoral Dealignment and the 1980 Presidential Election," *Political Science Quarterly* Vol. 96 (Spring 1981), pp. 1–25.

18. Jack Dennis, "New Measures of Partisanship in Models of Voting," paper presented at the 1982 Annual Meeting of the Midwest Political Science Association, Milwaukee, Wisconsin, p. 16.

19. Carmines and Stimson, "Issue Evolution, Population Replacement, and Normal Partisan Change."

20. The exact wording of the question was:

Some people believe that we should spend much less money for defense. Others feel that defense spending should be greatly increased. Where would you place yourself on this scale, or haven't you thought much about this?

1. Greatly decrease defense spending

7. Greatly increase defense spending

21. The question read:

Some people think the government should provide fewer services, even in areas such as health and education, in order to reduce spending. Other people feel it is important for the government to continue the services it now provides even if it means no reduction in spending. Where would you place yourself on this scale, or haven't you thought much about this?

1. Government should provide many fewer services; reduce spending a lot

7. Government should continue to provide services; no reduction in spending

22. More specifically, those interviewed were asked:

Some people feel that the government in Washington should make every effort to improve the social and economic position of blacks and other minority groups, even if it means giving them preferential treatment. Suppose these people are at one end of the scale at point number 1. Others feel that the government should not make any special effort to help minorities because they should help themselves. Suppose these people are at the other end at point 7. And, of course, some other people have opinions somewhere in between at points 2, 3, 4, 5, and 6. Where would you place yourself on this scale or haven't you thought much about this?

23. The exact wording of the question was:

Some people are afraid the government in Washington is getting too powerful for the good of the country and the individual person. Others feel that the government in Washington is not getting too strong. Do you have an opinion on this or not? (If yes) what is your feeling, do you think the government is getting too powerful or do you think the government is not getting too strong?

24. Everyone interviewed was asked:

Some people feel the federal government should take action to reduce the inflation rate, even if it means that unemployment would go up a lot. Others feel the government should take action to reduce the rate of unemployment, even if it means that inflation would go up a lot. Where would you place yourself on this scale, or haven't you thought much about this?

1. Reduce inflation even if unemployment goes up a lot
7. Reduce unemployment even if inflation goes up a lot

25. The exact wording of the question was:

Some people feel the government in Washington should see to it that every person has a job and a good standard of living. Others think the government should just let each person get ahead on his own. Where would you place yourself on this scale, or haven't you thought much about this?

1. Government see to a job and good standard of living
7. Government let each person get ahead on own

26. The question read:

Some say that the civil rights people have been trying to push too fast. Others feel they haven't pushed fast enough. How about you? Do you think that civil rights leaders are trying to push too fast, are going too slowly, or are they moving at about the right speed?

27. Controlling for race tended to lower the correlations between partisan direction and feelings about civil rights.

28. The precise wording of the question was:

Do you approve or disapprove of the proposed Equal Rights Amendment to the Constitution, sometimes called the ERA Amendment? Do you approve/disapprove strongly or not strongly?

29. Whenever possible, a respondent's position on an issue was weighted by the issue's importance to the respondent. However, this had little effect on our findings. Other issues examined in this investigation included energy, abortion, busing, environmental regulation, the proposed 30 percent tax cut, the treatment of women, prayer in the public schools, and U.S. relations with the Soviet Union. Analyses of party identification and views on these issues generated either very weak relationships or findings similar to those already reported in respective sections of this chapter. These results were therefore omitted from the discussion.

30. Campbell, Converse, Miller, and Stokes, *The American Voter*, p. 192.
31. Ibid., pp. 192–93.
32. Ibid., pp. 249–50. Further research by Pierce showed that this figure had risen in 1960 and in 1964. Later, Pierce and Hagner demonstrated that the percentage of ideologues in the electorate stayed relatively level between 1964 and 1976. Also, Republicans were more likely than Democrats to be ideologues, regardless of the election year. John C. Pierce, "Party Identification and the Changing Role of Ideology in American Politics," pp. 25–42; and John C. Pierce and Paul R. Hagner, "Conceptualization and Party Identification: 1956–1976," *American Journal of Political Science* Vol. 26 (May 1982), pp. 377–87.

33. Philip E. Converse, "The Nature of Belief Systems in Mass Publics," in *Ideology and Discontent*, ed. David Apter (New York: Free Press, 1964), pp. 206–61.
34. Ibid., p. 207.
35. James A. Stimson, "Belief Systems: Constraint, Complexity, and the 1972 Election," *American Journal of Political Science* Vol. 19 (August 1975), pp. 393–417.
36. Ibid., p. 415.
37. Campbell, Converse, Miller, and Stokes, *The American Voter*; and Converse, "The Nature of Belief Systems in Mass Publics."
38. For instance, see: Converse, "The Nature of Belief Systems in Mass Publics"; Harry Wilker and Lester Milbrath, "Political Belief Systems and Political Behavior," *Social Science Quarterly* Vol. 51 (December 1970), pp. 477–93; George E. Marcus, David Tabb, and John L. Sullivan, "The Application of Individual Differences Scaling to the Measurement of Political Ideologies," *American Journal of Political Science* Vol. 18 (May 1974), pp. 405–20; and William H. Flanigan and Nancy H. Zingale, *Political Behavior of the American Electorate*, Fourth Edition (Boston: Allyn and Bacon, 1979), pp. 117–26.
39. Stimson, "Belief Systems."
40. Ibid., p. 400.

5
PARTY AND CANDIDATE EVALUATIONS

Chapter Four analyzed the relationship between party identification, views on groups and issues, and ideological self-identification. We found a considerable number of differences between partisans' and nonpartisans' positions on various groups and issues. Moreover, Democrats were more likely than Republicans to think of themselves as liberals. The investigation also provided important evidence concerning the dimensionality of partisan strength and political independence and the separate party identification measures.

Chapter Five focuses on party and candidate evaluations and continues to examine the attitudes of party identifiers, whether partisan strength and independence are unidimensional, and the interchangeability of the standard and alternative party identification measures. Party and candidate evaluations are beliefs which voters hold about the parties and the candidates. These beliefs generally pertain to the personality of the candidates, and the experience and ability of the parties and the candidates. Before analyzing the data on party identification and party and candidate images, we will review the literature on the processes through which such images develop and change.

PARTY EVALUATIONS

There is reason to believe that current party identification is related to expected future party performance. As we pointed out in Chapter One, Morris Fiorina defined party identification as a weighted sum of past evaluations of the two parties.[1] Upon analyzing survey data from the 1976 election study, he found that "expectations about the party most capable of handling inflation and unemployment in the future depend a great deal on judgments about the parties' handling of inflation and unemployment in the past. . . . "[2] In other words, previous assessments affect anticipated party performance on economic issues. Using the standard party identification questions, he also found a close tie between party orientation and expected party performance. If current party identification is the product of retrospective evaluations, as Fiorina maintained, then we too should find a relationship between present party affiliation and the predicted ability of the two parties to handle salient issues.

Americans often remark that "the Democrats get us out of depressions and into wars while the Republicans get us out of wars and into depressions." Those espousing this viewpoint usually cite as evidence the entrance of the United States into World Wars I and II under the Democratic Administrations of Wilson and Roosevelt, the Panic of 1929 and the start of the Great Depression during Hoover's Republican Administration, and Roosevelt's successful effort to put the country back on the road to economic recovery in the 1930s. Support for this conventional wisdom is more than likely the result of chance and circumstance rather than of any inherent ability of the two parties to produce leaders with distinguishable talents. Nevertheless, based on their own past experiences, partisans will probably contend that their party can handle the difficulties associated with war and the economy better than the opposing party. Let us see if this is the case.

In 1980 respondents were asked: "Looking ahead, do you think the problem of keeping out of war would be handled better in the next four years by the Republicans, or by the Democrats, or about the same by both?" "Better by the Democrats" was coded 1, "the same by both" was coded 2, and "better by Republicans" was coded 3. Similar items on inflation and unemployment were also included in the questionnaire, and responses to these items were scored in the same manner.[3] As we predicted, the data in Table 5–1 reveal substantial partisan division over the perceived ability of each party to handle the problems of war and the economy. Clearly, Republican identifiers believe their party can deal with these problems better than the Democratic party, while Democratic identifiers hold the opposite view. Weak but significant relationships exist between partisan strength, political independence, and party evaluations. While strong partisans are inclined to feel that the Democratic party can handle these problems better than the Republican party, Independents tend to say that the Republican party is better equipped to manage these problems. The fact that strong Democrats outnumber strong Republicans in the electorate probably explains the relationship between partisan strength and respondents' position on the two questions. This makes it difficult to make any observations about the dimensionality of partisan strength and independence. The correlations between the individual party identification measures and views on the perceived ability of each party to handle war and the economy do not vary significantly.

Table 5-1
TAU-C Correlations between Party Identification and Handling of War and the Economy by Parties, Pre-Election Survey, 1980[a]

Items and Dimensions	War	Inflation	Unemployment
Partisan Direction			
Party Difference Index	-.46***	-.58***	-.54***
	(1322)	(1314)	(1322)
Party Closeness Scale	-.44***	-.51***	-.49***
	(1459)	(1454)	(1457)
Party Support Scale	-.36***	-.43***	-.41***
	(1456)	(1449)	(1451)
Democratic Party Feeling Thermometer	-.34***	-.47***	-.43***
	(1435)	(1432)	(1437)
Republican Party Feeling Thermometer	.34***	.38***	.37***
	(1434)	(1431)	(1435)
Seven-Point Party Identification Scale	-.42***	-.49***	-.48***
	(1485)	(1477)	(1480)
Strength of Partisanship			
Folded Party Closeness Scale	-.07**	-.04*	-.05*
	(1459)	(1454)	(1457)
Folded Party Support Scale	-.05*	-.03	-.06**
	(1456)	(1449)	(1451)
Four-Point Strength of Identification Scale	-.10***	-.09***	-.12***
	(1485)	(1477)	(1480)
Independence			
Strength of Independence Scale	.00	.07***	.05**
	(1468)	(1464)	(1465)
Independents Feeling Thermometer	.04*	.07**	.05*
	(1330)	(1326)	(1326)

a - Figures in parentheses are numbers of cases.

* Significant at the .05 level.
** Significant at the .01 level.
*** Significant at the .001 level.

CANDIDATE EVALUATIONS

We have long been familiar with the impact of candidate evaluations on the vote. Angus Campbell and his associates demonstrated their importance in the 1952 and 1956 presidential elections.[4] Donald Stokes, in a later study, extended this analysis to the 1960 and 1964 elections and again found a strong relationship between candidate evaluations and the vote.[5] John Kessel's recent study of candidate images between 1952 and 1976 yielded similar findings.[6]

Even though there is wide consensus on the significance of candidate evaluations in the vote choice process, there still exists an ongoing debate over the manner in which they develop and change. The debate centers on whether these judgments are stimulus-determined or perceiver-determined. The former view maintains that voters' assessments of the candidates are more directly a function of what they actually see, hear, or read (on television, radio, or in the newspapers or magazines) about the nominees. In other words, "candidate images are stimulus determined in the sense that the image is a direct representative of the stimuli or information presented by the candidate, e.g., his speeches, actions, and press coverage."[7] This implies that contenders have a large measure of control over voters' assessments of them. The perceiver-determined position asserts that citizens' candidate evaluations are mediated by their own predispositions (e.g., party identification) and "that selective processes help maintain cognitive consistency."[8] To elaborate, when individuals hold beliefs that are in conflict or are incongruent with each other, they experience stress and discomfort. The need to achieve and maintain "perceptual balance" forces people to modify their inconsistent beliefs so that they become consistent. Subsequent behavior usually reflects this change in beliefs.

Researchers' findings have been used to support both sides of the controversy. In an early study, Joseph and Marion McGrath found that Republicans and Democrats agreed in their evaluations of the 1960 presidential candidates on a number of personal characteristics such as "sensitivity" and "aggressiveness."[9] Even though their investigation also uncovered a number of partisan differences in candidate assessments, they concluded that their findings on the whole supported the stimulus-determined thesis.

Roberta Sigel strongly disagreed with the McGraths and offered, instead, a perceptual balance theory of image formation.[10] Also focusing on the 1960 election, she found that partisans' attitudes toward their own candidate tended to be more closely related to their images of the ideal President than were their images of the opposing party's candidate. That is, Democrats believed Kennedy was closer to their ideal than Nixon while Republicans felt the opposite. She interpreted these findings as support for the perceptual balance explanation and the perceiver-determined view. Yet she, too, found considerable agreement among partisans' evaluations of both contenders. According to Pamela Conover, the evidence uncovered by the McGraths and Sigel did not support unequivocally either side of the debate.[11] Later studies also failed to settle this controversy.

Because of these conflicting findings, some researchers tried to develop a theoretical framework combining the two approaches. Dan Nimmo and Robert Savage, for instance, explained that candidate evaluations are the product of "stimulus-perceiver transactions" involving symbolic exchanges between voters and candidates.[12] Their analysis of the 1972 presidential election suggested that elements of both theories help explain candidate image formation.

Herbert Asher postulated that the applicability of the two theories will vary at different stages of the presidential campaign.[13] He wrote:

> It is certainly the case that one's perceptual defenses are lower during the primaries than during the general election, and hence images of the candidates formed during the primary season, especially early on, are more likely to be stimulus-determined. In the gen-

eral election as people have more information about the candidates and as the perceptual screen function of party identification comes into play, images may be less stimulus-determined.[14]

Presently, empirical support for his hypothesis is lacking.

In a recent study, Conover used attribution theory to explain the development of candidate images.[15] This theory "focuses on the manner in which people attempt to discern the causes of their own and other's behavior. It is based on the assumption that, when confronted with a person's behavior, the perceiver must determine if it was caused by some aspect of the situation, by chance, or by some underlying personal disposition of the actor."[16] When information is missing or ambiguous, voters will rely on their dispositions and beliefs to generate the information necessary to make an assessment about the candidate. Her analysis of survey data collected during the Watergate affair offered some support for attribution theory as a possible explanation.

Another way voters may evaluate candidates is by reviewing the record of the incumbent President. A "retrospective vote," according to Morris Fiorina and Paul Abramson, John Aldrich, and David Rohde, represents a summary judgment of the incumbent's performance and is cast even if the previous Vice President is running for the White House in the current election.[17] Naturally, the voter must link the candidate of one party (such as the Vice President) with the actions taken by the incumbent. As Abramson and his colleagues said, "a 'pure' retrospective voter evaluates what has been done, not what might be done."[18] Proponents of this theory assume that voters closely follow the actions of the past administration and can make a rational judgment about its performance before deciding whom to support on election day.

Of course, this study is concerned with the relationship between party identification and candidate evaluations. We already reviewed Sigel's findings concerning this relationship.[19] Later studies conducted by Jerrold Rusk and Herbert Weisberg, and Gregory Markus and Philip Converse also showed party identification to be closely related to candidate images.[20] Even though these researchers employed only the standard seven-point measure, from a theoretical standpoint, we too expect to find an association between these variables.

Carter's Economic Program

President Carter's handling of the economy received a great deal of attention during the 1980 campaign. Kennedy, in the primaries, and Reagan and Anderson in the general election frequently criticized the President's economic program and pointed to the double-digit inflation and "high" unemployment rates as reasons why he should not be reelected. Carter staunchly defended his economic program, often citing the "large number" of jobs his policies had created.

In the pre-election survey respondents were asked how strongly they ap-

Table 5-2
TAU-C Correlations between Party Identification and Carter's Handling of Inflation and Unemployment, Pre-Election Survey, 1980[a]

Items and Dimensions	Inflation[b]	Unemployment[b]
Partisan Direction		
Party Difference Index	.35***	.32***
	(1236)	(1161)
Party Closeness Scale	.32***	.29***
	(1370)	(1280)
Party Support Scale	.27***	.23***
	(1362)	(1271)
Democratic Party Feeling Thermometer	.33***	.29***
	(1343)	(1257)
Republican Party Feeling Thermometer	-.18***	-.17***
	(1338)	(1254)
Seven-Point Party Identification Scale	.31***	.26***
	(1386)	(1297)
Strength of Partisanship		
Folded Party Closeness Scale	.05**	.07**
	(1370)	(1280)
Folded Party Support Scale	.03	.07***
	(1362)	(1271)
Four-Point Strength of Identification Scale	.09***	.11**
	(1386)	(1297)
Independence		
Strength of Independence Scale	-.05**	-.07**
	(1369)	(1276)
Independents Feeling Thermometer	-.04*	-.06**
	(1245)	(1167)

a - Figures in parentheses are numbers of cases.

b - The coefficients to the right of the folded party closeness and four-point strength of identification scales are tau-b correlations.

* Significant at the .05 level.

** Significant at the .01 level.

*** Significant at the .001 level.

proved or disapproved of the way Carter was handling the problems of inflation and unemployment.[21] Possible responses to the two questions were "strongly disapprove" (coded 1), "not strongly disapprove" (coded 2), "not strongly approve" (coded 3), and "strongly approve" (coded 4). As Table 5–2 shows, partisan direction is related to public opinion on the way Carter was handling inflation and unemployment. Not surprisingly, Democrats were more likely to believe that the President was managing the economy well while Republicans were more likely to disagree. There are also weak but significant relationships between partisan strength, political independence, and evaluations of the incumbent's economic policies. While strong partisans tended to voice approval of the way Carter was handling inflation and unemployment, Independents tended to disapprove of his performance. The preponderance of Democrats among strong party identifiers may explain strong partisans' opinion on how Carter managed the economy. Finally, only one significant difference was uncovered between the correlations for the individual party identification measures and responses to the two questions. Disregarding the direction of the relationships, the correlation between the standard seven-point measure and judgments about Carter's handling of inflation is significantly stronger (at the .05 level) than the correlation between the Republican thermometer and views on this issue. All and all, the data in Table 5–2 indicate that evaluations of Carter's ability to manage the economy were affected by party identification.[22]

Carter's Foreign Policy Decisions

President Carter faced two major foreign policy problems during his Administration, the taking of American hostages in Iran and the Soviet Union's invasion of Afghanistan. In November 1979, Iranian students seized American hostages in the U.S. Embassy in Teheran, and one month later the Soviet Union invaded Afghanistan. The Carter Administration reacted to the latter incident by placing an embargo on grain shipments and American technology and ordering a boycott of the 1980 Summer Olympics in Moscow. Both events received a great deal of media attention, and, as often happens in times of crises, public support for the President increased sharply. The fact that Americans were directly involved in the Iranian hostage crisis gave that issue added prominence. However, the length of the ordeal, coupled with the daring but ill-fated rescue attempt, raised serious doubts about the President's leadership ability. Ironically, Iran freed the hostages on the last day of the Carter presidency, 444 days after they were taken captive. The Iranian hostage crisis was the most difficult and persistent problem Carter faced while in office, and his failure to bring home the hostages sooner probably cost him the election.

Respondents interviewed prior to the election were asked about Carter's handling of both foreign policy problems. The following question addressed the President's reaction to the Soviet Union's invasion of Afghanistan:

As you may know, in late December Soviet troops moved into Afghanistan. So far the President has protested this Soviet action by cutting back on American trade, diplomatic and cultural ties with the Soviet Union. Considering the U.S. response thus far, would you say that Jimmy Carter has reacted too strongly to the Soviet Union, not strongly enough, or has the response been about right?

Respondents who said the President reacted "too strongly" were coded 1, those who said his response was "about right" were coded 2, and those who felt he reacted "not strongly enough" were coded 3. Interestingly, only five percent (n=75) of the respondents who had an opinion on this question believed Carter's actions were "too strong." The rest of the sample was evenly divided over whether his actions were "about right" or "not strong enough." In addition, those interviewed were asked how strongly they approved or disap-

Table 5-3
TAU-C Correlations between Party Identification and Carter's Handling of the Soviet Union's Invasion of Afghanistan and the Iranian Hostage Crisis, Pre-Election Survey, 1980[a]

Items and Dimensions	Afghanistan Invasion	Iranian Hostage Crisis[b]
Partisan Direction		
Party Difference Index	-.20*** (1292)	.30*** (1292)
Party Closeness Scale	-.16*** (1439)	.28*** (1434)
Party Support Scale	-.14*** (1436)	.24*** (1427)
Democratic Party Feeling Thermometer	-.18*** (1412)	.29*** (1410)
Republican Party Feeling Thermometer	.12*** (1411)	-.16*** (1407)
Seven-Point Party Identification Scale	-.15*** (1455)	.27*** (1448)
Strength of Partisanship		
Folded Party Closeness Scale	.00 (1439)	.10*** (1434)
Folded Party Support Scale	.00 (1436)	.05** (1427)
Four-Point Strength of Identification Scale	-.02 (1455)	.12*** (1448)
Independence		
Strength of Independence Scale	-.01 (1446)	-.04* (1436)
Independents Feeling Thermometer	-.02 (1321)	-.05* (1302)

a - Figures in parentheses are numbers of cases.

b - The coefficients to the right of the folded party closeness and four-point strength of identification scales (in the Iranian Hostage Crisis column) are tau-b correlation

* Significant at the .05 level.

** Significant at the .01 level.

*** Significant at the .001 level.

proved of the way Carter was handling the Iranian hostage crisis.[23] This item was coded the same way as the two items in Table 5-2.

Table 5-3 reports the tau-c correlations between party identification and attitudes toward Carter's decisions on both issues. An analysis of the cross-tables between partisan direction and Carter's response to the Soviet invasion of Afghanistan reveals that Democrats and Republicans were equally divided over whether the President had responded "too strongly." However, Democrats tended to say that the President's reaction was "about right" while Republicans felt that his reaction had not been "strong enough." No relationship was found between partisan strength, political independence, and views on this question.

Similarly, partisans were split over the way Carter was handling the Iranian hostage crisis. Democrats were more likely to approve of his actions, while Republicans were more likely to disapprove of them. Also, weak but significant correlations exist between partisan strength, independence, and perceptions of Carter's performance on this issue. More specifically, strong partisans were more supportive of the President's policies while Independents were more inclined to disapprove of them. The numerical advantage of Democrats over Republicans among strong partisans in the electorate may account for the relationship between partisan strength and how Carter managed the Iranian hostage crisis. In addition, only one significant difference exists between the correlations for the various party identification measures and beliefs about Carter's performance on the two foreign policy issues. Examining the absolute values of the correlations, the relationship between the standard seven-point measure and the President's handling of the Iranian hostage crisis is significantly stronger (at the .05 level) than the relationship between the Republican feeling thermometer and this same question.

CARTER'S PERFORMANCE OVERALL

In addition to évaluating Carter's performance on specific domestic and foreign policy issues, respondents were asked to rate his overall performance as President. This question was worded and coded in the same manner as the other approval/disapproval items examined thus far, and, from a retrospective evaluation standpoint, it sought to elicit a summary judgment of all aspects of the Carter presidency.[24] Table 5-4 reports the tau-c correlations between party identification and responses to this question. Clearly, Democrats and Republicans differed sharply in their assessments. As one would suspect, Democrats were more likely to give the President a higher approval rating than Republicans. Although the correlations are much smaller, strong partisans tended to approve of Carter's performance whereas Independents were less supportive. The numerical advantage of strong Democrats over strong Republicans in the electorate may account for the relationship between partisan strength and evaluations of the Carter presidency. This prevents us from making any statements about whether partisan strength and independence fall along a single continuum. Furthermore, the correlation between the standard seven-point measure and Carter's job approval rating is significantly higher (at the .01 level) than the absolute value of the correlation between the Republican feeling thermometer and this item. No other significant differences exist between the various party identification measures and views on this question. In conclusion, the findings in Table 5-4 suggest that partisan direction exerts an important influence over evaluations of presidential performance.

Table 5-4
TAU-C Correlations between Party Identification and Carter's Job Approval Rating, Pre-Election Survey, 1980[a]

Items and Dimensions	Carter's Job Approval Rating[b]
Partisan Direction	
Party Difference Index	.44*** (1267)
Party Closeness Scale	.40*** (1408)
Party Support Scale	.34*** (1401)
Democratic Party Feeling Thermometer	.42*** (1381)
Republican Party Feeling Thermometer	-.21*** (1376)
Seven-Point Party Identification Scale	.37*** (1431)
Strength of Partisanship	
Folded Party Closeness Scale	.06** (1408)
Folded Party Support Scale	.04* (1401)
Four-Point Strength of Identification Scale	.12*** (1431)
Independence	
Strength of Independence Scale	-.09*** (1414)
Independents Feeling Thermometer	-.05** (1274)

a - Figures in parentheses are numbers of cases.

b - The coefficients to the right of the folded party closeness and four-point strength of identification scales are tau-b correlations.

*   Significant at the .05 level.

**   Significant at the .01 level.

*** Significant at the .001 level.

Personal Qualities

In addition to evaluating incumbents on the way they have handled specific issues and their job, Americans may also form opinions on the presidential candidates' personal qualities. These images "contribute to a candidate's personal attractiveness, but unlike competence, executive ability, intelligence, and so on, these qualities are relatively distinct from characteristics that encompass personal capabilities. Pure personality or physical attributes probably are not captured by performance evaluations and future expectations."[25] However, Arthur Miller and Warren Miller found that personal attributes mattered little to voters in the 1972 election.[26] After making a similar observation about the 1960 and 1976 elections, Fiorina concluded, "The available evidence suggests that such qualities are of minor importance empirically despite the emphasis given them in popular commentary and casual academic discussion."[27]

Despite these findings, this study will analyze the relationship between party identification and the personal qualities of the candidates. The reader may wonder why we have decided to include these variables in our analysis when other researchers have found them to have little effect on the vote. Unlike the investigations mentioned above, this study is more concerned with correlates of party identification. As will soon be demonstrated, assessments of the candidates' personal qualities are closely related to party identification. A possible explanation for this finding lies in the fact that these kinds of characteristics are quite ambiguous and are open to total subjective evaluation. A lack of accurate information about the "true" personality of the candidate probably forces voters to use party orientation as a guide. As a result, partisans are seemingly more impressed with their party's candidate than the one from the opposing party. Most importantly, this condition allows us to make valuable comparisons between the different party identification measures. Those characteristics that are more germane to governing will be examined afterwards.

In the pre-election survey respondents were asked whether Reagan, Carter, and Anderson made them feel either "angry," "hopeful," "afraid," "proud," "disgusted," "sympathetic," or "uneasy."[28] A "no" response was coded zero, and a "yes" response was coded 1. The correlations between party identification and Anderson's evaluations are close to zero and are therefore not reported. The highest correlations exist between party identification and whether Reagan and Carter made respondents feel "hopeful," "proud," or "disgusted." These relationships are shown in Tables 5-5 and 5-6.

Based on the data in the two tables, partisan direction has a strong impact on attitudes toward the two candidates.[29] Not surprisingly, Republicans were more likely than Democrats to say that Reagan made them feel "hopeful," "proud," and not "disgusted." Conversely, Democrats tended to judge Carter more favorably on these three characteristics than did Republicans. Although strong partisans tended to be "proud" of both candidates, only Carter tended to make them feel "hopeful" and not "disgusted." While Reagan was more likely to instill "hope" in Independents, Carter was less likely to do so. Interestingly, Independents tended to be "disgusted" with *both* candidates.

There are a large number of significant differences between the correlations for the partisan direction measures and the personal qualities of the candidates. For instance, the correlations between the party difference index and whether Reagan and Carter made respondents feel "hopeful" ($r = -.48$ and $.36$, respectively) are significantly higher (at the .001 level) than the correlations between the standard seven-point measure and this attribute of the two candidates ($r = -.43$ and $.31$, respectively). The party difference index is also more closely related to the other two characteristics of the candidates than is the standard

Table 5-5
Pearson Correlations between Party Identification and Personal Qualities of Reagan, Pre-Election Survey, 1980[a]

Items and Dimensions	Hopeful	Proud	Disgusted
Partisan Direction			
Party Difference Index	-.48***	-.39***	.28***
	(1345)	(1341)	(1340)
Party Closeness Scale	-.42***	-.32***	.24***
	(1512)	(1508)	(1507)
Party Support Scale	-.36***	-.30***	.24***
	(1505)	(1501)	(1500)
Democratic Party Feeling Thermometer	-.29***	-.19***	.17***
	(1468)	(1465)	(1464)
Republican Party Feeling Thermometer	.39***	.38***	-.27***
	(1465)	(1461)	(1460)
Seven-Point Party Identification Scale	-.43***	-.34***	.22***
	(1527)	(1524)	(1523)
Strength of Partisanship			
Folded Party Closeness Scale	-.01	.06*	.03
	(1512)	(1508)	(1507)
Folded Party Support Scale	.01	.11***	.07**
	(1505)	(1501)	(1500)
Four-Point Strength of Identification Scale	-.03	.04	.02
	(1527)	(1524)	(1523)
Independence			
Strength of Independence Scale	.05*	.01	.09***
	(1513)	(1510)	(1509)
Independents Feeling Thermometer	.08**	.02	-.01
	(1354)	(1350)	(1349)

a - Figures in parentheses are numbers of cases.

* Significant at the .05 level.
** Significant at the .01 level.
*** Significant at the .001 level.

seven-point measure (significant at the .001 level in all cases). Moreover, the relationship between the party closeness scale and "disgust" toward Carter ($r = -.33$) is significantly stronger (at the .05 level) than the relationship between the traditional seven-point scale and this item ($r = -.29$). Yet, the correlations between the seven-point measure and whether Reagan instilled "hope" and "pride" ($r = -.43$ and $-.34$, respectively) are significantly larger (at the .001 and .05 levels, respectively) than those between the party support scale and these two qualities ($r = -.36$ and $-.30$, respectively). In nearly every case, the absolute values of the correlations between the two party thermometers and the candidates' evaluations differ significantly (at least at the .05 level) from the absolute values of the correlations between the old seven-point scale and these evaluations.

Comparisons can also be made between the correlations for the other party

Table 5-6
Pearson Correlations between Party Identification and Personal Qualities of Carter, Pre-Election Survey, 1980[a]

Items and Dimensions	Hopeful	Proud	Disgusted
Partisan Direction			
Party Difference Index	.36*** (1344)	.31*** (1338)	-.37*** (1343)
Party Closeness Scale	.33*** (1510)	.28*** (1505)	-.33*** (1509)
Party Support Scale	.31*** (1503)	.28*** (1499)	-.32*** (1502)
Democratic Party Feeling Thermometer	.37*** (1467)	.36*** (1462)	-.37*** (1466)
Republican Party Feeling Thermometer	-.15*** (1463)	-.11*** (1458)	.19*** (1463)
Seven-Point Party Identification Scale	.31*** (1526)	.25*** (1521)	-.29*** (1525)
Strength of Partisanship			
Folded Party Closeness Scale	.06** (1510)	.09*** (1505)	-.08*** (1509)
Folded Party Support Scale	.06** (1503)	.12*** (1499)	-.07** (1502)
Four-Point Strength of Identification Scale	.09*** (1526)	.16*** (1521)	-.11*** (1525)
Independence			
Strength of Independence Scale	.01 (1511)	-.03 (1506)	.14*** (1511)
Independents Feeling Thermometer	-.02 (1352)	-.07** (1345)	.08*** (1352)

a - Figures in parentheses are numbers of cases.

* Significant at the .05 level.
** Significant at the .01 level.
*** Significant at the .001 level.

identification measures and the personal qualities of the candidates. The relationship between the standard four-point partisan strength measure and whether respondents were "proud" of Carter (r = .16) is significantly stronger (at the .01 level) than the relationship between the folded party closeness scale and responses to this question (r = .09). In contrast, the correlations between the folded party support scale and whether voters felt "proud" of and "disgusted" with Reagan are significantly higher (at the .01 and .05 levels, respectively) than the correlations between the traditional four-point partisan strength measure and these items. In addition, there is a significant discrepancy (at the .01 level) between the correlations for the independence measures and "disgust" toward Reagan. As the data in Tables 5-5 and 5-6 show, the standard party identification questions are not always the best predictors of voters' feelings about the candidates' personal qualities.[30]

Personal Qualifications

In addition to evaluating the presidential candidates' personal attributes, respondents were asked to judge them on characteristics more relevant to their ability to perform in office. Respondents were asked how well the following words and phrases described Reagan, Carter, and Anderson: "moral," "dishonest," "weak," "knowledgeable," "power-hungry," "inspiring," "he would solve our economic problems," "he would develop good relations with other countries," and "he would provide strong leadership."[31] Possible responses to these items were "not well at all" (coded 1), "not too well" (coded 2), "quite well" (coded 3), and "extremely well" (coded 4). As before, the correlations between party identification and Anderson's evaluations are near zero and are not included in the analysis.[32] The highest correlations exist between party identification and assessments of Reagan and Carter on "he would solve our economic problems," "he would develop good relations with other countries," and "he would provide strong leadership." These relationships are reported in Tables 5–7 and 5–8.

As one might predict, there is a close association between partisan direction and evaluation of Reagan's and Carter's personal qualifications. Republicans were more likely than Democrats to say that Reagan would "solve our economic problems," "develop good relations with other countries," and "provide strong leadership," whereas Democrats were more likely than Republicans to feel that Carter would do these things. Almost no relationship exists between partisan strength, political independence, and judgments about Reagan. However, there are weak but significant correlations between partisan strength, political independence, and evaluations of Carter. The data in Table 5–8 show that strong partisans tended to view Carter favorably on the three characteristics, while Independents tended to be more critical of him. The higher number of strong Democrats in the electorate more than likely explains the relationship between partisan strength and feelings about Carter. Overall, our findings indicate that partisan direction plays an important role in shaping evaluations of the candidates' qualifications.[33]

There are few significant differences between the tau-c correlations for the various party identification measures and assessments of the candidates' ability to govern. In Table 5–7, the relationship between the standard seven-point measure and whether Reagan "would provide strong leadership" as President ($r = -.38$) is significantly stronger (at the .05 level) than the relationship between the Democrat thermometer and this evaluation ($r = -.25$). Similarly, the correlations between the seven-point measure and beliefs about Carter's qualifications are significantly higher (at least at the .05 level) than the absolute values of the correlations between the Republican party thermometer and these same judgments. Moreover, the standard four-point partisan strength measure is more closely related to whether Carter "would solve our economic problems" than

Table 5-7
TAU-C Correlations between Party Identification and Qualifications of Reagan, Pre-Election Survey, 1980[a]

Items and Dimensions	Solve Economic Problems[b]	Develop Good Foreign Relations[b]	Provide Strong Leadership[b]
Partisan Direction			
Party Difference Index	-.41*** (1234)	-.37*** (1207)	-.42*** (1259)
Party Closeness Scale	-.35*** (1357)	-.34*** (1328)	-.38*** (1391)
Party Support Scale	-.29*** (1348)	-.29*** (1319)	-.32*** (1382)
Democratic Party Feeling Thermometer	-.25*** (1341)	-.24*** (1312)	-.25*** (1372)
Republican Party Feeling Thermometer	.36*** (1340)	.33*** (1311)	.37*** (1371)
Seven-Point Party Identification Scale	-.34*** (1371)	-.31*** (1342)	-.38*** (1407)
Strength of Partisanship			
Folded Party Closeness Scale	.03 (1357)	.00 (1328)	-.01 (1391)
Folded Party Support Scale	.04* (1348)	.03 (1319)	.02 (1382)
Four-Point Strength of Identification Scale	.00 (1371)	.00 (1342)	-.03 (1407)
Independence			
Strength of Independence Scale	-.03* (1357)	-.05** (1328)	-.01 (1392)
Independents Feeling Thermometer	.03 (1254)	.00 (1231)	.05* (1280)

a - Figures in parentheses are numbers of cases.
b - The coefficients to the right of the folded party closeness and four-point strength of identification scales are tau-b correlations.
* Significant at the .05 level.
** Significant at the .01 level.
*** Significant at the .001 level.

is the folded party closeness scale (significant at the .05 level). The correlations between the other party identification measures and the candidates' qualifications do not differ significantly.[34]

PERCEIVED OUTCOME OF ELECTION

There is a good chance that party identification also influences voters' perceptions concerning the outcome of presidential races. As already demonstrated, voters tend to use party orientation as a cue in their evaluations of political figures, especially when hard information is lacking. Except for the results of public opinion polls (which are often inconclusive), the electorate has little

Table 5-8
TAU-C Correlations between Party Identification and Qualifications of Carter, Pre-Election Survey, 1980[a]

Items and Dimensions	Solve Economic Problems[b]	Develop Good Foreign Relations[b]	Provide Strong Leadership[b]
Partisan Direction			
Party Difference Index	.39*** (1305)	.34*** (1314)	.39*** (1318)
Party Closeness Scale	.36*** (1444)	.31*** (1450)	.36*** (1456)
Party Support Scale	.32*** (1436)	.29*** (1442)	.33*** (1448)
Democratic Party Feeling Thermometer	.41*** (1423)	.35*** (1430)	.41** (1435)
Republican Party Feeling Thermometer	-.16*** (1420)	-.16*** (1426)	-.16*** (1431)
Seven-Point Party Identification Scale	.34*** (1464)	.30*** (1467)	.35*** (1476)
Strength of Partisanship			
Folded Party Closeness Scale	.09*** (1444)	.06** (1450)	.08*** (1456)
Folded Party Support Scale	.10*** (1436)	.05** (1442)	.08*** (1448)
Four-Point Strength of Identification Scale	.17*** (1464)	.09*** (1467)	.14*** (1476)
Independence			
Strength of Independence Scale	-.11*** (1443)	-.03 (1452)	-.09*** (1457)
Independents Feeling Thermometer	-.09*** (1320)	-.04* (1322)	-.07** (1329)

a - Figures in parentheses are numbers of cases.

b - The coefficients to the right of the folded party closeness and four-point strength of identification scales are tau-b correlations.

* Significant at the .05 level.

** Significant at the .01 level.

*** Significant at the .001 level.

to go on in judging the outcome of an election. This is most likely to be true in tight races. Based on the findings reported in the preceding sections, we anticipate that voters will pick their party's candidates to triumph.

Prior to the 1980 election respondents were asked which presidential candidate would carry their state and the nation.[35] Respondents who thought Carter would win were coded zero while those who believed Reagan would win were coded 1. Table 5-9 reveals the Pearson correlations between party identification and perceived outcome of the election in the respondents' home state and in the nation. The data clearly show that partisan direction shades respondents' predictions; partisans felt their party's candidate would carry both their state and the country. The correlations between the partisan direction measures and whether Reagan or Carter would win the election are noticeably higher than

Table 5-9
Pearson Correlations between Party Identification and Perceived Outcome of the Presidential Election, Pre-Election Survey, 1980[a]

Items and Dimensions	Respondent's State	Nation
Partisan Direction		
Party Difference Index	-.26*** (1180)	-.43*** (1195)
Party Closeness Scale	-.22*** (1301)	-.36*** (1319)
Party Support Scale	-.23*** (1293)	-.35*** (1312)
Democratic Party Feeling Thermometer	-.26*** (1284)	-.37*** (1303)
Republican Party Feeling Thermometer	.11*** (1282)	.23*** (1301)
Seven-Point Party Identification Scale	-.25*** (1322)	-.38*** (1344)
Strength of Partisanship		
Folded Party Closeness Scale	-.06* (1301)	-.05* (1319)
Folded Party Support Scale	-.03 (1293)	-.02 (1312)
Four-Point Strength of Identification Scale	-.07** (1322)	-.07** (1344)
Independence		
Strength of Independence Scale	.05 (1300)	.02 (1321)
Independents Feeling Thermometer	.06* (1191)	.08** (1214)

a - Figures in parentheses are numbers of cases.

*   Significant at the .05 level.
**   Significant at the .01 level.
***   Significant at the .001 level.

those between the partisan direction measures and which candidate would win in the respondent's state. Perhaps voters are more knowledgeable about their state's political climate than the political climate of the rest of the nation. This information probably displaces some of the effect partisanship has on projected outcome of the election in the state. In addition, increased partisan strength tends to be related to the perception that Carter would be victorious. However, the correlations between the Independents thermometer and predicted result of the election indicate that Independents felt Reagan would triumph.

These findings provide us with a meaningful context in which to analyze the interchangeability of the separate party identification measures. The absolute values of the correlations between the standard seven-point measure and perceived outcome of the election in one's state and in the nation are significantly higher (at the .001 level) than the correlations between the Republican thermometer and these forecasts. Also, there is a significant difference between the correlations for the party difference index, the seven-point measure, and projected outcome of the national election. Stated another way, *the relationship between the party difference index and whether Reagan or Carter will win (r= −.43) is stronger (significant at the .001 level) than the relationship between the old seven-point measure and this question (r= −.38)*. The correlations involving the remaining party identification measures are about equal in size.

SUMMARY

This chapter analyzed the relationship between party identification and party and candidate evaluations. The chapter began with a review of the literature in this area. An analysis of the data followed and showed that partisans tended to evaluate their party and presidential candidate more positively than the other party and candidate. For example, Republicans and Democrats felt that their party could handle war and the economy better than the opposing party. Partisanship also shaded respondents' assessments of Reagan's and Carter's personal qualities and qualifications as well as their predictions on who would win the election. On the surface, it appeared that strong partisans were more likely to view Carter favorably than those with loose party attachments. However, the strong influence of partisanship and the numerical superiority of Democrats among strong partisans in the electorate probably best explains this finding.

For the most part, the correlations between the political independence measures and party and candidate evaluations were low. Increasing independence tended to be accompanied by favorable assessments of the Republican party's ability to manage the economy. Independents were most likely to give Carter low marks on his handling of the economy, the Iranian hostage crisis, and the presidency on the whole. They also questioned his ability to provide strong leadership. There was some evidence to indicate that Independents may actually have been "disgusted" with both presidential candidates. The strong influence of partisanship over strength of identification made it difficult to explore the dimensionality of partisan strength and independence.

The investigation provided additional evidence concerning the interchangeability of the standard and alternative party identification measures. *In contexts in which we would normally consider partisanship to be very important, we found the party difference index to be a superior measure of partisan direction.* For example, the party difference index was more closely related to evaluations of Reagan's and Carter's personal qualities and perceived outcome of the presidential election on the national level than the standard seven-point scale. In contrast, the data on the equivalence of the partisan strength and independence measures tended to be inconclusive. The next chapter analyzes the relationship between party identification and electoral behavior.

NOTES

1. Morris Fiorina, *Retrospective Voting in American National Elections* (New Haven: Yale University Press, 1981).
2. Ibid., p. 147.
3. The two items were phrased in the following manner:

Do you think inflation would be handled better by the Democrats, by the Republicans, or about the same by both?
Do you think the problems of unemployment would be handled better by the Democrats, by the Republicans, or about the same by both?

4. Angus Campbell, Philip E. Converse, Warren E. Miller, and Donald E. Stokes, *The American Voter* (New York: John Wiley and Sons, 1960), pp. 66–75.
5. Donald E. Stokes, "Some Dynamic Elements of Contests for the Presidency," *American Political Science Review* Vol. 60 (March 1966), pp. 19–28.
6. John H. Kessel, *Presidential Campaign Politics: Coalition Strategies and Citizen Responses* (Homewood, Ill.: The Dorsey Press, 1980), Chap. 8. Also see: Stanley Kelley, Jr. and Thad W. Mirer, "The Simple Act of Voting," *American Political Science Review* Vol. 68 (June 1974), pp. 572–91; Eugene Declercq, Thomas L. Hurley, and Norman R. Luttbeg, "Voting in American Presidential Elections: 1956–1972," *American Politics Quarterly* Vol. 3 (July 1975), pp. 222–46; Samuel A. Kirkpatrick, William Lyons, and Michael R. Fitzgerald, "Candidates, Parties and Issues in the American Electorate: Two Decades of Change," *American Politics Quarterly* Vol. 3 (July 1975), pp. 247–83; and David E. RePass, "Comment: Political Methodologies in Disarray: Some Alternative Interpretations of the 1972 Election," *American Political Science Review* Vol. 70 (September 1976), pp. 814–31.
7. Pamela J. Conover, "The Perception of Political Figures: An Application of Attribution Theory," in *The Electorate Reconsidered*, ed. John C. Pierce and John L. Sullivan (Beverly Hills, Calif.: Sage Publications, 1980), p. 92.
8. Herbert B. Asher, *Presidential Elections and American Politics: Voters, Candidates, and Campaigns Since 1952*, Revised Edition (Homewood, Ill.: The Dorsey Press, 1980), p. 250.
9. Joseph P. McGrath and Marion F. McGrath, "Effects of Partisanship on Perceptions of Political Figures," *Public Opinion Quarterly* Vol. 26 (Summer 1962), pp. 236–48.
10. Roberta S. Sigel, "Effect of Partisanship on the Perception of Political Candidates," *Public Opinion Quarterly* Vol. 28 (Fall 1964), pp. 483–96.
11. Conover, "The Perception of Political Figures," p. 93.
12. Dan Nimmo and Robert L. Savage, *Candidates and Their Images: Concepts, Methods, and Findings* (Pacific Palisades, Calif.: Goodyear, 1976).
13. Asher, *Presidential Elections and American Politics*.
14. Ibid., p. 250.
15. Conover, "The Perception of Political Figures."

16. Ibid., pp. 94–95.

17. Fiorina, *Retrospective Voting in American National Elections*; and Paul R. Abramson, John H. Aldrich, and David W. Rohde, *Change and Continuity in the 1980 Elections* (Washington, D.C.: Congressional Quarterly Press, 1982). Fiorina's study was actually a modification and extension of Anthony Down's work in this area. Anthony Downs, *An Economic Theory of Democracy* (New York: Harper and Row, 1957).

18. Abramson, Aldrich, and Rohde, *Change and Continuity in the 1980 Elections*, p. 142. Fiorina argued more explicitly for the need to maintain a conceptual distinction between retrospective voting and "prospective voting" even though a relationship between retrospective and prospective evaluations exists. Fiorina, *Retrospective Voting in American National Elections*, pp. 6–11.

19. Sigel, "Effect of Partisanship on the Perception of Political Candidates."

20. Herbert F. Weisberg and Jerrold G. Rusk, "Dimensions of Candidate Evaluation," *American Political Science Review* Vol. 64 (December 1970), pp. 1167–85; Jerrold G. Rusk and Herbert F. Weisberg, "Perceptions of Presidential Candidates: Implications for Electoral Change," *Midwest Journal of Political Science* Vol. 16 (August 1972), pp. 388–410; and Gregory B. Markus and Philip E. Converse, "A Dynamic Simultaneous Equation Model of Electoral Choice," *American Political Science Review* Vol. 73 (December 1979), pp. 1055–70.

21. The questions were worded in the following manner:

In general, do you approve or disapprove of the way Jimmy Carter is handling inflation? Do you approve/disapprove strongly or not strongly?

In general, do you approve or disapprove of the way Jimmy Carter is handling unemployment? Do you approve/disapprove strongly or not strongly?

22. Those interviewed in the pre-election survey were also requested to rate Carter's management of the energy problem. An analysis of party identification and this item led to findings similar to those reported in Table 5–2.

23. Respondents were asked:

Do you approve or disapprove of Jimmy Carter's handling of the crisis brought about by the taking of Americans as hostage in Iran? Do you approve/disapprove strongly or not strongly?

24. Specifically, the question read:

Do you approve or disapprove of the way Jimmy Carter is handling his job as President? Do you approve/disapprove strongly or not strongly?

25. Fiorina, *Retrospective Voting in American National Elections*, p. 150.

26. Arthur H. Miller and Warren E. Miller, "Ideology in the 1972 Election: Myth or Reality—A Rejoinder," *American Political Science Review* Vol. 70 (September 1976), pp. 832–49.

27. Fiorina, *Retrospective Voting in American National Elections*, pp. 153–54.

28. Respondents were asked the following question:

Now we would like to know something about the feelings you have toward the candidates for President. I am going to name a candidate, and I want you to tell me whether something about that person, or something he has done has made you have certain feelings like "anger" or "pride," or others I will mention. Think about Ronald Reagan (John Anderson, Jimmy Carter). Now, has Reagan (Anderson, Carter)—because of the kind of person he is, or because of something he has done—ever made you feel . . . ?

29. An analysis of party identification and the other personal qualities of the candidates generated similar results.

30. Similar differences also exist between the correlations for the separate party identification measures and the other personal attributes of the candidates.

31. The question read:

I am going to read a list of words and phrases people use to describe political figures. For each, please tell me whether the word or phrase describes the candidate I name extremely well, quite well, not too well, or not well at all. Think about Ronald Reagan (John Anderson, Jimmy Carter). The first word on our list is "moral." In your opinion does the word "moral" describe Reagan (Anderson, Carter) extremely well, quite well, not too well, or not well at all? You can just tell me the number of your choice.

32. Weak but significant relationships do exist between political independence and beliefs about Anderson's personal attributes and qualifications. In other words, Independents tended to give him positive evaluations.

33. An analysis of party identification and the other personal qualifications of the candidates reaffirms this conclusion.

34. Analogous differences exist between the correlations for the various party identification measures and the other characteristics of the candidates related to governing.

35. The questions were worded in the following manner:

Which candidate for President do you think will carry this state?

Who do you think will be elected President in November?

A majority of respondents who had a prediction thought Carter would be reelected President. Only seven people believed Anderson would win.

6
ELECTORAL BEHAVIOR

The last three chapters have concentrated on party identification and political attitudes. Chapter Three addressed orientations toward the political system, and Chapters Four and Five examined feelings about groups, issues, parties, and candidates. Our analysis has allowed us to learn more about the thought processes of partisans, ardent party loyalists, and Independents. Also, of equal importance, we have been able to draw meaningful comparisons between the various party identification measures. At this juncture it appears that the party difference index and the standard seven-point party identification scale are not interchangeable in certain important contexts. In most cases, the correlations between the traditional four-point strength of identification scale, the alternative partisan strength measures, and the criterion variables have been about equal in size. We still do not know which of the independence measures is a better estimate of political independence. However, there is substantial evidence that suggests strength of identification and political independence are two separate components of party identification and not one as generally believed. The study now moves into its final sphere, electoral behavior.

Chapter Six investigates the relationship between party identification and electoral behavior. In comparison to previous chapters, we are now less concerned about how a person thinks and more concerned about what a person does. This chapter primarily focuses on how party orientation influences campaign activities, voter registration, turnout, and the vote choice. From a theoretical standpoint, these relationships have received considerable attention in the literature, and their importance to the understanding of voting behavior cannot be overstated. Of course, only the standard party identification measures have been used in research in this area. The following analysis will permit us to gain valuable insights into the behavioral patterns of partisans, strong identifiers, and Independents and to gather additional evidence on the interchangeability of the party identification measures and the dimensionality of partisan strength and independence.

CAMPAIGN ACTIVITIES

Sidney Verba and Norman Nie conducted an intensive study of political participation and reported their findings in *Participation in America*.[1] One of the questions they sought to answer was, how much do Americans participate? They found the level of participation across a variety of different activities to be quite low. They summarized their findings by saying:

1. Few, if any, types of political activity beyond the act of voting are performed by more than a third of the American citizenry.
2. Activities that require the investment of more than trivial amounts of time and energy as well as those that have a short time referent (such as a single election) tend to be performed by no more than 10 to 15 percent of the citizens.
3. Less demanding activities as well as those with longer time referents (i.e., longer than a single election campaign) are performed by between 15 and 30 percent of the citizenry.[2]

Lester Milbrath and M. Lal Goel reached similar conclusions in their study.[3] Based on their data and those collected in the SRC/CPS election studies over the years, they offered the following profile of the American public:

Only about 8 percent belong to a political club or organization. About 10 to 12 percent make monetary contributions, about 10 to 15 percent contact public officials, and about 15 percent display a button or sticker. Around 25 to 30 percent try to proselytize others to vote a certain way, around 30 percent have tried to work on some community problem, and from 40 to 70 percent vote in any given election.[4]

Clearly, their investigation and the one conducted by Verba and Nie show that few citizens are actively involved in political affairs.[5]

Verba and Nie's factor analysis of a large number of diverse activities revealed the existence of four modes of participation: voting, campaign activity, communal activity, and particularized contacting.[6] After analyzing the relationship between party identification and level of activity within each participatory mode, they found that partisan direction and especially increased partisan strength tended to lead to higher campaign involvement rates irrespective of socioeconomic status.[7] As far as partisanship was concerned, they observed that Republicans participated more in elections than Democrats. According to them, "one's preference on issues relates more strongly to political activity among Republicans than among Democrats. And, as one would guess, the political beliefs of

Republicans that are having this effect on participation rates are conservative in direction."[8]

One would expect party identification to have a greater effect on participation in activities more directly related to the electoral process than on participation in general types of political activities (e.g., membership in community groups). Verba and Nie found this to be the case, though they employed the standard party identification questions in their study. Such an expectation is warranted because of the nonpartisan nature of acts outside the electoral process. Understandably, Republicans, Democrats, and strong identifiers see greater benefits in pursuing activities that more directly pertain to elections. Other factors (e.g., level of education) can better explain why people become involved in nonpartisan forms of activity.

In the 1980 election study, respondents were asked whether during the election they had tried to persuade others how to vote, had contributed money to a party or candidate, had attended any political meetings or rallies, had worked for a party or candidate, or had worn a button or placed a sticker on their car.[9] Respondents who said "no" were coded zero, while those who said "yes" were coded 1. In line with previous findings, 36 percent reported they had tried to persuade others how to vote, and less than 10 percent admitted engaging in the remaining campaign acts. Tables 6–1, 6–2, and 6–3 contain the Pearson correlations between party identification and participation in these different campaign activities.

For the most part, there is a weak but significant relationship between partisan direction and campaign activity. The data show that Republicans were somewhat more likely than Democrats to participate actively in the election. With the possible exception of contributing money to a party or candidate, the correlations between strength of identification and campaign involvement are somewhat higher. We find that as partisan strength increases, so does propensity to persuade others how to vote, attend political meetings or rallies, work for a party or candidate, and wear a button or put a sticker on a car. In contrast, political independence is only related to whether respondents tried to influence others how to vote and contributed money to a candidate. In other words, increased independence is accompanied by increased engagement in only these two activities. Also, the correlations between partisan strength, independence, whether respondents tried to persuade others how to vote, and whether they contributed to a candidate are in the same direction. At the same time the correlations between the partisan strength measures and the other activities tend to be noticeably higher than the correlations between the independence measures and the same activities. These findings suggest that partisan strength and independence are two separate dimensions and not one as commonly thought.

Several significant differences exist between the correlations for the various party identification measures and participation in the six campaign acts. For instance, the correlation between the standard seven-point measure and whether respondents contributed money to a candidate ($r = -.12$) is significantly higher

Table 6-1
Pearson Correlations between Party Identification and Whether Respondents Tried to Persuade Others to Vote a Certain Way, Post-Election Survey, 1980[a]

Items and Dimensions	Tried to Influence the Votes of Others
Partisan Direction	
Party Difference Index	-.09*** (1217)
Party Closeness Scale	-.07** (1358)
Party Support Scale	-.06* (1355)
Democratic Party Feeling Thermometer	-.08** (1331)
Republican Party Feeling Thermometer	.04 (1327)
Seven-Point Party Identification Scale	-.09*** (1376)
Strength of Partisanship	
Folded Party Closeness Scale	.17*** (1358)
Folded Party Support Scale	.22*** (1355)
Four-Point Strength of Identification Scale	.14*** (1376)
Independence	
Strength of Independence Scale	.11*** (1367)
Independents Feeling Thermometer	.02 (1232)

a - Figures in parentheses are numbers of cases.

*   Significant at the .05 level.
**   Significant at the .01 level.
***   Significant at the .001 level.

(at the .05 level) than the correlation between the party support scale and persuance of this activity ($r = -.07$). Similarly, the absolute value of the correlation between the seven-point measure and whether people gave money to a candidate is significantly higher (at the .01 level) than the correlation between the Republican feeling thermometer and this question. The traditional seven-point measure is also more closely related (significant at the .05 level) to working for a campaign ($r = -.09$) than is the party difference index ($r = -.05$). Further-

Table 6-2
Pearson Correlations between Party Identification and Campaign Contributions, Post-Election Survey, 1980[a]

Items and Dimensions	Contributed to A Candidate	Contributed to A Party
Partisan Direction		
Party Difference Index	-.09*** (1214)	-.14*** (1215)
Party Closeness Scale	-.09*** (1356)	-.16*** (1357)
Party Support Scale	-.07** (1353)	-.18*** (1354)
Democratic Party Feeling Thermometer	-.10*** (1328)	-.13*** (1329)
Republican Party Feeling Thermometer	.05* (1324)	.13*** (1325)
Seven-Point Party Identification Scale	-.12*** (1373)	-.17*** (1374)
Strength of Partisanship		
Folded Party Closeness Scale	.04 (1356)	.11*** (1357)
Folded Party Support Scale	.08** (1353)	.21*** (1354)
Four-Point Strength of Identification Scale	.05* (1373)	.13*** (1374)
Independence		
Strength of Independence Scale	.06* (1364)	-.03 (1365)
Independents Feeling Thermometer	.05* (1228)	-.01 (1229)

a - Figures in parentheses are numbers of cases.

* Significant at the .05 level.
** Significant at the .01 level.
*** Significant at the .001 level.

more, the relationship between the strength of independence scale and whether respondents attempted to proselytize others to vote a certain way is significantly stronger (at the .01 level) than the relationship between the Independents thermometer and this behavior. In addition, the folded party support scale is more highly correlated with participation in four of the six campaign activities than is the standard four-point strength measure. The correlations between the folded party support measure and whether citizens tried to influence others to vote a certain way, contributed money to a party, attended a political meeting or rally, and displayed a button or sticker are significantly larger (at least at the .05 level) than the correlation between the four-point partisan strength measure and par-

Table 6-3
Pearson Correlations between Party Identification and Campaign Activity, Post-Election Survey, 1980[a]

Items and Dimensions	Attended Meetings	Worked for A Campaign	Displayed Button or Sticker
Partisan Direction			
Party Difference Index	-.03 (1219)	-.05* (1217)	-.07* (1218)
Party Closeness Scale	-.04 (1360)	-.10*** (1358)	-.08*** (1359)
Party Support Scale	-.01 (1357)	-.08*** (1355)	-.05* (1356)
Democratic Party Feeling Thermometer	-.03 (1333)	-.06* (1331)	-.05* (1332)
Republican Party Feeling Thermometer	.00 (1329)	.04 (1327)	.08** (1328)
Seven-Point Party Identification Scale	-.05* (1377)	-.09*** (1375)	-.07** (1377)
Strength of Partisanship			
Folded Party Closeness Scale	.09*** (1360)	.09*** (1358)	.07** (1359)
Folded Party Support Scale	.18*** (1357)	.13*** (1355)	.14*** (1356)
Four-Point Strength of Identification Scale	.10*** (1377)	.11*** (1375)	.08** (1377)
Independence			
Strength of Independence Scale	.01 (1368)	-.01 (1366)	-.02 (1367)
Independents Feeling Thermometer	.03 (1233)	-.03 (1231)	.04 (1232)

a - Figures in parentheses are numbers of cases.

* Significant at the .05 level.
** Significant at the .01 level.
*** Significant at the .001 level.

ticipation in these same four acts. It appears that, in the context of campaign activity, how much one "supports" a political party is a better predictor of involvement than how much one "identifies" with a party. Although the difference between the two measures' points of reference is slight, it is important in the realm of participation in elections.

VOTER REGISTRATION AND TURNOUT

A major criticism of the American electoral system has been its failure to achieve the high voter turnout rates common in many foreign countries. While turnout in the presidential elections in the United States has only exceeded 60 percent in the twentieth century, other democracies have reported turnout rates as high as 90 percent. However, William Flanigan and Nancy Zingale say that such comparisons are unfair because of the different ways turnout is computed in other nations.[10] In some countries, such as Australia, voting is compulsory, and their turnout is often above 90 percent. Also, those who comment on turnout rates in the United States often ignore the substantial limitations of eligibility associated with residence requirements and other restrictions. Raymond Wolfinger and Steven Rosenstone contend that if certain registration law reforms were enacted, the turnout rate would increase by approximately nine percent.[11] When these factors are taken into account, our turnout rate is almost as high as in many foreign countries.[12]

Eligibility to vote as well as whether and how often Americans visit the polls on election day is dependent on a number of variables. The variables that influence turnout can be divided into three categories: institutional, social background, and attitudinal. Although we are most concerned with the relationship between party identification (an attitude) and turnout, a brief discussion of the factors within each category will provide the reader with a fuller understanding of why citizens vote.

Institutional

History shows that laws governing suffrage and eligibility have had a significant effect on voter turnout rates. Even though black males were granted the right to vote by Constitutional amendment in 1870, only a small percentage of them voted until the mid–1960s. As mentioned earlier in the book, many southern states used methods such as the poll tax, literacy tests, "white" primaries, discriminatory administrative measures, and intimidation to prevent blacks from voting.[13] Since most blacks lived in the South, the numerical impact of their enfranchisement was rather slight nationwide. Their turnout rate increased dramatically after the passage of the Voting Rights Act in 1965 (which was extended with minor revisions in 1982). In addition, the enfranchisement of women by Constitutional amendment in 1920 nearly doubled the electorate's size. Yet many women, especially those of foreign stock, did not immediately take advantage of this newly won right until the elections of 1928, 1932, and 1936.[14] The last major change took place in the early 1970s when the required age to vote was lowered from twenty-one to eighteen. In summary, the granting of suffrage to different segments of the population and the expansion of voting rights have affected turnout rates in the past.

Additional examples of the impact of institutional factors on turnout can be found in the literature. Walter Dean Burnham, Philip Converse, and Jerrold Rusk were involved in a lively debate over the reasons for the elevated turnout rates in the late 1800s and their decline at the turn of the century.[15] Burnham claimed that a high level of partisan loyalty and political involvement in the late 1800s resulted in high turnout and straight ticket voting. However, this political fervor ended because of increasing friction (brought on by the Industrial Revolution) between corporate power and the strong democratic and pluralist forces in the political system. Converse disagreed and argued that poor bookkeeping in the nineteenth century, widespread corruption at the polls, and the absence of personal-registration requirements explain changes in electoral behavior during this time. Rusk, siding with Converse, added that the introduction of the Australian ballot form between 1889 and 1896, replacing the Massachusetts ballot, caused a decrease in turnout (among other things). The Massachusetts ballot listed candidates by party whereas the Australian ballot listed candidates by office. The Massachusetts type ballots were prepared and distributed by the parties with the express purpose of attracting voters. The ease with which these ballots could be marked and cast and a lack of strict supervision at the polls propped up turnout rates. Voting became more private and more difficult after the Australian ballot was adopted, thus decreasing the influence of the party over electoral behavior. In a later study Burnham found that several of the contentions voiced by Converse and Rusk were indeed warranted, as well as some support for his proposition that the erosion of the mass base of American politics immediately following the realignment of 1896 "was a consequence of the tension between capitalism and democracy, and of the ascendancy of capitalism."[16] The dispute between these three scholars underscores the significant impact of election laws on voting behavior.

Social Background

Social background variables also influence voter turnout. For instance, life cycle has a curvilinear relationship with turnout.[17] Most studies show that propensity to vote increases with age until the middle years. At that point turnout rates peak and then decline in later years.[18] Married citizens are more likely to vote than unmarried ones, too. Although at one time men voted far more often than women, the difference has narrowed considerably in recent years. Moreover, whites demonstrate higher turnout rates than blacks and other minorities. In addition, income, occupational prestige, and education account for variation in turnout rates. In fact, Wolfinger and Rosenstone found that education is the best predictor of whether citizens vote when age, income, and occupation are held constant.[19]

Attitudinal

Personal attitudes play an important role in determining whether people vote. Angus Campbell, Philip Converse, Warren Miller, and Donald Stokes found that an increased sense of citizen duty and political efficacy is associated with elevated turnout rates.[20] Moreover, they showed that a high degree of interest in the campaign and concern over the election outcome raises the likelihood people will vote. Furthermore, those who perceive the race is close are more likely to vote than those who feel the election will be a landslide. Of course, these attitudes are likely to vary from one election to another.

Party identification also explains variation in turnout rates. Based on Verba and Nie's study, Republicans and Democrats tend to vote in roughly equal percentages after socioeconomic status is controlled.[21] Yet, they did find that as strength of identification increases, so does the turnout rate. Campbell and his colleagues found this to be true in their investigation, too.[22] Naturally, those who strongly identify with a party will follow their party and candidates closely during the campaign. Similar to loyal sports fans who frequently go to the ball park to root for their team, most strong identifiers visit the polls on election day to help their side win.

Past Frequency of Voting

In the pre-election survey respondents were asked how often they have voted in past presidential elections. The exact wording of the question was: "In the elections for president since you have been old enough to vote, would you say you have voted in all of them, most of them, some of them, or none of them?" Responses to this question were coded from 1 for "none" to 4 for "all."

Table 6-4 reveals the tau-c correlations between party identification and past frequency of voting. The data show that no relationship exists between partisan direction and previous turnout rate. But, as we anticipated, there is a significant relationship between partisan strength and how often respondents voted in the past. In other words, as partisan strength increases, so does the frequency with which people voted before. A weak but significant correlation exists between the strength of independence scale and turnout record, indicating that increased independence from politics is associated with a greater tendency to turnout in the past. These findings support the position that partisan strength and independence are bidimensional and not unidimensional. No significant differences were uncovered between the correlations for the individual party identification measures and past frequency of voting.

Voter Registration in 1980

As noted in Chapter Two, the SRC/CPS attempted to validate respondents' statements about their registration status and voting behavior in 1980. After the election, members of the SRC field staff visited the local government offices responsible for maintaining registration and voting records in the 108 sample districts to verify respondents' reports. At the same time, the CPS staff checked the records of individuals who said they lived outside the sampling domain over the telephone. Of the 1,614 people interviewed, only thirty-five respondents could not be validated.

The data gathered in the validation study provide us with the most accurate

Table 6-4
TAU-C Correlations between Party Identification and Past Frequency of Voting, Pre-Election Survey, 1980[a]

Items and Dimensions	Frequence of Past Voting[b]
Partisan Direction	
Party Difference Index	-.03 (1271)
Party Closeness Scale	-.02 (1429)
Party Support Scale	.02 (1424)
Democratic Party Feeling Thermometer	.01 (1387)
Republican Party Feeling Thermometer	.03 (1384)
Seven-Point Party Identification Scale	-.03 (1442)
Strength of Partisanship	
Folded Party Closeness Scale	.15*** (1429)
Folded Party Support Scale	.17*** (1424)
Four-Point Strength of Identification Scale	.14*** (1442)
Independence	
Strength of Independence Scale	.05** (1428)
Independents Feeling Thermometer	.03 (1274)

a - Figures in parentheses are numbers of cases.

b - The coefficients to the right of the folded party closeness and four-point strength of identification scales are tau-b correlations.

*   Significant at the .05 level.

**   Significant at the .01 level.

*** Significant at the .001 level.

information attainable on voter registration and turnout. In the past, researchers had to rely on respondents' reports which are prone to error. Since the validation study eliminates this source of error, we can now have more confidence in our conclusions concerning this behavior.[23]

More specifically, the SRC/CPS investigators obtained information on whether respondents were registered to vote and, if so, with which party they were registered, whether they voted in a primary election and, if so, in which primary, and whether they voted in the general election. Of course, the SRC/CPS investigators could not find out the actual vote choices of respondents since this information is kept confidential by law. The following analyses will address the

Table 6-5
Pearson Correlations between Party Identification and Voter Registration, Validation Study, 1980[a]

Items and Dimensions	Registered to Vote	Party Registration
Partisan Direction		
Party Difference Index	-.06* (1232)	.67*** (433)
Party Closeness Scale	-.02 (1379)	.62*** (465)
Party Support Scale	-.01 (1375)	.61*** (465)
Democratic Party Feeling Thermometer	-.03 (1344)	.44*** (464)
Republican Party Feeling Thermometer	.05* (1340)	-.44*** (465)
Seven-Point Party Identification Scale	-.05* (1395)	.75*** (478)
Strength of Partisanship		
Folded Party Closeness Scale	.16*** (1379)	.03 (465)
Folded Party Support Scale	.15*** (1375)	.01 (465)
Four-Point Strength of Identification Scale	.16*** (1395)	.07 (478)
Independence		
Strength of Independence Scale	.02 (1390)	.02 (471)
Independents Feeling Thermometer	-.02 (1240)	-.09* (431)

a - Figures in parentheses are numbers of cases.

* Significant at the .05 level.
** Significant at the .01 level.
*** Significant at the .001 level.

relationships between party identification and the items included in the validation study.

Table 6–5 shows the correlations between party identification, whether respondents were registered to vote in 1980 and, if they were, with which party they were registered. Respondents who were not registered to vote were coded zero while those who were registered were coded 1. Citizens who were listed as Republicans were coded zero and those who were listed as Democrats were coded 1. Although there is some evidence that Republicans are more likely to register to vote than Democrats in Table 6–5, controlling for education erases this relationship. In addition, partisan strength tends to increase with greater inclination to register; however, the small size of the correlations suggest that other factors may better explain this behavior. Not surprisingly, the data reveal that partisans are most likely to register with their own party. Yet, this relationship is far from perfect, indicating that some crossover is taking place. In many states nonpartisans must register with a party if they wish to vote in the party's primary, and this, too, may account for the size of the correlations.[24] There is also a weak but significant relationship between the Independents thermometer and party registration, which suggests that Independents tend to register as Republicans. The difference in the size of the correlations between the partisan strength and independence measures and whether respondents were registered to vote in 1980 implies that partisan strength and independence are two distinct entities.

There are a number of significant disparities between the correlations for the party identification measures, whether respondents were registered to vote, and with which party they were registered. The correlation between the standard seven-point measure and whether respondents were eligible to vote ($r = -.05$) is significantly higher (at the .05 level) than the correlation between the party support scale and this variable ($r = -.01$). The relationship between the standard seven-point measure and party registration is significantly stronger (at the .001 level in every case) than the relationships between the party difference index, the party closeness scale, the party support scale, the Democrat thermometer, and this behavior. In addition, the correlation between the seven-point measure and party registration is significantly higher (at the .001 level) than the absolute value of the correlation between the Republican thermometer and this item. Finally, there is a significant discrepancy (at the .05 level) between the correlations for the independence measures and with which party respondents were registered.

Voting Turnout in 1980

Within the last two decades important changes have taken place in the number of presidential primaries held across the country and the turnout rates in presidential elections. Reforms in the nomination process initiated by the Democratic party in the late 1960s resulted in greater use of the primary by the states. While only fifteen states used the primary to select delegates to the national conventions in 1968, thirty-seven used the primary in 1980.[25] The remaining states held caucuses or conventions to choose their representatives to the national conventions. Because primary elections are less salient than general elections, fewer people vote in them. Consequently, one would expect primaries to be dominated by intense partisans. At the very least, partisans will be more likely to vote in their party's primaries than in those of the opposing party.

Turnout in presidential elections has fallen steadily over the years. While 63 percent of all eligible citizens voted in 1960, only 53 percent voted in 1980. Since the size of the electorate has grown substantially over time, a greater number

Table 6-6
Pearson Correlations between Party Identification and Voting Behavior in Primaries, Validation Study, 1980[a]

Items and Dimensions	Turnout	Party Primary
Partisan Direction		
Party Difference Index	.00 (698)	.73*** (247)
Party Closeness Scale	-.02 (774)	.64*** (258)
Party Support Scale	-.02 (773)	.62*** (257)
Democratic Party Feeling Thermometer	-.01 (758)	.49*** (261)
Republican Party Feeling Thermometer	.01 (758)	-.43*** (261)
Seven-Point Party Identification Scale	-.01 (797)	.76*** (268)
Strength of Partisanship		
Folded Party Closeness Scale	.07* (774)	-.05 (258)
Folded Party Support Scale	.11*** (773)	-.06 (257)
Four-Point Strength of Identification Scale	.14*** (797)	.02 (268)
Independence		
Strength of Independence Scale	-.08** (782)	.03 (262)
Independents Feeling Thermometer	-.04 (699)	-.02 (240)

a - Figures in parentheses are numbers of cases.

*   Significant at the .05 level.
**   Significant at the .01 level.
***   Significant at the .001 level.

of people are not voting now than ever before. Despite these figures, studies by Wolfinger and Rosenstone, and Paul Abramson and his associates revealed few major differences in partisanship and policy preferences between voters and non-voters in 1972 and 1980.[26] Still, low turnout levels pose a potential threat to the stability of a democracy. If the turnout rate continues to decline, it could undermine the legitimacy of the two parties and elected leaders and lead to political upheaval.

Table 6-7
Pearson Correlations between Party Identification and Voter Turnout in General Election, Validation Study, 1980[a]

Items and Dimensions	Turnout
Partisan Direction	
Party Difference Index	-.07** (1381)
Party Closeness Scale	-.03 (1544)
Party Support Scale	-.01 (1540)
Democratic Party Feeling Thermometer	-.05* (1507)
Republican Party Feeling Thermometer	.03 (1503)
Seven-Point Party Identification Scale	-.06** (1563)
Strength of Partisanship	
Folded Party Closeness Scale	.14*** (1544)
Folded Party Support Scale	.14*** (1540)
Four-Point Strength of Identification Scale	.13*** (1563)
Independence	
Strength of Independence Scale	.04 (1551)
Independents Feeling Thermometer	.00 (1389)

a - Figures in parentheses are numbers of cases.

*   Significant at the .05 level.
**   Significant at the .01 level.
***   Significant at the .001 level.

Using information collected in the validation study, Tables 6-6 and 6-7 show the Pearson correlations between party identification, turnout in the presidential primaries, the party primary in which respondents voted, and turnout in the general election. Although partisan direction is not related to turnout in the primaries, it appears to be related to turnout in the general election. However, this relationship disappears after controlling for education. In addition, the correlations between the partisan direction measures and the primary in which respondents voted are quite high. As we predicted, Republicans and Democrats tend to vote in their party's primaries rather than in those of the opposing party. The data also demonstrate that increased partisan strength is associated with greater propensity to vote in both the primary and general elections. As with registration, the small size of the correlations indicates that other variables (e.g., level of education, sense of citizen duty, and political efficacy) may have a greater effect on turnout. Furthermore, there is a weak but significant relationship between the strength of independence scale and turnout in the primaries. That is, as independence increases, so does inclination to vote in the primaries. No relationship exists between independence and turnout in the 1980 general election.

The data in Tables 6-6 and 6-7 offer conflicting evidence as to whether partisan strength and independence fall along a single continuum. On the one hand, the similarity in size and opposite direction of the correlations between the partisan strength measures, the strength of independence scale, and primary turnout suggest that partisan strength and independence comprise one dimension. On the other hand, the difference in the size of the correlations between the partisan strength and independence measures and turnout in the general election implies that the two elements are separate dimensions. The latter finding represents an anomaly to those who theorize that strength of identification and political independence are the same thing.

The data in the two tables also provide a good setting in which to analyze the equivalency of the individual party identification measures. The correlation between the standard seven-point measure and the primary in which respondents voted is significantly higher (at the .001 level in every case) than the correlations between the party closeness scale, the party support scale, the two party thermometers, and this item. In contrast, the correlations between the seven-point measure, the party difference index, and whether citizens voted in a Republican or Democratic primary are about the same size. Moreover, the relationship between the old seven-point measure and turnout in the general election is significantly closer (at the .05 level) than the relationship between the party support scale and this behavior. Lastly, there is a stronger relationship (significant at the .05 level) between the standard four-point partisan strength measure and whether respondents voted in the primaries ($r = .14$) than between the folded party closeness scale and this question ($r = .07$). The correlations between the independence measures and the items in Tables 6-6 and 6-7 do not differ significantly.

THE VOTE CHOICE

The strong impact of party identification on the vote choice is well documented and there is no reason to belabor the point here. Party identification, of course, is not the only variable that influences the vote, and short-term forces such as issues and party and candidate images also have an effect. In fact, if it were not for these short-term forces, election outcomes would always resemble the distribution of party identification within the electorate. This observation inspired Converse to develop and operationalize the concept of a "normal" vote.[27] Although short-term pressures have probably played some role in every election, previous studies employing the usual party identification questions have concluded that party orientation has been the most powerful determinant of the vote since 1952.[28]

In brief review, a major finding (if not *the* major finding) of *The American Voter* was party identification's strong influence over the presidential party vote in 1952 and 1956.[29] Subsequent analyses found this variable to have a strong impact on voter preferences in the 1960 election as well.[30] Even though a larger portion of the electorate voted in line with their issue positions between 1964 and 1972, party identification remained the dominant force throughout the period. John Petrocik's study demonstrated that the impact of party affiliation actually rose in 1976, though not to the levels registered during the Eisenhower and Kennedy elections.[31] A rise in political independence in recent years, as we noted in Chapter One, has weakened the relationship between the two variables and has led to greater electoral volatility. Nevertheless, the theoretical and empirical significance accorded this relationship throws a spotlight on our effort to compare the different party identification measures. To be sure, the best measure of party identification will be the most precise estimate of the two-party vote.

Table 6–8 contains the Pearson correlations between party identification and respondents' House, Senate, and presidential vote choices.[32] Only those respondents whose turnout was validated were included in this table and in ensuing analyses where appropriate. As expected, partisan direction is closely related to the vote, indicating that partisans tended to vote for House, Senate, and presidential candidates from their own party. Observe how the correlations between the partisan direction measures and the vote increase with higher office. This finding is surprising given the lower saliency of congressional races and the greater opportunity for partisanship to act as a guide in the vote choice process in these races.[33] The result of the 1980 election combined with the data in the table suggest that an unusually high incidence of defections from the Democratic party helped the Republicans make dramatic inroads in the House and Senate. Although it is difficult to say whether partisan strength is related to voters' preferences for the House and Senate, it does appear that strong partisans were most likely to vote for Carter. The fact that Democrats outnumber Republicans in the electorate explains this finding. While political independence is not related to the two-party House and Senate vote, there is a weak but significant association between the Independents thermometer and the presidential vote, suggesting that Independents tended to support Reagan. Little can be said about the dimensionality of strength of identification and independence because of the obvious partisan nature of the criterion variables. Findings similar to those re-

Table 6-8
Pearson Correlations between Party Identification and Two-Party Vote Choice, Post-Election Survey, 1980[a]

Items and Dimensions	House	Senate	President
Partisan Direction			
Party Difference Index	.49*** (612)	.56*** (418)	.75*** (604)
Party Closeness Scale	.48*** (663)	.51*** (458)	.65*** (644)
Party Support Scale	.42*** (661)	.52*** (457)	.62*** (644)
Democratic Party Feeling Thermometer	.37*** (662)	.38*** (458)	.58*** (645)
Republican Party Feeling Thermometer	-.32*** (663)	-.45*** (458)	-.49*** (647)
Seven-Point Party Identification Scale	.49*** (677)	.54*** (469)	.65*** (664)
Strength of Partisanship			
Folded Party Closeness Scale	.07* (663)	.04 (458)	.20*** (644)
Folded Party Support Scale	.02 (661)	.03 (457)	.17*** (644)
Four-Point Strength of Identification Scale	.06 (677)	.08* (469)	.20*** (664)
Independence			
Strength of Independence Scale	.00 (670)	-.04 (459)	-.04 (653)
Independents Feeling Thermometer	-.06 (629)	.00 (432)	-.07* (605)

a - Figures in parentheses are numbers of cases.

*   Significant at the .05 level.
** Significant at the .01 level.
*** Significant at the .001 level.

ported in Table 6-8 were uncovered in an analysis of party orientation and strength of vote preference for the candidates for each office.

There are significant differences between the correlations for the standard and alternative partisan direction measures and the vote. First, the correlations between the standard seven-point measure and respondents' vote choices for all three offices are significantly higher (at least at the .05 level) than the absolute values of the correlations between the two party thermometers and these decisions. Second, the seven-point measure is more closely related to the House vote than is the party support scale (significant at the .01 level). Finally, and most importantly, there is a sizable split between the correlations for the party difference index, the seven-point measure, and respondents' presidential vote. More specifically, *the correlation between the party difference index and the*

Table 6-9
Proportion of Variance in Two-Party Presidential Vote Accounted for by Seven-Point Identification Scale and Party Difference Index, 1964–1980[a]

	1964	1968	1972	1976	1980	Average
Seven-Point Party Identification Scale	43.5	49.4	28.0	41.6	44.7	41.4
Party Difference Index	49.1	59.0	45.4	54.7	57.9	53.2

a - The cell entries are eta-squares. The figures between 1964 and 1976 were drawn from: Herbert F. Weisberg, "A Multidimensional Conceptualization of Party Identification," Political Behavior Vol. 2 No. 1 (1980), p. 46.

vote for president ($r = .75$) is significantly higher (at the .001 level) than the correlation between the traditional seven-point scale and this behavior ($r = .65$). This is a major finding and it deserves a closer look.

Herbert Weisberg conducted a similar analysis of the various party identification measures and the vote over time.[34] In particular, he examined how well the seven-point measure and the party difference index explained variation in the two-party presidential vote between 1964 and 1976. Table 6–9 reveals his findings along with the proportion of explained variance in the presidential vote accounted for by the two partisan direction measures in 1980 as computed by the author. As one can see, *the party difference measure consistently accounts for more variation in the vote than does the standard seven-point measure.* Hence, our finding that the party difference index is the best determinant of the vote in 1980 is not the exception but the rule.

Following this analysis Weisberg investigated whether the seven-point measure can account for some of the variance in the vote that the party difference measure leaves unexplained.[35] He did this by checking whether the seven-point measure affects the 1976 Republican presidential vote within categories of the party difference index. While the party difference index had a definite effect on the vote within the categories of the seven-point scale, the standard measure had only a minimal effect on the vote within the categories of the party difference measure. He therefore concluded; "Party identification seems to have little added impact upon the vote once party difference is taken into account . . . ," and "much of the effect of party identification seems due to its relationship with the party difference."[36] A similar analysis of data collected in the 1980 election study yielded the same results. An alternative explanation of the better fit for the party difference index is that it may gauge a more short-term attitude than does the seven-point scale, and, as Weisberg suggested, future research should concentrate on the comparative stability of the two measures over time.[37]

INDICATORS OF ELECTORAL VOLATILITY

In this final section of the chapter we analyze the relationship between party identification and two indicators of electoral volatility, vote switching and split ticket voting. David Hill and Norman Luttbeg tracked these two indicators over time and concluded that there has been a slow but consistent decline in party fidelity since the 1950s.[38] Although several variables may account for increases in voter defection (e.g., heightened issue awareness), the rise in psychological independence is thought to be a major factor. We begin by analyzing the association between party identification and vote switching.

Vote Switching

V.O. Key had reservations about some of the conclusions reached in *The American Voter*, particularly those concerning the dominant influence of party identification over the vote. Unlike Campbell and his colleagues, he believed that a significant number of Americans were moved by central questions of public policy and government performance. His book, *The Responsible Electorate*, contained a detailed analysis of three types of voters, "standpatters," "switchers," and "new voters."[39] Standpatters were citizens who voted for candidates of the same party in two successive elections. Switchers were individuals who would vote for a given party in one election and the opposing party in the next election. New voters, who are not included in this analysis, were simply first time voters.[40] Respondents were classified as standpatters or switchers based on their recall which, of course, can be inaccurate. But, upon comparing the divisions between the remembered vote and the actual vote over a twenty year period, he found that the recall of the vote was close enough to the actual vote to give him some confidence in the contrasts between the different groups of voters. His study of the attitudes of these voters led him to conclude that a sizeable portion of the electorate do indeed react to their perceptions and appraisals of policy and performance.[41]

Nevertheless, at the end of his book, Key admitted that partisan loyalty was a crucial factor in determining whether voters stand pat or switch. His study showed that those who agreed with their party's issue positions were most inclined to support their party on election day. Moreover, standpatters tended to stay by their party even when they agreed with the stands of the opposing party. The attitudes and characteristics of switching voters, however, differed from election to election in response to the changing political conditions of the various contests. He concluded that many of his findings tended to confirm the strong impact of party orientation on the vote.[42]

Several questions included in the 1980 election study make it possible for us to investigate the relationship between party identification and tendency to switch votes in presidential elections, and to see whether certain party identification

Table 6-10
Pearson Correlations between Party Identification and Past Party Voting for President, Pre-Election Survey, 1980[a]

Items and Dimensions	Voted for Same or Different Party for President	Two-Party Vote
Partisan Direction		
Party Difference Index	.22*** (1109)	.87*** (486)
Party Closeness Scale	.17*** (1226)	.76*** (518)
Party Support Scale	.19*** (1222)	.71*** (517)
Democratic Party Feeling Thermometer	.19*** (1200)	.65*** (512)
Republican Party Feeling Thermometer	-.15*** (1197)	-.53*** (512)
Seven-Point Party Identification Scale	.19*** (1248)	.89*** (528)
Strength of Partisanship		
Folded Party Closeness Scale	.35*** (1226)	.02 (518)
Folded Party Support Scale	.31*** (1222)	.04 (517)
Four-Point Strength of Identification Scale	.37*** (1248)	.12** (528)
Independence		
Strength of Independence Scale	-.23*** (1228)	-.08* (526)
Independents Feeling Thermometer	-.10*** (1103)	-.11** (468)

a - Figures in parentheses are numbers of cases.

* Significant at the .05 level.
** Significant at the .01 level.
*** Significant at the .001 level.

measures predict defection better than others. In the pre-election wave, respondents were asked: "Have you always voted for the same party or have you voted for different parties for president?" Those who said they have voted for different parties were coded zero while those who said they have voted for the same party were coded 1. Table 6–10 shows the Pearson correlations between party identification and reported past party voting for president. There is a weak but significant relationship between partisan direction and whether respondents have voted for the same party. The direction of the correlations reveals that Democrats are more likely than Republicans to support their own party. The data also show that as voters' partisan strength increases, so does their willingness to back their party every four years. This relationship is stronger than the one between partisan direction and propensity to stand pat. As logic would dictate, independence tends to be accompanied by a desire to switch. The disparity in the size of the correlations between the partisan strength and independence measures and the tendency to stand pat indicates, however, that partisan strength and independence are unique components of party identification.

Following this question, standpatters were asked which major party's presidential candidates they have supported over the years.[43] Those who stated the "Republican party" were coded zero whereas those who responded the "Democratic party" were coded 1. As one might expect, the correlations in Table 6–10 between partisan direction and party vote are very high, revealing strong agreement between standpatters' party allegiance and their endorsement of their party's candidates. There is also a weak but significant relationship between the four-point partisan strength measure and party vote, suggesting that strong partisanship is associated with Democratic party support. However, the correlation between these two items probably reflects the numerical superiority of Democrats in the electorate more than anything else. Furthermore, the data show a slight tendency for Independents to vote consistently for Republican party nominees. This finding might be the product of a coincidental pattern of short term forces which could change in the future.

Significant discrepancies exist between the correlations for the party identification measures, whether respondents have always voted for the same party, and which party they have supported in the past. Our analysis reveals there is a significant difference between the correlations for the standard four-point partisan strength measure, the folded party support scale, and whether respondents are standpatters or switchers. In other words, the correlation between the standard four-point partisan strength measure and inclination to back the same party ($r = .37$) is significantly higher (at the .05 level) than the correlation between the folded party support measure and this variable ($r = .31$). Also, the relationship between the strength of independence scale and tendency to stand pat ($r = -.23$) is significantly stronger (at the .001 level) than the relationship between the Independents thermometer and this action ($r = -.10$). Moreover, the correlation between the traditional seven-point partisan direction measure and the party vote for standpatters is significantly greater (at the .001 level) than the correlations between the party closeness scale, the party support scale, the two feeling thermometers, and this item. The correlations between the old seven-point measure, the party difference index, and standpatters' party vote, however, are about the same size. Finally, the relationship between the standard four-point partisan strength measure and party vote is significantly closer (at the .05 level) than the relationship between the folded party closeness scale and this behavior.

Table 6-11
Pearson Correlations between Party Identification and Vote Switching, Post-Election Survey, 1980[a]

Items and Dimensions	Whether Respondents Switched Their Vote	Two-Party Vote
Partisan Direction		
Party Difference Index	.03 (499)	.86*** (403)
Party Closeness Scale	.04 (533)	.74*** (423)
Party Support Scale	.03 (532)	.72*** (422)
Democratic Party Feeling Thermometer	.04 (533)	.64*** (425)
Republican Party Feeling Thermometer	-.03 (536)	-.57*** (427)
Seven-Point Party Identification Scale	-.07 (547)	.78*** (434)
Strength of Partisanship		
Folded Party Closeness Scale	.24*** (533)	.23*** (423)
Folded Party Support Scale	.26*** (532)	.19*** (422)
Four-Point Strength of Identification Scale	.23*** (547)	.23*** (434)
Independence		
Strength of Independence Scale	-.03 (537)	-.07 (427)
Independents Feeling Thermometer	-.01 (499)	-.07 (399)

a - Figures in parentheses are numbers of cases.

* Significant at the .05 level.
** Significant at the .01 level.
*** Significant at the .001 level.

Respondents were also asked whom they voted for in the 1976 presidential election as well as in the 1980 election.[44] Those who voted for presidential candidates from the Republican and Democratic parties in the two elections were considered vote switchers and were coded zero, while those who voted for candidates from the same party were considered standpatters and were coded 1. Again, the validation study was used to verify turnout in 1980. Based on the data in Table 6–11, there is no relationship between partisan direction, political independence, and whether respondents switched their party vote in the Reagan-Carter election. Yet, partisan strength is related to whether voters stand pat; as partisan strength increases, so does tendency to stand pat. The noticeable dissimilarity in the size of the correlations between the strength of identification and independence measures and willingness to stand pat suggests that partisan strength and independence do not fall along a single continuum as commonly assumed.

There are significant differences between the correlations for the standard and alternative partisan direction measures and whether respondents switched their party vote. The standard seven-point measure is more closely related to propensity to defect than are the party difference index, the party closeness scale, the party support scale, and the Democrat thermometer (significant at least at the .01 level). The correlations between the partisan strength measures, the independence measures, and likelihood to switch do not vary significantly.

In order to provide a meaningful context in which to compare the party identification measures, we analyzed the relationship between party affiliation and the direction of the two-party presidential vote in 1976 and 1980. One would normally expect Republicans and Democrats to vote for their own party's nominees in two succeeding elections. Respondents who supported Ford and Reagan were coded zero and those who supported Carter both times were coded 1. The findings of this analysis are reported in Table 6–11. The relationship between partisan direction and the 1976 and 1980 party vote is very strong. As anticipated, Republicans and Democrats tended to vote for their party's candidate in both elections. The fact that the correlations are not perfect demonstrates that other variables besides partisan direction affected voters' preferences. On the surface, there appears to be a significant relationship between partisan strength and two-party vote. However, the predominance of Democrats in the electorate probably explains this finding. No relationship exists between political independence and whether respondents backed the Republicans or Democratic candidates in the two elections.

A number of significant disparities exist between the correlations for the various partisan direction measures and the two-party vote. For instance, the relationship between the standard seven-point measure and which party Americans voted for in the 1976 and 1980 elections is significantly stronger (at least at the .05 level) than the relationships between the party closeness scale, the party support scale, the Democrat thermometer, and this variable. The correlation between the standard seven-point measure and the party vote is also significantly higher than the absolute value of the correlation between the Republican thermometer and this behavior. This is not true, however, for the correlations between the party difference index, the seven-point measure, and which party standpatters supported in the two contests. In other words, the association between the party difference index and the party vote is significantly closer (at the .001 level) than the association between the traditional seven-point measure and this decision. *At least in the two elections under investigation, the party difference measure is a better predictor of standpatters' party vote than is the old seven-point scale.*

Split Ticket Voting

The debate between Burnham, Converse, and Rusk also centered on trends in split ticket voting (as one indicator of party infidelity) since the late 1800s and revealed how ballot reform accounted for variations in this type of behavior.[45] Rusk argued that the Massachusetts ballot forms, which were produced and distributed by the political parties, made it virtually impossible to ticket split.[46] But the introduction of the Australian office block ballot in the 1890s allowed voters to split their ticket more easily, thus explaining the sudden increase in this activity at the turn of the century.[47] Similarly, Campbell and Miller showed that straight ticket voting was most common in states which permitted voters to mark a party circle or pull a party lever in the voting machine.[48] They also found a close relationship between strength of partisanship and tendency to vote a straight ballot. That is, as partisan strength increased, so did willingness to vote a straight ticket. In fact, for strong party identifiers, the ballot form had no discernible effect on whether they voted a straight ticket.[49] In a later study, Campbell offered additional evidence which reaffirmed the importance of partisan strength as a motivational force in straight ticket voting.[50]

One must exercise caution when interpreting data on split ticket voting. A popular political figure, the ballot form, a scandal involving a candidate, and other salient, short-term forces can affect the way citizens vote in a given election. What may seem to be a surge or decline in party defection may actually represent a series of idiosyncratic events. Moreover, reports on ticket splitting are usually based on a collection of aggregate data, and it is dangerous to draw inferences about individual behavior from aggregate results.[51] In addition, Campbell and Miller discussed how voters can split their ballot in various patterns and how these patterns have different political implications.[52] The manner in which split ticket voting is conceptualized and measured may therefore influence one's conclusions. We will keep these things in mind as we analyze the relationship between party identification and ticket splitting.

Following the 1980 election respondents were asked whether they had cast a straight or split ticket ballot at the state and local level.[53] Those who stated they had voted a split ticket were coded zero, while those who stated they had voted a straight ticket were coded 1. Respondents who reported they had supported only one party were asked which party.[54] Republican straight ticket voters were coded zero, and Democratic straight ticket voters were coded 1. The Pearson correlations between party identification and responses to these two questions are shown in Table 6–12. With the exception of the Republican feeling thermometer, there is a weak but significant relationship between partisan direction and whether voters split their ticket. In other words, Democrats were more likely than Republicans to vote for all their party's candidates at the state and local

Table 6-12
Pearson Correlations between Party Identification and Split Ticket Voting at the State and Local Level, Post-Election Survey, 1980[a]

Items and Dimensions	Split Ticket or Straight Ticket	Straight Ticket Party Vote
Partisan Direction		
Party Difference Index	.09* (655)	.91*** (264)
Party Closeness Scale	.07* (710)	.77*** (271)
Party Support Scale	.11** (708)	.74*** (271)
Democratic Party Feeling Thermometer	.12*** (712)	.71*** (278)
Republican Party Feeling Thermometer	.00 (713)	-.58*** (279)
Seven-Point Party Identification Scale	.09** (730)	.84*** (284)
Strength of Partisanship		
Folded Party Closeness Scale	.34*** (710)	.15** (271)
Folded Party Support Scale	.25*** (708)	.19*** (271)
Four-Point Strength of Identification Scale	.29*** (730)	.19*** (284)
Independence		
Strength of Independence Scale	-.23*** (717)	-.09 (279)
Independents Feeling Thermometer	-.06 (673)	-.12* (260)

a - Figures in parentheses are numbers of cases.

* Significant at the .05 level.
** Significant at the .01 level.
*** Significant at the .001 level.

level in 1980. The relationship between partisan strength and inclination to ticket split is stronger. The data indicate that heightened party allegiance is accompanied by a tendency to vote for candidates from the same party. Furthermore, the direction of the correlation between the strength of independence scale and whether respondents had cast a straight or split ballot suggests that increased independence is associated with a greater likelihood to ticket split. This makes sense theoretically. These findings imply that partisan strength and independence are one and the same thing.

Not surprisingly, there is a strong relationship between partisan direction and the straight ticket party vote at the state and local level. The data clearly show that Republicans and Democrats who voted a straight ticket supported their party's nominees. Moreover, there appears to be a relationship between partisan strength and party vote, implying that strong partisans were most likely to endorse Democrats at the polls. However, this finding probably reflects the high percentage of loyal Democrats in the electorate. Finally, there is some evidence that Independents tended to support Republican candidates at the state and local level.

There are significant differences between the correlations for the individual party identification measures and the two items in Table 6–12. For example, the correlation between the standard seven-point measure and propensity to vote a split ticket on the state and local level is significantly higher (at the .05 level) than the correlation between the Republican thermometer and this action. Also, the correlation between the strength of independence scale and tendency to ticket split ($r = -.23$) is significantly higher (at the .001 level) than the correlation between the Independents thermometer and this decision ($r = -.06$). In addition, the relationship between the standard seven-point measure and party vote is significantly stronger (at the .001 level) than the relationships between the party closeness scale, the party support scale, the Democrat feeling thermometer, and this behavior. The same can be said about the absolute value of the correlations between the seven-point measure, the Republican thermometer, and which party straight ticket voters endorsed. One cannot draw this conclusion, however, about the correlations between the seven-point scale, the party difference index, and party vote. *According to the data, the party difference index is more closely related to the party vote than is the traditional seven-point measure (significant at the .001 level).*

Besides questioning respondents about the vote choice for president in 1980, interviewers also asked respondents about their vote choices for candidates for other federal government offices. Using this information we developed a measure of split ticket voting at the national level by comparing the party vote for president with the party vote for the House of Representatives. Researchers have traditionally construed split ticket voting this way.[55] Specifically, respondents who voted for candidates from opposing parties were coded zero, and those who voted for candidates from the same party were coded 1. The findings of an analysis between party identification and split ticket voting are reported in Table 6–13. The data show that there is a very weak correlation between the Republican thermometer and whether voters split their ballot ($r = -.07$), suggesting that Republicans tended to ticket split. The other five partisan direction items, however, are not related to engagement in this behavior. Furthermore, there is a relationship between partisan strength and split ticket voting. That is, as partisan strength increases, so does inclination to cast a straight ballot. Campbell and Miller, you will recall, also found this to be the case in their study of the American electorate in the 1950s. Moreover, the table shows that there is a correlation between the strength of independence scale and whether voters split their ticket ($r = -.11$). As one would imagine, increased indepen-

Table 6-13
Pearson Correlations between Party Identification and Split Ticket Voting at the National Level, Post-Election Survey, 1980[a]

Items and Dimensions	Split Ticket or Straight Ticket	Two-Party Vote
Partisan Direction		
Party Difference Index	.07 (548)	.84*** (390)
Party Closeness Scale	.02 (585)	.75*** (417)
Party Support Scale	.00 (584)	.69*** (416)
Democratic Party Feeling Thermometer	.07 (584)	.63*** (420)
Republican Party Feeling Thermometer	-.07* (587)	-.54*** (422)
Seven-Point Party Identification Scale	.02 (599)	.77*** (429)
Strength of Partisanship		
Folded Party Closeness Scale	.18*** (585)	.19*** (417)
Folded Party Support Scale	.11** (584)	.13** (416)
Four-Point Strength of Identification Scale	.17*** (599)	.20*** (429)
Independence		
Strength of Independence Scale	-.11** (593)	-.03 (427)
Independents Feeling Thermometer	-.05 (554)	-.11* (396)

a – Figures in parentheses are numbers of cases.

* Significant at the .05 level.
** Significant at the .01 level.
*** Significant at the .001 level.

dence leads to a greater tendency to ticket split. The size and direction of the correlations between the partisan strength measures, the strength of independence scale, and split ticket voting support the position that partisan strength and independence are unidimensional.

Similar to previous analyses, we again selected out straight ballot voters for the purpose of comparing the various partisan direction measures. Republicans who voted a straight ticket were scored zero, and Democrats who did likewise were scored 1. Table 6–13 indicates that there is a strong relationship between partisan direction and party voting. Stated another way, partisans who voted a straight ballot did so down their own party line. The relationship between partisan strength and this behavior is undoubtedly due to the numerical advantage of Democrats. As in Table 6–12, the correlation between the Independents thermometer and the party vote suggests that Independents who voted a straight ballot were most likely to support the Republican party.

There are several significant differences between the correlations for the six partisan direction measures and the two items in the table. The party difference index is more closely related (significant at the .05 level) to whether respondents split their ballot than is the standard seven-point measure. In addition, the correlation between the standard seven-point measure and party vote is significantly higher (at the .001 level) than the correlations between the party support scale, the Democrat thermometer, and this variable. The correlation between the seven-point measure and party vote is also significantly greater (at the .001 level) than the absolute value of the correlation between the Republican thermometer and this behavior. In contrast, however, *the relationship between the party difference index and whether straight ticket voters supported the Republican or Democratic party in 1980 ($r = .84$) is significantly stronger (at the .001 level) than the relationship between the traditional seven-point measure and this item ($r = .77$)*. No other differences were uncovered between the individual party identification measures and the two variables in Table 6–13.

SUMMARY

This chapter examined the relationship between party identification and voting behavior. While previous chapters investigated the social background and political attitudes of partisans, strong identifiers, and Independents, this segment of the study focused on the electoral activities of these individuals. The close theoretical link between party orientation and behavior often discussed in the literature places added significance on the findings concerning the interchangeability of the various party identification measures reported in this chapter.

The results of our analysis unmasked a considerable number of differences in the behavioral patterns of partisans and nonpartisans in 1980. We found that strong identifiers and, to a lesser extent, Republicans and Independents were the most likely to proselytize others to vote a certain way. Strong identifiers and, to a lesser degree, Republicans were also more likely to partake in different campaign activities than their counterparts in the electorate. In addition, partisan strength was found to share a positive relationship with frequency of past voting, voter registration, and turnout in the primaries and general election. Moreover, Republicans and Democrats tended to support candidates from their own party in races for the House of Representatives, Senate, and White House. While Democrats and strong partisans demonstrated a tendency to vote for presidential candidates from the same party in the 1976 and 1980 elections, Independents tended to switch. The latter group was also more likely to ticket split at all levels of government, whereas Democrats only engaged in this behavior at the state and local level. Lastly, increased partisan strength was associated with a greater likelihood to stand pat and vote a straight party ballot.

The analysis of party identification and electoral behavior provided an opportunity for us to investigate further whether partisan strength and political independence fall along a single continuum as commonly assumed. The size and direction of the correlations between the partisan strength and independence measures, primary election turnout, and split ticket voting at the local, state, and national levels supported the view that strength of identification and independence are unidimensional. But more often than not we found evidence to the contrary. For example, strength of party attachment was related to whether respondents were registered to vote in 1980 while independence was not related to this behavior. An analysis of party orientation and vote switching yielded a similar result. At the same time the correlations between the indicators of partisan strength and independence, whether respondents tried to influence the votes of others, and whether they had contributed money to a candidate were in the same direction. These and other results indicate that partisan strength and independence are indeed two separate components of party identification.

Furthermore, we discovered significant differences between the correlations for the six partisan direction measures and the behaviors we studied. In several cases, the standard seven-point party identification scale was found to be a better predictor of behavior than the alternative measures. For example, the seven-point scale was more closely related to whether respondents had worked for a political campaign than was the party difference index. The standard measure was also more closely related to party registration than the new measures. With the exception of the party difference index, the old seven-point measure was a better predictor of the party primary vote. In addition, the seven-point measure was more strongly associated with respondents' vote choices for the House, Senate, and presidency than the two party thermometers. However, the party difference measure was found to be a more accurate estimate of the presidential vote. Upon extending this analysis, we found that the party difference measure explained more variation in the two-party presidential vote between 1964 and 1980 than did the seven-point scale. Moreover, the party difference index was a more accurate determinant of the two-party vote for standpatters and straight ticket voters than was the standard seven-point measure. These findings represent a serious challenge to those who advocate the continued use of the traditional seven-point scale.

We also uncovered significant differences between the correlations for the partisan strength measures and electoral behavior. For instance, the folded party support scale was found to be a better predictor of participation in four of the six campaign activities examined. This finding suggests that "party support" is more germane within the context of campaign activity than is "strength of identification." The standard four-point measure, however, was more closely related to whether respondents had voted for the same party for president in the past than was the folded party support measure. Moreover, the relationship between the traditional four-point measure and primary election turnout was stronger than the relationship between the folded party closeness scale and this variable.

A few significant disparities were found between the correlations for the two independence measures and electoral behavior. Most notably, the correlations between the strength of independence scale, whether respondents had voted for the same party for president over the years, and whether they had split their ticket on the state and local level in 1980 were higher than the correlations between the Independence thermometer and these criterion variables. These findings are revealing because they involve items that directly address defection, a behavior thought to be closely associated with political independence. The fact that the strength of independence scale predicted defection more precisely makes it a superior measure of independence in the context of political behavior. Overall, we found no discrepancies in the direction of the (significant) correlations between the various party identification measures and the criterion variables analyzed in this chapter. The next and last chapter will provide some general observations about Republicans, Democrats, party enthusiasts, and Independents in 1980, comment on the dimensionality of partisan strength and independence, and discuss the implications of the study's findings for the use of the individual party identification measures in future research.

NOTES

1. Sidney Verba and Norman H. Nie, *Participation in America: Political Democracy and Social Equality* (New York: Harper and Row, 1972). Also refer to: Sidney Verba, Norman H. Nie, and Jae-on Kim, *Participation and Political Equality* (New York: Cambridge University Press, 1978).
2. Ibid., p. 32.
3. Lester Milbrath and M. Lal Goel, *Political Participation: How and Why Do People Get Involved in Politics?* Second Edition (Chicago: Rand McNally, 1977).
4. Ibid., p. 24.
5. Although Americans participate infrequently, few political scientists express great concern about the future of democracy in this country. Other devices and conditions, such as leader-citizen linkage mechanisms, help ensure the continued existence of our democratic form of government. For further elaboration of this point see: Robert A. Dahl, *A Preface to Democratic Theory* (Chicago: University of Chicago Press, 1956); V.O. Key, *Public Opinion and American Democracy* (New York: Knopf, 1961), Chap. 21.
6. Verba and Nie, *Participation in America*, pp. 60–73.
7. Ibid., Chap. 12.
8. Ibid., p. 225.
9. The questions were worded in the following manner:

We would like to find out about some of the things people do to help a party or a candidate win an election. During the campaign, did you talk to any people and try to show them why they should vote for one of the parties or candidates?

Did you go to any political meetings, rallies, fundraisers, or things like that?

Did you do any (other) work for one of the parties or candidates (during the campaign)?

Did you wear a campaign button or put a campaign sticker on your car?

Now a few questions about giving money during this last election campaign . . . Did you give any money this year to a candidate running for public office?

Apart from contributions to specific candidates, how about contributions to any of the political parties? Did you give money to a political party during this election year?

10. William H. Flanigan and Nancy H. Zingale, *Political Behavior of the American Electorate*, Fourth Edition (Boston: Allyn and Bacon, 1979), p. 14.

11. Raymond E. Wolfinger and Steven J. Rosenstone, *Who Votes*? (New Haven: Yale University Press, 1980), p. 73.

12. Flanigan and Zingale, *Political Behavior of the American Electorate*, p. 14. Also refer to: William G. Andrews, "American Voting Participation," *Western Political Quarterly* Vol. 19 (December 1966), pp. 639–52.

13. A study conducted by Jerrold Rusk and John Stucker showed that the poll tax was the most effective device. Jerold G. Rusk and John J. Stucker, "The Effect of the Southern System of Election Laws on Voting Participation: A Reply to V.O. Key, Jr.," in *The History of American Electoral Behavior*, ed. Joel Silbey, Allan Bogue, and William Flanigan (Princeton: Princeton University Press, 1978), pp. 198–250.

14. Kristi Andersen, "Generation, Partisan Shift, and Realignment: A Glance Back to the New Deal," in *The Changing American Voter*, ed. Norman H. Nie, Sidney Verba, and John R. Petrocik, Enlarged Edition (Cambridge: Harvard University Press, 1979), pp. 77, 89.

15. Walter Dean Burnham, "The Changing Shape of the American Political Universe," *American Political Science Review* Vol. 59 (March 1965), pp. 7–28; Walter Dean Burnham, *Critical Elections and the Mainsprings of American Politics* (New York: W.W. Norton, 1970); Jerrold G. Rusk, "The Effect of the Australian Ballot Reform on Split Ticket Voting: 1876–1908," *American Political Science Review* Vol. 64 (December 1970), pp. 1220–38; and Philip E. Converse, "Change in the American Electorate," in *The Human Meaning of Social Change*, ed. Angus Campbell and Philip E. Converse (New York: Russell Sage Foundation, 1972), pp. 263–337.

16. Walter Dean Burnham, "Theory and Voting Research: Some Reflections on Converse's 'Change in the American Electorate'," *American Political Science Review* Vol. 68 (September 1974), p. 1002. Also see comments by Converse and Rusk and Burnham's rejoinder in this issue of the *Review*, pp. 1024–57.

17. Verba and Nie, *Participation in America*, Chap. 9.

18. Ibid., p. 138; and Milbrath and Goel, *Political Participation*, p. 144.

19. Wolfinger and Rosenstone, *Who Votes*?, Chap. 2.

20. Angus Campbell, Philip E. Converse, Warren E. Miller, and Donald E. Stokes, *The American Voter* (New York: John Wiley and Sons, 1960), Chap. 5.

21. Verba and Nie, *Participation in America*, pp. 214–15.

22. Campbell, Converse, Miller, and Stokes, *The American Voter*, pp. 96–101.

23. This does not imply that the validation study is completely error free. A few mistakes may have been made in recording and coding information. This source of error is always a problem.

24. A cross-tabular analysis shows that a large percentage of nonpartisans did indeed register with one of the two parties.

25. Paul R. Abramson, John H. Aldrich, and David W. Rohde, *Change and Conti-*

nuity in the 1980 Elections (Washington, D.C.: Congressional Quarterly Press, 1982), p. 13.

26. Ibid., pp. 89–90; and Wolfinger and Rosenstone, *Who Votes?*, Chap. 6.

27. Philip E. Converse, "The Concept of A Normal Vote," in *Elections and the Political Order*, ed. Angus Campbell et al. (New York: John Wiley and Sons, 1966), pp. 9–39.

28. For example see: Norman H. Nie, Sidney Verba, and John R. Petrocik, *The Changing American Voter*, Enlarged Edition (Cambridge: Harvard University Press, 1979), pp. 373–78.

29. Campbell, Converse, Miller, and Stokes, *The American Voter*.

30. Philip E. Converse, Angus Campbell, Warren E. Miller, and Donald E. Stokes, "Stability and Change in 1960: A Reinstating Election," in *Elections and the Political Order*, ed. Angus Campbell et al., pp. 78–95.

31. John R. Petrocik, "Contextual Sources of Voting Behavior: The Changeable American Voter," in *The Electorate Reconsidered*, ed. John C. Pierce and John L. Sullivan (Beverly Hills, Calif.: Sage Publications, 1980), pp. 257–77.

32. The survey questions read:

Who did you vote for (in the election for the House of Representatives in Washington)?
Who did you vote for (for the United States Senate)?
Who did you vote for (in the election for president)?

Since only one-third of the Senate is elected every two years, not all the respondents had an opportunity to vote in a senatorial election.

33. This observation has been made about off-year Congressional elections in: Donald E. Stokes and Warren E. Miller, "Party Government and the Saliency of Congress," in *Elections and the Political Order*, ed. Angus Campbell et al., pp. 194–211; and Flanigan and Zingale, *Political Behavior in the American Electorate*, pp. 42–47.

34. Herbert F. Weisberg, "A Multidimensional Conceptualization of Party Identification," *Political Behavior* Vol. 2 No. 1 (1980), pp. 33–60.

35. Ibid.

36. Ibid., p. 48.

37. Ibid., p. 58, footnote 12. Questions concerning the reliability and stability of the party difference index are raised in: Michael D. McDonald and Susan E. Howell, "Reconsidering the Reconceptualizations of Party Identification," *Political Methodology* Vol. 8 No. 4 (1982), pp. 73–91.

38. David Hill and Norman Luttbeg, *Trends in American Electoral Behavior*, Second Edition (Itasca, Ill.: F.E. Peacock Publishers, 1983), pp. 32–38. Also consult: Angus Campbell and Warren E. Miller, "The Motivational Basis of Straight and Split Ticket Voting," *American Political Science Review* Vol. 51 (June 1957), pp. 293–312; V.O. Key, *The Responsible Electorate: Rationality in Presidential Voting, 1936–1960* (Cambridge: Harvard University Press, 1966); Walter DeVries and V. Lance Tarrance, *The Ticket-Splitter: A New Force in American Politics* (Grand Rapids: William B. Eerdmans Publishing Company, 1972); Jack Dennis, "Trends in Public Support for the American Party System," *British Journal of Political Science* Vol. 5 Part 2 (April 1975), pp. 187–230; and Ruth K. Scott and Ronald J. Hrebenar, *Parties in Crisis* (New York: John Wiley and Sons, 1979).

39. V.O. Key, *The Responsible Electorate*.

40. Ibid., p. 16.

41. Ibid., p. 150.

42. Ibid.

43. The wording of the question was: "Which party was that (that R has always voted for, for president)?"

44. The following item was included in the pre-election survey: "Which one did you vote for (candidate in the 1976 presidential election)?"

45. Burnham, "The Changing Shape of the American Political Universe," and *Critical Elections and the Mainsprings of American Politics*; Rusk, "The Effect of the Australian Ballot Reform on Split Ticket Voting"; and Converse, "Change in the American Electorate."

46. Rusk, "The Effect of the Australian Ballot Reform on Split Ticket Voting."

47. Jack Walker has also demonstrated how the ballot form affects voting behavior. Jack L. Walker, "Ballot Forms and Voter Fatigue: An Analysis of the Office Block and Party Column Ballots," *Midwest Journal of Political Science* Vol. 10 (November 1966), pp. 448–63.

48. Campbell and Miller, "The Motivational Basis of Straight and Split Ticket Voting." Today twenty states allow voters to mark a party box or pull a party lever. Voters in Georgia and North Carolina have this option only in primary elections. Voters in Oklahoma can cast a straight party ticket only for each level of government. The Council of State Governments, *The Book of the States, 1980–81* Volume 23 (Lexington, Kentucky: Council of State Governments, 1980), p. 65.

49. Ibid., p. 307.

50. Angus Campbell, "Surge and Decline: A Study of Electoral Change," in *Elections and the Political Order*, ed. Angus Campbell et al., pp. 40–62.

51. Also see: Andrew T. Cowart, "A Cautionary Note on Aggregate Indicators of Split Ticket Voting," *Political Methodology* Vol. 1 (Winter 1974), pp. 109–30.

52. Campbell and Miller, "The Motivational Basis of Straight and Split Ticket Voting."

53. Specifically, respondents were asked: "How about the elections for other state and local offices—did you vote a straight ticket, or did you vote for candidates from different parties?"

54. The question simply read: "(If R voted a straight ticket) which party?"

55. For example, this approach is adopted in: Milton Cummings, Jr., *Congressmen and the Electorate: Elections for the U.S. House and the President, 1920–1964* (New York: Free Press, 1967), pp. 28–55. DeVries and Tarrance also made this point in: DeVries and Tarrance, *Ticket-Splitter*.

7
OBSERVATIONS AND CONCLUSIONS

This book has presented the findings of an extensive investigation of party identification. As indicated at the outset, recent studies have challenged the unidimensional conceptualization of party identification presented in *The American Voter* and adopted in subsequent works.[1] At issue is whether the concept is unidimensional or multidimensional. In favor of the latter position, we developed a multidimensional model of the concept using the old and new party identification items included in the 1980 National Election Study and examined the relationships between a large number of criterion variables and these items. Presumably, the most accurate measures of the concept would be those most closely related to the different external variables. The study also examined whether partisan strength and political independence are unidimensional, as assumed in the literature, or bidimensional. Along the way we were able to gain additional insights into the social background, political attitudes, and electoral behavior of Republicans, Democrats, strong party identifiers, and Independents.

Drawing upon the findings presented in this study, this chapter first presents some general observations about the social characteristics, attitudes, and behavior of partisans, intense partisans, and Independents in 1980. We then examine whether partisan strength and independence represent one or two dimensions. This is followed by a summary analysis of the various party identification measures and conclusions concerning their future usage. The limitations of our study and the areas in which additional research is needed are discussed at the end of the chapter.

MEMBERS OF THE ELECTORATE

This section reviews the social characteristics of Republicans, Democrats, strong party loyalists, and Independents and discusses how they think and behave. The employment of a three dimensional party identification model has allowed us to broaden our understanding of these members of the electorate. Because we primarily analyzed data collected in the 1980 election study, it should be kept in mind that our findings cannot be easily generalized beyond this time period. Republicans are examined first.

Republicans

Republicans possess a number of characteristics that set them apart from the rest of the electorate. They are predominantly white, Protestant, and support the Moral Majority. They are likely to be well educated and have prestigious jobs and high incomes. Both parents of Republicans tended to be Republicans as well. The data showed that Republicans were relatively knowledgeable about the presidential candidates running in 1980. In addition, Republicans watched the Carter-Reagan debate on television and felt that their candidate had performed better. Though they feel warm toward "big business," they hold less affection for "civil rights leaders" and "people on welfare."

Republicans hold fairly consistent views on policy issues. They favor more defense spending and less public services spending. Also, they oppose "aid to minorities," "big" government, the Equal Rights Amendment (ERA), and further expansion of civil rights protection. In general, these members of the electorate consider themselves to be more conservative than liberal. Many Republicans were dissatisfied with the Democratic party and President Carter's performance in office. In 1980 they felt that their party could handle the problems associated with war and the economy better than the Democrats. Moreover, they believed Carter had mishandled the economy, the Iranian hostage crisis, and the Soviet Union's invasion of Afghanistan. Overall, they disapproved of Carter's performance as President. Predictably, Reagan received high marks on his personal attributes and qualifications from them, and they thought he would win the election.

Republicans generally tend to participate in electoral activities. They contribute money to parties and candidates as well as engage in other activities (e.g., displaying a button or sticker). These voters register to vote with their party, vote in their party's primaries, and support their party's nominees in races for the House, Senate, and presidency. Finally, and not surprisingly, they are most likely to back their party's candidates when they stand pat or vote a straight party ticket.

Democrats

The composition of the Democratic party tends to be more heterogeneous than the Republican party. For instance, a much higher proportion of blacks than whites identify with the Democratic party. We also found that an equal percentage of Protestants and Catholics affiliated with the Democratic party in 1980. Democrats are likely to have a lower socioeconomic status and more trust in the federal government than Republicans and Independents. For the most part, their parents were Democrats too.

Compared to other voters, Democrats differ in their opinions on groups, issues, parties, and candidates. They tend to feel positively toward minorities, "older people," "labor unions," "civil rights leaders," and "people on welfare." They are likely to favor aid to minorities, decreases in defense spending, and increases in government services spending, and they believe the federal government has not become too strong. Based on our analysis, Democrats think of themselves as being more liberal than conservative. Furthermore, they feel that their party can handle matters pertaining to war and the economy better than the Republican party. Unlike other voters, they approved of the way Carter handled the economy, the Iranian hostage crisis, and the presidency in general. However, they were somewhat more split over the outcome of the Carter-Reagan debate than were Republicans. Carter's personal attributes and qualifications were evaluated positively by this group of voters, and they thought he would win the election.

Democrats also differ from Republicans in terms of their electoral behavior. While they are more likely to try to persuade others to vote a certain way, they are less likely to become actively involved in a campaign. As one would expect, they register to vote with the Democratic party and vote in their party's primaries. In addition, they have voted for the same party for president in previous elections and, in 1980, supported their party's candidates for the House, Senate, and presidency. Not surprisingly, they back their party's candidates when they stand pat and cast a straight party ballot.

Strong Party Identifiers

A third group of voters examined in this study is strong party identifiers. Blacks and the old tend to be overrepresented among these voters. Strong partisans are interested in politics, concerned about the outcome of elections, and follow the campaign on television. Many reported that they saw the Carter-Reagan debate. They are somewhat politically efficacious and support the party system. In addition, they hold favorable attitudes toward "blacks," "older people," "people on welfare," "labor unions," "big business," and "civil rights leaders." These opinions, however, are probably influenced by other factors (e.g., race and party identity) rather than partisan strength per se.

As one would guess, intense party loyalists are actively involved in election campaigns. They attempt to affect the votes of others and participate in a variety of campaign activities (e.g., attending meetings and rallies). They were more likely to turn out regularly in the 1980 primaries and general election than were weak partisans. Strong party identifiers also tend to stand pat and vote a straight ticket.

Independents

Independents now make up a substantial portion of the electorate. Because of the comparatively small size of the Republican party and lower turnout rates among Democrats, it is becoming increasingly difficult for candidates from either party to win elections without the backing of Independents. In other words, they represent the potential "swing vote" in every election and, if their numbers continue to grow in the future, there will likely be even greater competition for their votes. This study's findings concerning Independents take on added significance for these reasons.

According to our analysis, Independents possess a unique and interesting set of social and political attributes. They tend to be young and white, and, like Republicans, they are well educated, hold prestigious jobs, and earn good incomes. Their high level of education probably explains why they prefer to follow the campaign through the printed media, and were reasonably informed about the presidential candidates in 1980. Although they were interested in the presidential election, they did not care which candidate won. Further analysis revealed that Independents did not particularly like either Carter or Reagan. While they have negative feelings about the Moral Majority, their attitudes toward other segments of the electorate are mixed.

Independents' views on issues, parties, and candidates vary from those held by other voters. They believe that the government has become too strong, and they favor decreases in appropriations for national defense and government services. At the same time they support the passage of the ERA and continued expansion of civil rights protection. Generally speaking, they perceive themselves as being closer to the liberal than the conservative end of the spectrum. Independents think that the Republican party can better deal with the nation's economic maladies, but they clearly do not support the party system. Furthermore, this group of voters disagreed with the manner in which Carter handled inflation and unemployment, the Iranian hostage crisis, and the presidency. They also questioned his ability to solve the country's economic problems and provide strong leadership. Lastly, they were "disgusted" with both candidates running for the White House in 1980, but said that Reagan gave them "hope."

In addition, we analyzed the electoral behavior of Independents. These citizens tried to proselytize others to vote a specific way and contributed money to a candidate. They did not vote for either party in the House and Senate elections; however, there is some evidence that they supported Reagan for president. They also exhibited a propensity to switch their party vote for president in the past and split their ballot in 1980. Based on these findings, the disinterested and uninvolved Independents of the 1950s are being replaced by a more politically aware and active generation of Independents in the 1980s.

PARTISAN STRENGTH AND POLITICAL INDEPENDENCE

A major goal of this study was to investigate whether strength of partisanship and political independence represent one dimension or two dimensions. Both elements are assumed to be inverse in the voting behavior literature. In order to see whether this is true, we compared the size and direction of the correlations between the partisan strength and independence measures and the criterion variables. If partisan strength and independence fall along the same continuum, then we would expect to find these correlations to be in the opposite direction and about the same size. However, if the two are distinct entities, then we should find these correlations to be either in the same direction or differ noticeably in size. The large number and varied nature of the criterion variables enabled us to conduct an extensive examination of this issue. Taken together, the study's findings indicate that partisan strength and independence are indeed two different things. There are many instances in which the correlations between the partisan strength and independence measures and the criterion variables were either in the same direction or differed noticeably in magnitude. We found correlations of the same sign between these measures and, for example, class self-identification, interest in the campaign, attention to the campaign in newspapers and the electronic media, knowledge about the presidential candidates, whether respondents watched the Carter-Reagan debate and tried to influence the votes of others, attitudes toward civil rights leaders, and contributions to a candidate. And even when the correlations had opposite signs, we found a substantial gap between the correlations involving the partisan strength and independence items and, for example, family income, the Duncan SEI, level of education, concern over the outcome of the election, attention to the campaign in magazines, ideological self-identification, party system support, and various forms of electoral behavior. *These findings challenge the prevailing assumption in the literature that strength of identification is inverse to independence, and they strongly suggest that partisan strength and independence are two separate components of party orientation.*

MEASURES OF PARTY IDENTIFICATION

The following discussion will focus on the various party identification measures analyzed throughout this study. Our analysis has examined a large number of relationships between party identification and different criterion variables, many of which vary in their theoretical significance. Assessments governing the future employment of the individual party orientation measures will be primarily based on the closeness (both empirically and theoretically) of the relationships between these indicators and the most important criterion variables. The assumption behind this strategy is that the best measures of the concept will be those most strongly correlated with the most important external variables. We begin by examining the standard and alternative partisan direction items.

The Partisan Direction Measures

In Chapter Two we analyzed the relationships between a host of social background characteristics and the standard and alternative partisan direction measures. Race and income were more closely correlated with the standard seven-point party identification scale than with the Republican party thermometer. The Duncan SEI was also more strongly related to the traditional seven-point measure than to the party support scale and the Republican thermometer. The same findings were obtained in an analysis of education and partisan direction; however, education tended to be a more accurate predictor of Democrat thermometer scores than of scores on the seven-point measure. More importantly, the party affiliation of respondents' parents was a better predictor of position on the old seven-point scale than of position on all the new partisan direction measures. Equally illuminating was the finding that the most significant social background variables were able to explain the highest percentage of the variance in the standard seven-point measure. It therefore appears that the seven-point measure is the best indicator of partisan direction within the context of the social environment.

Another set of criterion variables analyzed in this study was attitudes toward groups, issues, parties, and candidates. Although the correlations between opinions on "blacks," "people on welfare," "civil rights leaders," and the standard seven-point measure proved to be stronger than the correlations between opinions on these groups and the Republican thermometer, both the Democrat thermometer and the party difference index were better estimates of views on these individuals. In addition, feelings about "labor unions" and "big business" were more closely related to the Democrat and Republican thermometers, respectively, than to the traditional seven-point measure. While the standard seven-point scale was a more accurate determinant of perceived outcome of the Carter-Reagan debate than was the Republican thermometer, the party difference index was more closely related to this item. The party difference index also excelled in its ability to predict views on most of the policy issues addressed in this study. However, the relationship between ideological self-classification and the seven-point measure was stronger than the relationships between the party thermometers and this criterion variable. In most cases we found the correlations between retrospective evaluations of Carter, the professional qualifications of Carter and Reagan, and the standard and alternative partisan direction measures to be about equal. In contrast, the party difference index and the two party thermometers were better predictors of views on the presidential candidates' personal qualities in 1980. There was also a higher correlation between the party difference index and who would win the presidential election than between the usual seven-point scale and this question. Hence, according to these results, *the traditional seven-point measure is not always interchangeable with the alternative partisan direction items, and in many cases the party thermometers and especially the party difference index clearly outperform the old measure.*

The sixth chapter reported the findings of an analysis between electoral behavior and the various partisan direction measures. These findings are crucial to our assessment of the separate partisan direction items because of the close theoretical relationship between partisanship and voting behavior. Data collected in the validation study showed that the standard seven-point measure was a more precise estimate of voter registration with a party than were the new partisan direction measures. Excluding the party difference index, the same findings were uncovered in our analysis of the party primary vote, past party voting for president, the seven-point scale, and the alternative partisan direction items. Moreover, the standard seven-point measure was a better predictor of the two-party vote for the House, Senate, and presidency than were the party thermometers. More significantly, however, *the party difference index was a better estimate of the two-party presidential vote in 1980 than was the often used seven-point measure*. Furthermore, a longitudinal analysis revealed this to be the case in *every* presidential election since 1964. We also found the party difference index to be a more accurate gauge of the two-party vote when respondents stood pat in 1976 and 1980 and voted a straight ticket on the local, state, and national levels. *Thus, the party difference index is a superior measure of partisan direction within the context of electoral behavior.*

After examining the relationships between partisan direction and the most prominent criterion variables, we must conclude that the party difference index is the best indicator of partisanship. The degree to which this measure outperformed the standard seven-point scale on questions relating to groups, issues, presidential candidates, and electoral behavior is striking and cannot be ignored. Researchers should therefore seriously consider replacing the old measure of partisan direction with this new one. Those who often conduct time-series analyses will take comfort in the fact that the two party thermometer items used to construct the party difference index have been included in the SRC/CPS National Election Studies since 1964. This also allows analysts to investigate whether this study's findings and conclusions concerning the party difference and seven-point measures hold up prior to 1980. But let us not totally disregard the strong correlations found between the seven-point measure and some of the criterion variables, as well as its close association with social background. These findings and the fact that it has been widely used in surveys since 1952 warrant its inclusion in future surveys. Its continued employment will provide researchers greater analytical flexibility, particularly in instances where they wish to study changes in a relationship between partisan direction and another variable since the early 1950s. Overall, however, the party difference index is a more accurate measure of partisan direction.[2]

The Partisan Strength Measures

Our findings concerning the standard and alternative partisan strength measures differed markedly from those involving the partisan direction measures. The correlations between the three partisan strength measures, interest in the campaign, concern over the election outcome, whether respondents were registered to vote, turnout in the general election, tendency to stand pat, and likelihood of casting a straight party ballot at all levels of government were similar in strength. The only major challenge to the standard four-point strength of identification scale came from the rival folded party support measure in the context of campaign activity. Location on the folded party support scale was a more accurate determinant of whether respondents tried to affect the votes of others, contributed money to a party, displayed a button or sticker, and attended meetings or rallies than was location on the traditional four-point partisan strength measure. In contrast, the old four-point measure was more closely related to the party system support scale, whether "the best rule in voting is to pick a candidate regardless of party label," whether "it is better to be a firm party supporter than to be a political independent," turnout in primary elections, and propensity to vote for the same party for president previously than were either one or both rival partisan strength measures. Moreover, social background accounted for a higher proportion of the variance in the four-point measure than in the folded party support and folded party closeness scales. *Thus, excluding the realm of campaign activity, the standard four-point scale is the best measure of partisan strength.* Students of politics who are interested in the relationship between partisan strength and participation in campaigns may wish to employ the folded party support scale in their analysis.

The Political Independence Measures

Research by Herbert Weisberg, and David Valentine and John Van Wingen has pointed to the failure of the standard party identification questions to measure political independence adequately.[3] Their studies' findings prompted them to call for the development of a new, unidimensional measure of independence. As a step in this direction, we have examined the relationships between two possible independence measures—an Independents feeling thermometer and a strength of independence scale—and several relevant outside variables. Let us now evaluate the predictive power of the independence measures and make a recommendation concerning their future use.

In this regard, the study's findings are clear-cut. We found that race, income, the Duncan SEI, and education were more strongly correlated with the strength of independence scale than with the Independents thermometer. In addition, the social environment explained a higher percentage of the variance in the strength of independence measure than in the Independents thermometer. We also found the strength of independence measure to be a more accurate predictor of knowledge about the presidential candidates. Far more revealing, however, was that this measure was more closely related to the party system support scale, whether "the best rule in voting is to pick a candidate regardless of party label," whether "it is better to be a firm party supporter than to be a political independent," willingness to vote for different parties for president before 1980, and tendency to ticket split on the state and local level. *Clearly, the data show that the strength of independence scale is the best measure of party independence.*

CLOSING REMARKS

In summarizing a study such as this there is always a temptation to state the findings definitively, as if they were now engraved in stone. As much as I might like to do this, I am fully aware that this study has several limitations. For instance, the data examined were primarily collected in one year, 1980. To what extent are this investigation's findings applicable to other time periods? Also, how stable are the party difference index and the strength of independence scale over time, and how will they behave under varying political conditions? Subsequent studies should address these questions.

If we have learned anything here it is that the concept of party identification is not unidimensional as originally thought but is multidimensional. After evaluating the results of this study it appears that partisan direction, partisan strength, and independence—the three dimensions of party identification—can best be measured by using the party difference index, the four-point strength of identification scale, and the strength of independence scale, respectively. Such an approach will allow researchers to capture multiple identifications which might exist among voters (as Weisberg maintained).[4] Thus, an outgrowth of this investigation is a parsimonious and complete multidimensional model of party identification.

Of course, I have only developed one possible model of the concept, and others exist. For example, William Claggett argued that partisan strength is probably composed of two separate dimensions—partisan acquisition and partisan intensity—and not just one, as many (including myself) have assumed.[5] His hypothesis deserves serious consideration and testing, particularly in light of the findings uncovered in this analysis. Although I have taken the first step, alternative theories and measures of party identification need to be developed and analyzed if we are to continue to make progress in this area.

NOTES

1. Angus Campbell, Philip E. Converse, Warren E. Miller, and Donald E. Stokes, *The American Voter* (New York: John Wiley and Sons, 1960).

2. Questions concerning the reliability and stability of the party difference index are raised in: Michael D. McDonald and Susan E. Howell, "Reconsidering the Reconceptualizations of Party Identification," *Political Methodology* Vol. 8 No. 4 (1982), pp. 73–91. McDonald and Howell's findings also challenge the validity of the party difference measure; however, their analysis is flawed in two respects. First, the assumptions on which their causal model is based are questionable. They assume, for example, that the relation between party identification and the two-party presidential vote in 1976 is reciprocal and the causal direction of party identification and vote choice in 1972 cannot be specified. Second, their criterion variables are very limited in scope. One cannot therefore have a high degree of confidence in their results.

3. Herbert F. Weisberg, "A Multidimensional Conceptualization of Party Identification," *Political Behavior* Vol. 2 No. 1 (1980), pp. 33–60; and David C. Valentine and

John R. Van Wingen, "Partisanship, Independence, and the Partisan Identification Question," *American Politics Quarterly* Vol. 8 (April 1980), pp. 165–86.

4. Weisberg, "A Multidimensional Conceptualization of Party Identification."

5. William Claggett, "Partisan Acquisition Versus Partisan Intensity: Life-Cycle, Generation, and Period Effects, 1952–1976," *American Journal of Political Science* Vol. 25 (May 1981), pp. 193–214.

BIBLIOGRAPHY

Aberbach, Joel. "Alienation and Political Behavior." *American Political Science Review* Vol. 63 (March 1969), 86–99.

Abramowitz, Alan. "The Impact of a Presidential Debate on Voter Rationality." *American Journal of Political Science* Vol. 22 (August 1978), pp. 680–90.

Abramson, Paul R. "Generational Change in the American Electorate." *American Political Science Review* Vol. 68 (March 1974), pp. 93–105.

Abramson, Paul R. "Generational Change and the Decline of Party Identification in America: 1952–1974." *American Political Science Review* Vol. 70 (June 1976), pp. 469–78.

Abramson, Paul R. "Developing Party Identification: A Further Examination of Life-Cycle, Generational, and Period Effects." *American Journal of Political Science* Vol. 23 (February 1979), pp. 78–96.

Abramson, Paul R. and Ada W. Finifter. "On the Meaning of Political Trust: New Evidence from Items Introduced in 1978." *American Journal of Political Science* Vol. 25 (May 1981), pp. 297–307.

Abramson, Paul R., John H. Aldrich, and David W. Rohde. *Change and Continuity in the 1980 Elections* (Washington, D.C.: Congressional Quarterly Press, 1982).

Agger, Robert E., Marshall N. Goldstein, and Stanley A. Pearl. "Political Cynicism: Measurement and Meaning." *Journal of Politics* Vol. 23 (August 1961), pp. 477–506.

American Political Science Review. Vol. 66, Articles on Issue Voting (June 1972), pp. 415–70.

Andersen, Kristi. "Generation, Partisan Shift, and Realignment: A Glance Back to the New Deal," in *The Changing American Voter* by Norman Nie, Sidney Verba, and John R. Petrocik, Enlarged Edition (Cambridge: Harvard University Press, 1979), Chap. 5.

Andersen, Kristi. *The Creation of A Democratic Majority, 1928–1936* (Chicago: University of Chicago Press, 1979).

Andrews, William G. "American Voting Participation." *Western Political Quarterly* Vol. 19 (December 1966), pp. 639–52.

Asher, Herbert B. *Presidential Elections and American Politics: Voters, Candidates, and Campaigns Since 1952*, Revised Edition (Homewood, Ill.: The Dorsey Press, 1980).

Baker, Kendall. "Generational Differences in the Role of Party Identification in German Political Behavior." *American Journal of Political Science* Vol. 22 (February 1978), pp. 106–29.

Balch, George I. "Multiple Indicators in Survey Research: The Concept 'Sense of Political Efficacy.'" *Political Methodology* Vol. 1 (Spring 1974), pp. 1–43.

Beck, Paul Allen. "A Socialization Theory of Partisan Realignments," in *The Politics of Future Citizens*, ed. Richard G. Niemi et al. (San Francisco: Josey-Bass, 1974), pp. 200–206.

Belknap, George and Angus Campbell. "Political Party Identification and Attitudes Toward Foreign Policy." *Public Opinion Quarterly* Vol. 15 (Winter 1952), pp. 601–23.

Berelson, Bernard, Paul F. Lazarsfeld, and William McPhee. *Voting: A Study of Opinion Formation in a Presidential Election* (Chicago: University of Chicago Press, 1954).

Bishop, George F., Alfred J. Tuchfarber, and Robert W. Oldendick. "Change in the Structure of American Political Attitudes: The Nagging Question of Question Wording." *American Journal of Political Science* Vol. 22 (May 1978), pp. 250–69.

Bishop, George F., Alfred J. Tuchfarber, Robert W. Oldendick, and Stephen E. Bennett. "Questions About Question Wording: A Rejoinder to Revisiting Mass Belief Systems Revisited." *American Journal of Political Science* Vol. 23 (February 1979), pp. 187–92.

Bishop, George F., Robert W. Oldendick, and Alfred J. Tuchfarber. "Effects of Question Wording and Format on Political Attitude Consistency." *Public Opinion Quarterly* Vol. 42 (Spring 1978), pp. 81–92.

Bishop, George F., Robert W. Oldendick, Alfred J. Tuchfarber, and Stephen E. Bennett. "The Changing Structure of Mass Belief Systems: Fact or Artifact." *Journal of Politics* Vol. 40 (August 1978), pp. 781–87.

Blank, Robert. *Political Parties* (Englewood Cliffs: Prentice-Hall, 1980).

Broder, David S. *The Party's Over: The Failure of Party Politics in America* (New York: Harper, 1971).

Brody, Richard A. "Stability and Change in Party Identification: Presidential to Off-Years," presented at the 1977 Annual Meeting of the American Political Science Association, Washington, D.C.

Brody, Richard A. and Lawrence S. Rothenberg. "Dynamics of Partisanship During the 1980 Election," presented at the 1983 Annual Meeting of the American Political Science Association, Chicago, Illinois.

Brunk, Gregory G. "The 1964 Attitude Consistency Leap Reconsidered." *Political Methodology* Vol. 5 No. 3 (1978), pp. 347–59.

Burnham, Walter Dean. "The Changing Shape of the American Political Universe." *American Political Science Review* Vol. 59 (March 1965), pp. 7–28.

Burnham, Walter Dean. *Critical Elections and the Mainsprings of American Politics* (New York: W. W. Norton, 1970).

Burnham, Walter Dean. "Theory and Voting Research: Some Reflections on Converse's 'Change in the American Electorate.'" *American Political Science Review* Vol. 68 (September 1974), pp. 1002–23.

Butler, David and Donald E. Stokes. *Political Change in Britain* (New York: St. Martin's Press, 1969).

Campbell, Angus. "Surge and Decline: A Study of Electoral Change," in *Elections and the Political Order*, ed. Angus Campbell, Philip E. Converse, Warren E. Miller, and Donald E. Stokes (New York: John Wiley and Sons, 1966), pp. 40–62.

Campbell, Angus, Philip E. Converse, Warren E. Miller, and Donald E. Stokes. *The American Voter* (New York: John Wiley and Sons, 1960).

Campbell, Angus and Warren E. Miller. "The Motivational Basis of Straight and Split Ticket Voting." *American Political Science Review* Vol. 51 (June 1957), pp. 293–312.

Carmines, Edward G. and James A. Stimson. "The Two Faces of Issue Voting." *American Political Science Review* Vol. 74 (March 1980), pp. 78–91.

Carmines, Edward G. and James A. Stimson. "Issue Evolution, Population Replacement, and Normal Partisan Change." *American Political Science Review* Vol. 75 (March 1981), pp. 107–18.

Centers, Richard. *The Psychology of Social Classes* (Princeton: Princeton University Press, 1949).

Citrin, Jack. "Comment: The Political Relevance of Trust in Government." *American Political Science Review* Vol. 68 (September 1974), pp. 973–88.

Claggett, William. "Partisan Acquisition versus Partisan Intensity: Life-Cycle, Generation, and Period Effects, 1952–1976." *American Journal of Political Science* Vol. 25 (May 1981), pp. 193–214.

Clarke, Peter and Eric Fredin. "Newspapers, Television and Political Reasoning." *Public Opinion Quarterly* Vol. 42 (Summer 1978), pp. 143–60.

Clubb, Jerome M., William H. Flanigan, and Nancy H. Zingale. *Partisan Realignment: Voters, Parties, and Government in American History* (Beverly Hills, Calif.: Sage Publications, 1980).

Cohen, Jacob and Patricia Cohen. *Applied Multiple Regression/Correlation Analysis for the Behavioral Sciences* (Hillsdale: Lawrence Erlbaum Associates, 1975).

Conover, Pamela J. "The Perception of Political Figures: An Application of Attribution Theory," in *The Electorate Reconsidered*, ed. John C. Pierce and John L. Sullivan (Beverly Hills, Calif.: Sage Publications, 1980), pp. 91–109.

Converse, Philip E. "A Major Political Realignment in the South?" in *Change in the Contemporary South*, ed. A.P. Sindler (Durham: Duke University Press, 1963).

Converse, Philip E. "The Nature of Belief Systems in Mass Publics," in *Ideology and Discontent*, ed. David Apter (New York: Free Press, 1964), pp. 206–61.

Converse, Philip E. "The Concept of a Normal Vote," in *Elections and the Political Order*, ed. Angus Campbell, Philip E. Converse, Warren E. Miller, and Donald E. Stokes (New York: John Wiley and Sons, 1966), pp. 9–39.

Converse, Philip E. "Information Flow and the Stability of Partisan Attitudes," in *Elections and the Political Order*, ed. Angus Campbell, Philip E. Converse, Warren E. Miller, and Donald E. Stokes (New York: John Wiley and Sons, 1966), pp. 136–57.

Converse, Philip E. "Religion and Politics: The 1960 Election," in *Elections and the*

Political Order, ed. Angus Campbell, Philip E. Converse, Warren E. Miller, and Donald E. Stokes (New York: John Wiley and Sons, 1966), pp. 96–124.

Converse, Philip E. "Of Time and Partisan Stability." *Comparative Political Studies* Vol. 2 (July 1969), pp. 139–71.

Converse, Philip E. "Change in the American Electorate," in *The Human Meaning of Social Change*, ed. Angus Campbell and Philip E. Converse (New York: Russell Sage Foundation, 1972), pp. 263–337.

Converse, Philip E. *The Dynamics of Party Support* (Beverly Hills, Calif.: Sage Publications, 1976).

Converse, Philip E. "Rejoinder to Abramson." *American Journal of Political Science* Vol. 23 (February 1979), pp. 97–100.

Converse, Philip E., Angus Campbell, Warren E. Miller, and Donald E. Stokes. "Stability and Change in 1960: A Reinstating Election," in *Elections and the Political Order*, ed. Angus Campbell, Philip E. Converse, Warren E. Miller, and Donald E. Stokes (New York: John Wiley and Sons, 1966), pp. 78–95.

Converse, Philip E. and George Dupeux. "The Politicization of the Electorate in France and the United States," in *Elections and the Political Order*, ed. Angus Campbell, Philip E. Converse, Warren E. Miller, and Donald E. Stokes (New York: John Wiley and Sons, 1966), pp. 269–91.

Cowart, Andrew T. "A Cautionary Note on Aggregate Indicators of Split Ticket Voting." *Political Methodology* Vol. 1 (Winter 1974), pp. 109–30.

Crewe, Ivor. "Party Identification Theory and Political Change in Britain," in *Party Identification and Beyond: Representations of Voting and Party Competition*, ed. Ian Budge, Ivor Crewe, and Dennis Farlie (New York: John Wiley and Sons, 1976), pp. 33–61.

Crotty, William J. and Gary C. Jacobson. *American Parties in Decline* (Boston: Little, Brown, 1980).

Cummings, Milton, Jr. *Congressmen and the Electorate: Elections for the U.S. House and the President, 1920–1964* (New York: Free Press, 1967).

Cutler, Neal E. "Generation, Maturation and Party Affiliation: A Cohort Analysis." *Public Opinion Quarterly* Vol. 33 (Winter 1970), pp. 583–88.

Dahl, Robert A. *A Preface to Democratic Theory* (Chicago: University of Chicago Press, 1956).

Dahl, Robert A. *Who Governs?* (New Haven: Yale University Press, 1961).

Dahrendorf, Ralf. *Class and Class Conflict in Industrial Society* (Stanford: Stanford University Press, 1959).

Declercq, Eugene, Thomas L. Hurley, and Norman R. Luttbeg. "Voting in American Presidential Elections: 1956–1972." *American Politics Quarterly* Vol. 3 (July 1975), pp. 222–46.

Dennis, Jack. "Support for the Party System by the Mass Public." *American Political Science Review* Vol. 60 (September 1966), pp. 600–615.

Dennis, Jack. "Trends in Public Support for the American Party System." *British Journal of Political Science* Vol. 5 Part 2 (April 1975), pp. 187–230.

Dennis, Jack. "New Measures of Partisanship in Models of Voting," paper presented at the 1982 Annual Meeting of the Midwest Political Science Association, Milwaukee, Wisconsin.

Dennis, Jack. "Toward A Theory of Political Independence," presented at the 1983 Annual Meeting of the American Political Science Association, Chicago, Illinois.

Dennis, Jack and Donald J. McCrone. "Pre-Adult Development of Political Party Identification in Western Democracies." *Comparative Political Studies* Vol. 3 (July 1970), pp. 243–63.

DeVries, Walter and V. Lance Tarrance. *The Ticket-Splitter: A New Force in American Politics* (Grand Rapids: William B. Eerdmans Publishing Company, 1972).

Dobson, Douglas and Douglas St. Angelo. "Party Identification and the Floating Vote: Some Dynamics." *American Political Science Review* Vol. 69 (June 1975), pp. 481–90.

Dobson, Douglas and Duane A. Meeter. "Alternative Markov Models for Describing Change in Party Identification." *American Journal of Political Science* Vol. 18 (August 1974), pp. 487–500.

Downs, Anthony. *An Economic Theory of Democracy* (New York: Harper and Row, 1957).

Dreyer, Edward C. "Media Use and Electoral Choices: Some Political Consequences of Information Exposure." *Public Opinion Quarterly* Vol. 35 (Winter 1971–72), pp. 544–53.

Dreyer, Edward C. "Change and Stability in Party Identification." *Journal of Politics* Vol. 35 (August 1973), pp. 712–23.

Easton, David. *A Systems Analysis of Political Life* (New York: John Wiley and Sons, 1965).

Ellsworth, John W. "Rationality and Campaigning: A Content Analysis of the 1960 Presidential Campaign Debates." *Western Political Quarterly* Vol. 18 (December 1965), pp. 794–802.

Epstein, Leon D. *Political Parties in Western Democracies* (New York: Praeger, 1967).

Erbring, Lutz, Edie Goldenberg, and Arthur H. Miller. "Front-Page News and Real-World Cues: A New Look at Agenda-Setting by the Media." *American Journal of Political Science* Vol. 24 (February 1980), pp. 16–49.

Erikson, Robert S. "The Influence of Newspaper Endorsements in Presidential Elections: The Case of 1964." *American Journal of Political Science* Vol. 20 (May 1976), pp. 207–33.

Erikson, Robert S. and Kent L. Tedin. "The 1928–1936 Partisan Realignment: The Case for the Conversion Hypothesis." *American Political Science Review* Vol. 75 (December 1981), pp. 951–62.

Erikson, Robert S., Norman R. Luttbeg, and Kent L. Tedin. *American Public Opinion: Its Origins, Content, and Impact*, Second Edition (New York: John Wiley and Sons, 1980).

Eulau, Heinz. *Class and Party in the Eisenhower Years* (New York: Free Press, 1962).

Field, John O. and Ronald E. Anderson. "Ideology in the Public's Conceptualization of the 1964 Election." *Public Opinion Quarterly* Vol. 33 (Fall 1969), pp. 380–98.

Finifter, Ada W. "Dimensions of Political Alienation." *American Political Science Review* Vol. 64 (June 1970), pp. 389–410.

Fiorina, Morris. "Formal Models in Political Science." *American Journal of Political Science* Vol. 19 (February 1975), pp. 133–59.

Fiorina, Morris. "An Outline for a Model of Party Choice." *American Journal of Political Science* Vol. 21 (August 1977), pp. 601–25.

Fiorina, Morris. *Retrospective Voting in American National Elections* (New Haven: Yale University Press, 1981).

Flanigan, William H. and Nancy H. Zingale. *Political Behavior of the American Electorate*, Fourth Edition (Boston: Allyn and Bacon, 1979).

Franklin, Charles H. "Issue Preferences, Socialization, and the Evolution of Party Identification," *American Journal of Political Science* Vol. 28 (August 1984), pp. 459–78.
Glenn, Norval D. "Aging, Disengagement and Opinionation." *Public Opinion Quarterly* Vol. 33 (Spring 1969), pp. 17–34.
Glenn, Norval D. and Michael Grimes. "Aging, Voting and Political Interest." *American Sociological Review* Vol. 33 (September 1968), pp. 563–75.
Glenn, Norval D. and Ted Hefner. "Further Evidence on Aging and Party Identification." *Public Opinion Quarterly* Vol. 36 (Spring 1972), pp. 31–47.
Goldberg, Arthur S. "Social Determinism and Rationality as Bases of Party Identification." *American Political Science Review* Vol. 63 (March 1969), pp. 5–25.
Graber, Doris. *Mass Media and American Politics* (Washington, D.C.: Congressional Quarterly Press, 1980).
Hamilton, Richard. *Restraining Myths: Critical Studies of U.S. Social Structure and Politics* (New York: John Wiley and Sons, 1975).
Hennessy, Bernard. *Public Opinion*, Fourth Edition (Monterey: Brooks/Cole Publishing Company, 1981).
Hill, David B. and Norman R. Luttbeg. *Trends in American Electoral Behavior*, Second Edition (Itasca, Ill.: F.E. Peacock Publishers, 1983).
Hodge, Robert W., Paul M. Siegel, and Peter H. Rossi. "Occupational Prestige in the United States, 1925–63." *American Journal of Sociology* Vol. 70 (November 1964), pp. 286–302.
Hofstetter, C. Richard and Terry F. Buss. "Politics and Last Minute Political Television." *Western Political Quarterly* Vol. 33 (March 1980), pp. 24–37.
Ippolito, Dennis S., Thomas G. Walker, and Kenneth L. Kolson. *Public Opinion and Responsible Democracy* (Englewood Cliffs: Prentice-Hall, 1976).
Jackman, Mary R. and Robert W. Jackman. *Class Awareness in the United States* (Berkeley: University of California Press, 1983).
Jacoby, William G. "Unfolding the Party Identification Scale: Improving the Measurement of an Important Concept." *Political Methodology* Vol. 8 No. 2 (1982) pp. 33–59.
Jennings, M. Kent and Richard G. Niemi. "The Transmission of Political Values From Parent to Child." *American Political Science Review* Vol. 62 (March 1968), pp. 169–84.
Jennings, M. Kent and Richard G. Niemi. "The Persistence of Political Orientations: An Over-Time Analysis of Two Generations." *British Journal of Political Science* Vol. 8 (July 1978), pp. 333–63.
Jennings, M. Kent and Richard G. Niemi. *Generations and Politics: A Panel Study of Young Adults and Their Parents* (Princeton: Princeton University Press, 1981).
Jensen, Richard F. *The Winning of the Midwest: Social and Political Conflict, 1888–1896* (Chicago: University of Chicago Press, 1971).
Kamieniecki, Sheldon and Robert O'Brien. "Are Social Class Measures Interchangeable?" *Political Behavior* Vol. 6 No. 1 (1984), pp. 41–59.
Katz, Richard S. "The Dimensionality of Party Identification: Cross-National Perspectives." *Comparative Politics* Vol. 11 (January 1979), pp. 147–63.
Keith, Bruce E., David B. Magleby, Candice J. Nelson, Elizabeth Orr, Mark C. Westlye, and Raymond E. Wolfinger. "Further Evidence on the Partisan Affinities of Independent 'Leaners,' " presented at the 1983 Annual Meeting of the American Political Science Association, Chicago, Illinois.

Kelley, Stanley, Jr. and Thad W. Mirer. "The Simple Act of Voting." *American Political Science Review* Vol. 68 (June 1974), pp. 572–91.
Kendall, Maurice G. *Rank Correlation Methods*, Fourth Edition (New York: Hafner, 1970).
Kessel, John H. *Presidential Campaign Politics: Coalition Strategies and Citizen Response* (Homewood, Ill.: The Dorsey Press, 1980).
Key, V.O. "A Theory of Critical Elections." *Journal of Politics* Vol. 17 (February 1955), pp. 3–18.
Key, V.O. *Public Opinion and American Democracy* (New York: Knopf, 1961).
Key, V.O. *The Responsible Electorate: Rationality in Presidential Voting, 1936–1960* (Cambridge: Harvard University Press, 1966).
King, Anthony. "Political Parties in Western Democracies: Some Skeptical Reflections." *Polity* Vol. 2 (Winter 1969), pp. 111–41.
Kirkpatrick, Samuel A., William Lyons, and Michael R. Fitzgerald. "Candidates, Parties and Issues in the American Electorate: Two Decades of Change." *American Politics Quarterly* Vol. 3 (July 1975), pp. 247–83.
Knoke, David. *Change and Continuity in American Politics: The Social Bases of Political Parties* (Baltimore: The Johns Hopkins University Press, 1976).
Knoke, David and David E. Long. "The Economic Sensitivity of the American Farm Vote." *Rural Sociology* Vol. 40 (Spring 1975), pp. 7–17.
Knoke, David and Michael Hunt. "Social and Demographic Factors in American Party Affiliation: 1952–1972." *American Sociological Review* Vol. 39 (October 1974), pp. 700–713.
Kraus, Sidney (ed.). *The Great Debates* (Bloomington: Indiana University Press, 1962).
Kraus, Sidney (ed.). *The Great Debates, 1976: Ford versus Carter* (Bloomington: Indiana University Press, 1979).
Ladd, Everett C. "The Brittle Mandate: Electoral Dealignment and the 1980 Presidential Election." *Political Science Quarterly* Vol. 96 (Spring 1981), pp. 1–25.
Ladd, Everett C. and Charles D. Hadley. "Party Definition and Party Differentiation." *Public Opinion Quarterly* Vol. 37 (Spring 1973–74), pp. 21–34.
Lazarsfeld, Paul F. "Problems in Methodology," in *Sociology Today: Problems and Prospects*, ed. Robert K. Merton, Leonard Broom, and Leonard S. Cottrell (New York: Harper and Row, 1959), pp. 39–78.
Lazarsfeld, Paul F., Bernard Berelson, and Hazel Gaudet. *The People's Choice* (New York: Columbia University Press, 1948).
LeBlanc, Hugh L. and Mary B. Merrin. "Mass Belief Systems Revisited." *Journal of Politics* Vol. 39 (November 1977), pp. 1082–87.
Leggett, John C. *Race, Class, and Political Consciousness* (Cambridge: Schenkman, 1972).
Lipset, Seymour Martin. "Class, Politics, and Religion in Modern Society: The Dilemma of the Conservatives," in *Revolution and Counterrevolution*, ed. Seymour Martin Lipset (New York: Basic Books, 1968).
Lipset, Seymour Martin. "Social Class," in *The International Encyclopedia of the Social Sciences*, Vol. 15, ed. D.L. Sills (New York:Macmillan, 1968), pp. 296–316.
Lipset, Seymour Martin. *Political Man: The Social Bases of Politics*, Expanded Edition (Baltimore: The Johns Hopkins University Press, 1981).
Lipset, Seymour Martin. "Labor, Democrats Are Hurting Themselves." *Los Angeles Times* October 7, 1983, Part II, p. 13.

Lowi, Theodore. "Toward Functionalism in Political Science: The Case of Innovation in Party Systems." *American Political Science Review* Vol. 57 (September 1963), pp. 570–83.

McDonald, Michael D. and Susan E. Howell. "Reconsidering the Reconceptualizations of Party Identification." *Political Methodology* Vol. 8 No. 4 (1982), pp. 73–91.

McGrath, Joseph E. and Marion F. McGrath. "Effects of Partisanship on Perceptions of Political Figures." *Public Opinion Quarterly* Vol. 26 (Summer 1962), pp. 236–48.

Maggiotto, Michael and James E. Piereson. "Partisan Identification and Electoral Choice: The Hostility Hypothesis." *American Journal of Political Science* Vol. 21 (November 1977), pp. 745–67.

Marcus, George E., David Tabb, and John L. Sullivan. "The Application of Individual Differences Scaling to the Measurement of Political Ideologies." *American Journal of Political Science* Vol. 18 (May 1974), pp. 405–20.

Margolis, Michael. "From Confusion to Confusion: Issues and the American Voter (1956–1972)." *American Political Science Review* Vol. 71 (March 1977), pp. 31–43.

Markus, Gregory B. and M. Kent Jennings. "Partisan Orientations over the Long Haul: Results from the Three-Wave Political Socialization Panel Study," presented at the 1983 Annual Meeting of the American Political Science Association, Chicago, Illinois.

Markus, Gregory B. and Philip E. Converse. "A Dynamic Simultaneous Equation Model of Electoral Choice." *American Political Science Review* Vol. 73 (December 1979), pp. 1055–70.

Marx, Karl. *Capital* Vols. 1–3 (Moscow: Foreign Languages Publishing House, 1962).

Meier, Kenneth J. "Party Identification and the Vote Choice: The Causal Relationship." *Western Political Quarterly* Vol. 28 (September 1975), pp. 496–505.

Michels, Robert. *Political Parties* (Glencoe: Free Press, 1949).

Milbrath, Lester and M. Lal Goel. *Political Participation: How and Why Do People Get Involved in Politics?* Second Edition (Chicago: Rand McNally, 1977).

Miller, Arthur H. "Political Issues and Trust in Government: 1964–1970." *American Political Science Review* Vol. 68 (September 1974), pp. 951–72.

Miller, Arthur H. "Rejoinder to 'Comment' by Jack Citrin: Political Discontent or Ritualism?" *American Political Science Review* Vol. 68 (September 1974), pp. 989–1001.

Miller, Arthur H. "Partisanship Reinstated? A Comparison of the 1972 and 1976 U.S. Presidential Elections." *British Journal of Political Science* Vol. 8 (April 1978), pp. 129–52.

Miller, Arthur H., Edie N. Goldenberg, and Lutz Erbring. "Type-Set Politics: Impact of Newspapers on Public Confidence." *American Political Science Review* Vol. 73 (March 1979), pp. 67–84.

Miller, Arthur H. and Martin P. Wattenberg. "Measuring Party Identification: Independent or No Partisan Preference?" *American Journal of Political Science* Vol. 27 (February 1983), pp. 106–21.

Miller, Arthur H. and Michael MacKuen. "Learning About the Candidates: The 1976 Presidential Debates." *Public Opinion Quarterly* Vol. 43 (Fall 1979), pp. 326–46.

Miller, Arthur H. and Warren E. Miller. "Ideology in the 1972 Election: Myth or Real-

ity—A Rejoinder." *American Political Science Review* Vol. 70 (September 1976), pp. 832–49.
Miller, Arthur H., Warren E. Miller, Alden S. Raine, and Thad A. Brown. "A Majority Party in Disarray: Policy Polarization in the 1972 Election." *American Political Science Review* Vol. 70 (September 1976), pp. 753–78.
Miller, Warren E. "The Cross-National Use of Party Identification," in *Party Identification and Beyond: Representations of Voting and Party Competition*, ed. Ian Budge, Ivor Crewe, and Dennis Farlie (New York: John Wiley and Sons, 1976), pp. 21–31.
Miller, Warren E. "Misreading the Public Pulse." *Public Opinion* Vol. 2 (October/November 1979), pp. 9–15, 60.
Nie, Norman H. and James N. Rabjohn. "Revisiting Mass Belief Systems Revisited: Or, Why Doing Research Is Like Watching A Tennis Match." *American Journal of Political Science* Vol. 23 (February 1979), pp. 139–75.
Nie, Norman H. and Kristi Andersen. "Mass Belief Systems Revisited: Political Change and Attitude Structure." *Journal of Politics* Vol. 36 (August 1974), pp. 540–91.
Nie, Norman H., Sidney Verba, and John R. Petrocik. *The Changing American Voter*, Enlarged Edition (Cambridge: Harvard University Press, 1979).
Niemi, Richard G., Richard S. Katz, and David Newman. "Reconstructing Past Partisanship: The Failure of the Party Identification Recall Questions." *American Journal of Political Science* Vol. 24 (November 1980), pp. 633–51.
Nimmo, Dan and Robert L. Savage. *Candidates and Their Images: Concepts, Methods, and Findings* (Pacific Palisades, Calif.: Goodyear, 1976).
Ostrogorski, Moisei. *Democracy and the Organization of Political Parties*, Volume Two (New York: Anchor, 1964).
Page, Benjamin I. *Choices and Echoes in Presidential Elections: Rational Man and Electoral Democracy* (Chicago: Chicago University Press, 1978).
Page, Benjamin I. and Richard A. Brody. "Policy Voting and the Electoral Process: The Vietnam War Issue." *American Political Science Review* Vol. 66 (September 1972), pp. 979–95.
Petrocik, John R. "An Analysis of Intransitivities in the Index of Party Identification." *Political Methodology* Vol. 1 (Summer 1974), pp. 31–47.
Petrocik, John R. "Comment: Reconsidering the Reconsiderations of the 1964 Change in Attitude Consistency." *Political Methodology* Vol. 5 No. 3 (1978), pp. 361–68.
Petrocik, John R. "Contextual Sources of Voting Behavior: The Changeable American Voter," in *The Electorate Reconsidered*, ed. John C. Pierce and John L. Sullivan (Beverly Hills, Calif.: Sage Publications, 1980), pp. 257–77.
Phillips, Kevin P. *The Emerging Republican Majority* (New Rochelle: Arlington House, 1969).
Pierce, John C. "Party Identification and the Changing Role of Ideology in American Politics." *Midwest Journal of Political Science* Vol. 14 (February 1970), pp. 25–42.
Pierce, John C., Kathleen M. Beatty, and Paul R. Hagner. *The Dynamics of American Public Opinion: Patterns and Processes* (Glenview: Scott, Foresman and Company, 1982).
Polsby, Nelson W. and Aaron Wildavsky. *Presidential Elections: Strategies of Ameri-*

can Electoral Politics, Fifth Edition (New York: Charles Scribner's Sons, 1980).
Pomper, Gerald M. "From Confusion to Clarity: Issues and American Voters, 1956–1968." *American Political Science Review* Vol. 66 (June 1972), pp. 415–28.
Pomper, Gerald M. *Voters' Choice: Varieties of American Electoral Behavior* (New York: Dodd, Mead and Company, 1975).
Ranney, Austin. *The Doctrine of Responsible Party Government: Its Origins and Present State* (Urbana: University of Illinois Press, 1962).
Ranney, Austin (ed.). *The American Elections of 1980* (Washington, D.C.: American Enterprise Institute, 1981).
Reiss, Albert J. (ed.). *Occupations and Social Status* (New York: Free Press, 1961).
RePass, David. "Issue Salience and Party Choice." *American Political Science Review* Vol. 65 (June 1971), pp. 389–400.
RePass, David E. "Comment: Political Methodologies in Disarray: Some Alternative Interpretations of the 1972 Election." *American Political Science Review* Vol. 70 (September 1976), pp. 814–31.
Reynolds, H.T. *The Analysis of Cross-Classifications* (New York: Free Press, 1977).
Robinson, Michael J. "Public Affairs Television and the Growth of Political Malaise: The Case of 'The Selling of the Pentagon.' " *American Political Science Review* Vol. 70 (June 1976), pp. 409–32.
Rose, Douglas D. "Citizen Users of the Ford-Carter Debates." *Journal of Politics* Vol. 41 (February 1979), pp. 214–21.
Rusk, Jerrold G. "The Effect of the Australian Ballot Reform on Split Ticket Voting: 1876–1908." *American Political Science Review* Vol. 64 (December 1970), pp. 1220–38.
Rusk, Jerrold G. and Herbert F. Weisberg. "Perceptions of Presidential Candidates: Implications for Electoral Change." *Midwest Journal of Political Science* Vol. 16 (August 1972), pp. 388–410.
Rusk, Jerrold G. and John J. Stucker. "The Effect of the Southern System of Election Laws on Voting Participation: A Reply to V.O. Key, Jr.," in *The History of American Electoral Behavior*, ed. Joel Silbey, Allan Bogue, and William Flanigan (Princeton: Princeton University Press, 1978), pp. 198–250.
Sandoz, Ellis and Cecil V. Crabb, Jr. (eds.) *A Tide of Discontent: The 1980 Elections and Their Meaning* (Washington, D.C.: Congressional Quarterly Press, 1981).
Schattschneider, E.E. *Party Government* (New York: Rinehart, 1942).
Scott, Ruth K. and Ronald J. Hrebenar. *Parties in Crisis* (New York: John Wiley and Sons, 1979).
Searing, Donald D., Joel J. Schwartz, and Alden E. Lind. "The Structuring Principle: Political Socialization and Belief Systems." *American Political Science Review* Vol. 67 (June 1973), pp. 415–32.
Shively, W. Phillips. "Identification Costs and the Partisan Cycle," presented at the 1977 Annual Meeting of the American Political Science Association, Washington, D.C.
Shively, W. Phillips. "The Development of Party Identification among Adults: Exploration of a Functional Model." *American Political Science Review* Vol. 73 (December 1979), pp. 1039–54.
Shively, W. Phillips. "The Relationship between Age and Party Identification: A Cohort Analysis." *Political Methodology* Vol. 6 No. 4 (1979), pp. 437–46.
Shively, W. Phillips. "The Nature of Party Identification: A Review of Recent Devel-

opments," in *The Electorate Reconsidered*, ed. John C. Pierce and John L. Sullivan (Beverly Hills, Calif.: Sage Publications, 1980), pp. 219–36.

Shyrock, Henry S., Jacob S. Siegel, and Associates. *The Methods and Materials of Demography* (Washington, D.C.: U.S. Government Printing Office, 1975).

Siegel, Paul M. "Prestige in the American Occupational Structure," unpublished Ph.D. dissertation, University of Chicago, 1971.

Sigel, Roberta S. "Effect of Partisanship on the Perception of Political Candidates." *Public Opinion Quarterly* Vol. 28 (Fall 1964), pp. 483–96.

Sorauf, Frank J. *Party Politics in America*, Fourth Edition (Boston: Little, Brown and Company, 1980).

State Governments, The Council of. *The Book of the States, 1980–81* Volume 23 (Lexington, Kentucky: Council of State Governments, 1980).

Steward, John G. *One Last Chance: The Democratic Party, 1974–1976* (New York: Praeger, 1974).

Stimson, James A. "Belief Systems: Constraint, Complexity, and the 1972 Election." *American Journal of Political Science* Vol. 19 (August 1975), pp. 393–417.

Stokes, Donald E. "Some Dynamic Elements of Contests for the Presidency." *American Political Science Review* Vol. 60 (March 1966), pp. 19–28.

Stokes, Donald E. and Warren E. Miller. "Party Government and the Saliency of Congress," in *Elections and the Political Order*, ed. Angus Campbell, Philip E. Converse, Warren E. Miller, and Donald E. Stokes (New York: John Wiley and Sons, 1966), pp. 194–211.

Stuart, Alan. "The Estimation and Comparison of Strengths of Association in Contingency Tables." *Biometrika* Vol. 40 Parts 1 and 2 (June 1953), pp. 105–10.

Sullivan, John L., James E. Piereson, and George E. Marcus. "Ideological Constraint in the Mass Public: A Methodological Critique and Some New Findings." *American Journal of Political Science* Vol. 22 (May 1978), pp. 233–49.

Tedin, Kent L. "The Influence of Parents on the Political Attitudes of Adolescents." *American Political Science Review* Vol. 68 (December 1974), pp. 1579–92.

Tedin, Kent L. "Assessing Peer and Parent Influence on Adolescent Political Attitudes." *American Journal of Political Science* Vol. 24 (February 1980), pp. 136–54.

Thomassen, Jacques. "Party Identification as a Cross-Cultural Concept: Its Meaning in the Netherlands," in *Party Identification and Beyond: Representations of Voting and Party Competition*, ed. Ian Budge, Ivor Crewe, and Dennis Farlie (New York: John Wiley and Sons, 1976), pp. 63–79.

Valentine, David C. and John R. Van Wingen. "Partisanship, Independence, and the Partisan Identification Question." *American Politics Quarterly* Vol. 8 (April 1980), pp. 165–86.

Verba, Sidney and Norman H. Nie. *Participation in America: Political Democracy and Social Equality* (New York: Harper and Row, 1972).

Verba, Sidney, Norman H. Nie, and Jae-on Kim. *Participation and Political Equality* (New York: Cambridge University Press, 1978).

Wald, Kenneth D. and Michael B. Lupfer. "The Presidential Debate As a Civics Lesson." *Public Opinion Quarterly* Vol. 42 (Fall 1978), pp. 342–59.

Walker, Jack L. "Ballot Forms and Voter Fatigue: An Analysis of the Office Block and Party Column Ballots." *Midwest Journal of Political Science* Vol. 10 (November 1966), pp. 448–63.

Weber, Max. "Class, Status, Party," in *Class, Status, and Power*, Second Edition, ed. Reinhard Bendix and Seymour Martin Lipset (New York: Free Press, 1966), pp. 21–28.

Weisberg, Herbert F. "A Multidimensional Conceptualization of Party Identification." *Political Behavior* Vol. 2 No. 1 (1980), pp. 33–60.

Weisberg, Herbert F. and Jerrold G. Rusk. "Dimensions of Candidate Evaluation." *American Political Science Review* Vol. 64 (December 1970), pp. 1167–85.

Wilker, Harry and Lester Milbrath. "Political Belief Systems and Political Behavior." *Social Science Quarterly* Vol. 51 (December 1970), pp. 477–93.

Wilson, James Q. *American Government: Institutions and Policies* (Lexington: D.C. Heath, 1980).

Wolfinger, Raymond E. and Steven J. Rosenstone. *Who Votes*? (New Haven: Yale University Press, 1980).

Zeller, Richard A. and Edward G. Carmines. *Measurement in the Social Sciences: The Link between Theory and Data* (New York: Cambridge University Press, 1980).

INDEX

Aberbach, Joel, 115 n.48, 116 n.65
Abramowitz, Alan, 114 n.26
Abramson, Paul R., 33-34 n.25; 49-50; 77 nn.29, 32, 34; 104-5; 116 nn.54, 58; 144 n.16; 151; 165 nn.17, 18; 180; 198 n.25
Adams, Robert McC., 12 n.1
Afghanistan, Soviet Union's invasion of, 153-55, 202
Age, 49-53, 72-74
Agger, Robert, 106, 116 n.64
Aid to minorities, opinions on, 130-32, 141, 202
Aldrich, John H., 144 n.16; 151; 165 nn.17, 18; 198 n.25
Andersen, Kristi, 5-6; 12 n.1; 31 n.9; 127; 142 n.6; 198 n.14
Anderson, John, 114 n.23; 151; 157; 160
Anderson, Ronald E., 143 n.6
Andrews, William G., 198 n.12
Asher, Herbert B., 12 n.4; 24-25; 35 n.46; 86; 113 n.8; 150-51; 165 nn.8, 13

Baker, Howard, 114 n.23
Baker, Kendall, 23; 35 n.42
Balch, George, 105; 116 n.60

Beatty, Kathleen M., 82; 98; 113 nn.5, 10; 114 n.34; 116 n.67
Beck, Paul Allen, 12 n.5, 33 n.25
Belknap, George, 31 n.2
Bendix, Reinhard, 78 n.60
Bennett, Stephen E., 143 n.8
Berelson, Bernard, 78 n.47
Bishop, George F., 143 n.8
Blacks, attitudes toward, 119-21, 141, 174, 206
Blank, Robert, 99, 115 n.42
Bogue, Allan, 198 n.13
Boyd, Richard W., 11
Broder, David S., 115 n.39
Brody, Richard A., 7-10; 12 n.5; 20; 32 nn.17, 18, 143 n.6
Brown, Jerry, 93, 114 n.23
Brown, Thad A., 143 n.6
Brunk, Gregory G., 143 n.8
Budge, Ian, 34 n.37
Burnham, Walter Dean, 57; 77 n.45; 115 n.39; 174-75; 191; 198 nn.15, 16; 200 n.45
Bush, George, 114 n.23
Business, attitudes toward, 121-23, 133, 141, 202-3, 206

224 *Index*

Buss, Terry, 86, 113 n.7
Butler, David, 23, 32 n.21, 34 n.36

Campaign activities, 168-73, 195-96, 202-5, 208
Campbell, Angus, 4; 12 n.2; 15; 19; 27; 29; 31 nn.2, 3; 32 nn.10, 21; 33 n.25; 43; 47; 70; 76 nn.18, 21, 23; 77 nn.27, 30; 78 n.48; 79 n.65; 80 n.71; 82; 84; 113 nn.1, 7; 115 nn.52, 53; 127; 138; 142 n.5; 145 n.30; 146 n.37; 149; 165 n.4; 175-76; 186; 191; 193; 198 nn.15, 20, 22; 199 nn.27, 29, 30, 33, 38; 200 nn.48, 50, 52; 209 n.1
Candidate evaluations, 149-51
Carmines, Edward G., 36 n.67; 74 n.3; 127-28; 143 nn.6, 9; 144 n.19
Carter, Jimmy, 19, 54, 67, 93-97, 104-5, 111-12, 114 n.23, 128-29, 133, 135, 162-64, 183, 190, 202-6; economic program of, 151-53, 202-4; foreign policy decisions of, 153-55, 202-4; overall performance of, 155, 202-4; personal qualifications of, 160-61, 164, 202-4, 206; personal qualities of, 156-59, 164, 202-4, 206
Castro, Jeanne, 12
Centers, Richard, 69-70; 80 n.68
Citrin, Jack, 105, 116 n.55
Civil rights, 20, 47, 51, 54, 105, 127, 139, 141, 202, 204; attitudes toward leaders, 125-26, 135, 141, 202-3, 206
Claggett, William, 12 n.5, 33 n.22, 34 n.25, 50, 77 n.35, 209, 210 n.5
Clarke, Peter, 87, 113 n.17
Class self-identification, 69-70, 74, 205
Clubb, Jerome M., 31 n.8
Connally, John, 114 n.23
Conover, Pamela J., 150-51; 165 nn.7, 11, 15
Converse, Philip E., 4; 12 nn.1, 2; 15; 19; 27; 31 n.3; 32 nn.10, 12, 21; 33 nn.21, 25; 34 n.25; 47; 50; 70; 76 nn.18, 21, 23; 77 nn.27, 30, 31, 38; 78 nn.48, 49; 79 n.65; 80 n.71; 84; 86; 113 nn.1, 7; 115 nn.52, 53; 116 nn.61, 63; 127; 138; 142 n.5; 145 n.30; 146 nn.33, 37, 38; 151; 165 n.4; 166 n.20; 174-75; 183;
191; 198 nn.15, 16, 20, 22; 199 nn.27, 29, 30; 200 n.45; 209 n.1
Cowart, Andrew T., 200 n.51
Crabb, Cecil V., Jr., 144 n.17
Crane, Philip, 114 n.23
Crewe, Ivor, 34 n.37
Crotty, William J., 79 n.65
Cummings, Milton, Jr., 200 n.55
Cutler, Neal E., 33 n.25

Dahl, Robert A., 77 n.43, 197 n.5
Dahrendorf, Ralf, 66, 78 n.60
Davis, James, 12 n.4
Debates, 81, 93-98, 111-12, 202-3, 206
Declercq, Eugene, 165 n.6
Defense spending, attitudes toward, 128-30, 141, 202-4
Dennis, Jack, 7-11; 12 n.5; 27; 32 n.21; 35 n.59; 98-100; 114 n.33; 115 nn.41, 45; 128; 144 n.18; 199 n.38
Depressions, economic, 19, 49, 67, 148
DeVries, Walter, 24, 35 n.44, 199 n.38; 200 n.55
Dobson, Douglas, 20-21, 32 n.13, 17
Dole, Robert, 114 n.23
Downs, Anthony, 34 n.31, 166 n.17
Dreyer, Edward, 20, 32 n.15, 86, 113 n.7
Dupeux, George, 33 n.21

Easton, David, 99, 115 n.40
Economy, opinions on, 132-35, 141, 202-4
Education, 68-69, 72-73, 202, 204-6, 208
Efficacy, political, 104, 109-11
Eisenhower, Dwight D., 16, 57, 128, 183
Elderly, attitudes toward, 123-25, 141, 203
Election outcome: concern over, 84-86, 111, 207; perceived winner, 161-64, 202-3, 206
Elections, types of, 19
Ellsworth, John W., 114 n.26
Epstein, Leon D., 115 n.44
Equal Rights Amendment (ERA). *See* Women's rights
Erbring, Lutz, 87; 113 n.18; 114 n.19; 115 n.49; 116 nn.56, 62, 66, 69
Erikson, Robert S., 31 n.9; 47; 76 n.25; 79 n.65; 87; 113 n.12
Eulau, Heinz, 5; 10; 12 nn.1, 4; 79 n.65

Falwell, Reverend Jerry, 58
Farlie, Dennis, 34 n.37
Fenno, Richard, 12 n.4
Field, John O., 142 n.6
Finifter, Ada, 104-6; 115 n.48; 116 nn.54, 58, 65
Fiorina, Morris, 22; 34 nn.31-34; 147-48; 151; 157; 165 n.1; 166 nn.17, 18, 25, 27
Fitzgerald, Michael R., 165 n.6
Flanigan, William H., 31 n.8; 76 n.25; 79 n.65; 146 n.38; 174; 198 nn.10, 12, 13; 199 n.33
Ford, Gerald, 54, 93, 114 n.23, 190
Franklin, Charles H., 78 n.58
Fredin, Eric, 87, 113 n.17

Gaudet, Hazel, 78 n.47
Glenn, Norval D., 33 n.25, 49-50, 77 n.29
Goel, M. Lal, 169, 197 n.3, 198 n.18
Goldberg, Arthur S., 32 n.21
Goldenberg, Edie, 87; 113 n.18; 114 n.19; 115 n.49; 116 nn.56, 62, 66, 69
Goldstein, Marshall, 106, 116 n.64
Government power, opinions on, 130-32, 141, 202-3
Graber, Doris, 86, 113 n.7
Grimes, Michael, 33 n.25
Grofman, Bernard, 12 n.5
Gurin, Gerald, 12 n.2
Guynes, Randall, 10, 12 n.5

Hadley, Charles, 24, 35 n.45
Hagner, Paul R., 82; 98; 113 nn.5, 10; 114 n.34; 116 n.67; 145 n.32
Hamilton, Richard, 79 n.65
Hefner, Ted, 33 n.25, 49-50, 77 n.29
Hennessy, Bernard, 113 n.11
Hill, David B., 31 n.1, 115 n.48, 186, 199 n.38
Hispanics, attitudes toward, 119-21, 141
Hodge, Robert W., 79 n.64
Hofstetter, C. Richard, 86, 113 n.7
Hooks, Benjamin, 125
Hoover, Herbert, 19, 67, 148
Howell, Susan E., 199 n.37, 209 n.2
Hrebenar, Ronald J., 199 n.38
Humphrey, Hubert, 87

Hunt, Michael, 33 n.21
Hurley, Thomas L., 165 n.6

Ideology, 138-41, 202-5
Income, 68-69, 72-73, 202, 204-6, 208
Interest in politics, 82-84, 111, 205, 207
Ippolito, Dennis S., 79 n.65
Iranian hostage crisis, 153-55, 164, 202-4
Issue voting, 127-28. *See also individual issues*

Jackman, Mary, 79 n.63
Jackman, Robert, 79 n.63
Jackson, John E., 7, 10, 12 n.5
Jacob, John E., 125
Jacobson, Gary C., 79 n.65
Jacoby, William, 35 n.56
Janda, Kenneth, 12 n.5
Jennings, M. Kent, 21; 32 n.21; 33 nn.23, 24; 66; 78 nn.57, 58
Jensen, Richard F., 77 n.44
Johnston, J. Paul, 12 n.5

Kamieniecki, Sheldon, 3-5, 8-11, 36 n.67
Katz, Richard, 8, 10-11, 12 n.5, 27-28, 31 n.9, 32 n.17, 36 n.60
Keith, Bruce, 26
Kelley, Stanley, Jr., 165 n.6
Kendall, Maurice G., 80 n.72
Kennedy, John, 57, 128, 150, 183
Kennedy, Ted, 114 n.23, 151
Kessel, John, 20, 32 n.19, 113 n.6, 114 n.22, 149, 165 n.6
Key, V. O., 31 n.8; 35 n.43; 186; 197 n.5; 198 n.13; 199 nn.38, 39
Kim, Jae-on, 197 n.1
Kinder, Donald, 10
King, Anthony, 115 n.44
King, Reverend Martin Luther, Jr., 125
Kirkpatrick, Samuel A., 165 n.6
Knoke, David, 12 n.5; 33 n.21; 53; 77 n.37; 78 nn.46, 60; 79 nn.61, 65; 80 n.67
Kolson, Kenneth L., 79 n.65
Kraus, Sidney, 114 n.26

Labor unions, attitudes toward, 121-23, 141, 203, 206

Index

Ladd, Everett, 24, 35 n.45, 144 n.17
Lazarsfeld, Paul F., 36 n.66, 78 n.47
LeBlanc, Hugh L., 143 n.8
Leggett, John C., 79 n.65
Levitin, Teresa, 12 n.2
Lind, Alden E., 33 n.21
Lipset, Seymour Martin, 66-67; 78 nn.46, 60; 79 n.62; 142 n.2
Lodge, Milton, 12 n.5
Long, David E., 80 n.67
Lowi, Theodore, 115 n.37
Lucey, Patrick, 114 n.23
Lupfer, Michael B., 114 n.26
Luttbeg, Norman R., 31 n.1, 47, 76 n.25, 79 n.65, 115 n.48, 165 n.6, 186, 199 n.38
Lyons, William, 165 n.6

McAllister, William T., 12 n.5
McCrone, Donald J., 32 n.21
McDonald, Michael D., 199 n.37, 209 n.2
McGrath, Joseph, 150, 165 n.9
McGrath, Marion, 150, 165 n.9
MacKuen, Michael, 93; 114 nn.26, 28
McPhee, William, 78 n.47
Maggiotto, Michael, 21, 34 n.26
Magleby, David B., 35 n.57
Marcus, George E., 143 n.8, 146 n.38
Margolis, Michael, 143 n.6
Markus, Gregory B., 33 n.24, 66, 78 n.58, 151, 166 n.20
Marx, Karl, 66-67, 70, 78 n.59
Media, 58, 86-90, 111, 205
Meeter, Duane A., 32 n.17
Meier, Kenneth, 20, 23, 32 n.17, 35 n.39
Merrin, Mary B., 143 n.8
Merton, Robert K., 36 n.66
Michels, Robert, 115 n.38
Milbrath, Lester, 146 n.38, 169, 197 n.3, 198 n.18
Miller, Arthur H., 32 n.12; 35 n.58; 87; 93; 105-6; 113 n.18; 114 nn.19, 26, 28; 115 nn.49, 53; 116 nn.55, 56, 62, 63, 66, 69; 143 n.6; 144 n.12; 156; 166 n.26
Miller, Warren E., 4; 12 nn.1, 2; 13 n.11; 15; 19; 27; 31 n.3; 33 n.25; 34 n.37; 47; 70; 76 nn.18, 21, 23; 77 nn.27, 30; 78 n.48; 79 n.65; 80 n.71; 84; 113 n.1; 115 n.52; 116 n.66; 127; 138; 142 n.5; 143 n.6; 145 n.30; 146 n.37; 156; 165 n.4; 166 n.26; 175; 191; 193; 198 nn.20, 22; 199 nn.29, 30, 33, 38; 200 nn.48, 50, 52; 209 n.1
Mirer, Thad W., 165 n.6
Mondale, Walter, 114 n.23
Moral Majority, 58, 62-63, 73-74, 202, 204

Nelson, Candice J., 35 n.57
Newman, David, 11, 31 n.9, 32 n.17
Nie, Norman, 20; 31 n.9; 32 nn.11, 16; 54; 58; 76 n.22; 77 nn.28, 39; 78 nn.51, 52; 79 n.65; 82; 113 n.3; 114 n.20; 127; 142 n.6; 143 nn.6, 8; 169-70; 176; 197 nn.1, 6; 198 nn.14, 17, 21; 199 n.28
Niemi, Richard G., 7-8; 11; 12 n.5; 21; 31 n.9; 32 nn.17, 21; 33 nn.23, 25; 66; 78 n.57
Nimmo, Dan, 150, 165 n.12
Nixon, Richard, 54, 87, 150
Normal vote, 19, 32 n.10, 183
Norpoth, Helmut, 12 n.5

O'Brien, Robert, 36 n.67
Occupation, 68-69, 202, 204-6, 208
Oldendick, Robert W., 143 n.8
Orr, Elizabeth, 35 n.57
Ostrogorski, Moisei, 115 n.38

Page, Benjamin I., 12 n.4, 143 n.6
Party evaluations, 147-48, 164, 202-4
Party identification, Tallahassee Conference on, 5-8; 10; 12 nn.5, 6
Party system support, 42-43, 98-104, 111, 205, 208
Pearl, Stanley, 106, 116 n.64
Perkins, Jerry, 12 n.5
Petrocik, John, 20; 25-26; 31 n.9; 32 nn.11, 16; 35 n.51; 54; 58; 76 n.22; 77 nn.28, 39; 78 nn.51, 52; 82; 113 n.3; 114 n.20; 128; 143 nn.6, 8; 144 nn.12, 13; 183; 198 n.14; 199 nn.28, 31
Phillips, Kevin, 54, 57, 77 n.40, 78 n.50
Pierce, John C., 82, 98, 106, 113 nn.5, 10, 114 n.34, 116 n.67, 127, 142 n.6, 143 n.8, 145 n.32, 199 n.31
Pierson, James E., 21, 34 n.26, 143 n.8

Polsby, Nelson W., 115 n.43
Pomper, Gerald M., 12 n.5, 79 n.65, 127, 142 n.6, 143 n.7
Presidential candidates, knowledge about, 90-93, 202, 204-5, 208
Public services spending, attitudes toward, 128-30, 141, 202-4

Rabjohn, James N., 143 n.8
Race, 47-49, 53, 72-74, 202-6, 208
Raine, Alden S., 143 n.6
Ranney, Austin, 115 n.37
Reagan, Ronald, 19, 47, 54, 58, 93-97, 111-12, 114 n.23, 128-29, 131, 133, 135, 151, 162-64, 183, 190, 202-6; personal qualifications of, 160-61, 202-4, 206; personal qualities of, 157-59, 202-4, 206
Region, 53-56
Reiss, Albert J., 79 n.64
Religion, 56-63, 72-73, 74, 202, 203
RePass, David, 127, 142 n.6, 165 n.6
Residence, place of, 56
Reynolds, H. T., 80 n.72
Rhode, David W., 144 n.16; 151; 165 nn.17, 18; 198 n.25
Richardson, Bradley, 12 n.5
Robinson, Ann, 12
Robinson, Michael, 87; 113 n.15, 16
Rood, Steven, 12 n.5
Roosevelt, Franklin D., 19, 47, 51, 57, 67, 148
Rose, Douglas D., 114 n.26
Rosenstone, Steven, 174-75; 180; 198 nn.11, 19; 199 n.26
Rossi, Peter H., 79 n.64
Rothenberg, Lawrence, 20, 32 n.18
Rusk, Jerrold, 151; 166 n.20; 174-75; 191; 198 nn.13, 15, 16; 200 nn.45, 46

St. Angelo, Douglas, 20-21, 32 n.13, 17
Sanchez, Maria, 12
Sandoz, Ellis, 144 n.17
Savage, Robert, 150, 165 n.12
Schattschneider, E. E., 115 n.37
Schlafly, Phyllis, 135
Schwartz, Joel J., 33 n.21
Scott, Ruth K., 199 n.38
Searing, Donald D., 33 n.21

Sears, David O., 7, 10, 12 n.4
Shanks, Merrill, 7, 10, 12 n.4
Shively, W. Phillips, 12 n.5; 20-23; 25; 32 nn.14, 17, 21; 33 n.22; 34 nn.25, 29; 35; 35 nn.40, 50; 50; 77 n.33
Shyrock, Henry S., 79 n.66
Siegel, Jacob S., 79 n.66
Siegel, Paul M., 79 n.64
Sigel, Roberta, 93, 114 n.27, 150, 165 n.10, 166 n.19
Silbey, Joel, 198 n.13
Sills, D. L., 79 n.60
Smelser, Neil J., 12 n.1
Smith, Al, 57
Socialization, political, 21, 63-66, 72-73, 202-3, 206
Socioeconomic status, 66-70, 74, 203. See also Class self-identification; Education; Income; Occupation
Sorauf, Frank, 98, 115 n.36
Sprague, John, 12 n.4
Steinem, Gloria, 135
Steward, John G., 115 n.39
Stimson, James A., 12 n.5; 127-28; 138; 143 nn.6, 9; 144 n.19; 146 nn.35, 39
Stokes, Donald E., 4, 12 n.2; 15; 19; 23; 27; 31 n.3; 33 n.25; 34 n.36; 47; 70; 76 nn.18, 21, 23; 77 nn.27, 30; 78 n.48; 79 n.65; 80 n.71; 84; 113 n.1; 115 n.52; 127; 138; 142 n.5; 145 n.30; 146 n.37; 149; 165 nn.4, 5; 175; 198 nn.20, 22; 199 nn.29, 30, 33; 209 n.1
Stuart, Alan, 80 n.72
Stucker, John, 198 n.13
Sullivan, John L., 143 n.8, 146 n.38, 199 n.31

Tabb, David, 146 n.38
Tallahassee Conference. See Party identification
Tarrance, V. Lance, 24, 35 n.44, 199 n.38, 200 n.55
Tedin, Kent L., 31 n.9, 33 n.21, 47, 76 n.25, 79 n.65
Thomassen, Jacques, 23, 34 n.38
Ticket splitting, 191, 202, 208; at national level, 193-96, 207-8; at state and local level, 191-93, 196-97, 207-8

Treiman, Donald J., 12 n.1
Trust, political, 104-8, 111
Tuchfarber, Alfred J., 143 n.8
Tufte, Edward R., 12 n.4

Valentine, David, 10, 12 n.5, 26, 28, 35 n.52, 116 n.69, 209 n.3
Verba, Sidney, 20; 31 n.9; 32 nn.11, 16; 54; 58; 76 n.22; 77 nn.28, 39; 78 nn.51, 52; 79 n.65; 82; 113 n.3; 114 n.20; 143 n.6; 169-70; 176; 197 nn.1, 6; 198 nn.14, 17, 21; 199 n.28
Vidal, Gore, 93
Vietnam War, 20, 105, 127
Vote choice, the two-party, 168, 182-85, 195, 202-4, 207
Vote switching, 186-91, 195-97, 202-4, 208
Voter registration, 168, 176-79, 195-96, 202-4, 206
Voter turnout, 168, 179-82, 195-97, 202-4, 207-8; factors behind, 173-76
Voting, past frequency of, 176, 195

Wald, Kenneth D., 114 n.26
Walker, Jack L., 200 n.47
Walker, Thomas G., 79 n.65
Wallace, George, 87

Wattenberg, Martin P., 35 n.58
Weber, Max, 66, 78 n.60
Weisberg, Herbert, 7-11; 12 n.5; 13 n.9; 27-31; 36 n.61; 37-42; 44; 46; 73; 74 nn.1, 4; 75 n.7; 98; 106; 114 n.32; 116 n.68; 151; 166 n.20; 185; 199 n.34; 209; 209 n.3; 210 n.4
Welfare recipients, attitudes toward, 123-25, 141, 202-3, 206
Westlye, Mark C., 35 n.57
Wildavsky, Aaron, 115 n.43
Wilker, Harry, 146 n.38
Wilkins, Roy, 125
Wilson, James Q., 142 n.3
Wilson, Woodrow, 148
Wingen, John Van, 10, 12 n.5, 26, 28, 35 n.52, 116 n.69, 210 n.3
Wolfinger, Raymond E., 35 n.57; 174-75; 180; 198 nn.11, 19; 199 n.26
Women's rights, attitudes toward, 135-38, 141, 202, 204

Young, Whitney, 125

Zeller, Richard A., 36 n.67, 74 n.3
Zingale, Nancy H., 31 n.8; 76 n.25; 79 n.65; 146 n.38; 174; 198 nn.10, 12; 199 n.33

About the Author

SHELDON KAMIENIECKI is Assistant Professor of Political Science at the University of Southern California. He is the author of *Public Representation in Environmental Policy Making,* coauthor of *The Politics of Referendums,* and the coeditor of *Controversies in Environmental Policy.* His articles have appeared in numerous political science periodicals.